The Joy of Not Knowing

The Joy of Not Knowing takes every aspect of the curriculum and school life and transforms it into a personalised, meaningful and enjoyable experience for all. It offers readers an innovative, theoretical and practical guide to establish a values-based, enquiry-led and challenge-rich *learning to learn* approach to teaching and learning and to school leadership.

This thought-provoking guide provides the reader with a wealth of whole-class, easy-to-implement, malleable, practical ideas and case studies that can be personalised to the vision of each setting, age group and curriculum. It brings together, as a whole-school framework, the strategies that have been shown to have the greatest impact on the practitioner's professional fulfilment and on children's life chances, love of learning, intrinsic motivation and enthusiasm for *wanting* to know. *The Joy of Not Knowing*

- enables schools to launch the academic year with a bespoke JONK Learning to Learn Week that enables every student to succeed across all areas of the curriculum
- develops philosophical, creative and critical problem-solving thinking skills and embraces a multilingual and multicultural approach to learning
- establishes collaborative cultures of thinking, learning and leadership
- informs practice through teachers engaging in action research
- incorporates a values-led democratic approach to school life and to thriving when uncertain
- nurtures school–pupil–family–community partnerships

Designed for school leaders and practitioners at all levels and across all ages, this practical guide shows how all students can thrive and develop the dispositions of successful lifelong learners and global citizens.

Marcelo Staricoff is the creator of the Joy of Not Knowing (JONK) approach, founder and director of JONK Thinking and Learning Ltd, a School Tutor in Education at the University of Sussex and an educational consultant, speaker and trainer working with schools nationally and internationally on applying the principles contained in this book. He is the author of *Start Thinking* and a former scientist who became a primary school teacher and headteacher. He is a Founding Fellow of the Chartered College of Teaching (elected in 2019).

'This is a wonderful book packed with practical examples of how to build an authentic learning culture within an early years setting or primary school. The author draws upon his own extensive research experience as a teacher and headteacher in helping the reader to develop their own deep understanding of learning discovery, the importance of challenge and the insight of being able to explain thinking. This is a book to dip into and to delight in whether you are starting out on your career as a teacher or whether you have spent many years observing and learning with children. There is much here to remind us about the purpose and wonder of learning as a truly collective endeavor. I recommend this work to you and hope that as you are guided through the text by Staricoff you discover much that resonates with your existing philosophy and even more that spurs you not only to be inspired but to act.'

Dame Alison Peacock, Chief Executive
of The Chartered College of Teaching

'The Joy of Not Knowing provides readers with a philosophically informed festival of teaching ideas and strategies to fundamentally rethink how to inspire and foster the curiosity of learners. Whether you are an experienced school leader, or a beginning professional engaged in initial teacher education, this book offers a thought-provoking guide to unleashing a radical classroom culture of engagement in uncertainty and nurturing a commitment to lifelong learning. Rooted in both pedagogic wisdom and practice rich exemplification, JONK moves from establishing values led principles and ethos to sharing structured models for personalised learning, cross-curricula development and whole school approaches whereby a love of learning becomes not only a source of pleasure and inspiration but a way of being and knowing.'

Simon James Thompson, Head of Education,
National Teaching Fellowship Award 2016

'If it is true that "the mind is not a vessel to be filled but a fire to be kindled" then The Joy of Not Knowing is a bonfire. Marcelo Staricoff has produced a resource that is radical and reassuring, challenging and supportive. JONK offers a deeply thought out, integrated and coherent model that focuses on securing optimal learning for every member of the school community but particularly every child. This is a highly inclusive strategy that supports academic success, personal development and building cultural capital.'

John West-Burnham, Independent Writer, Teacher,
Author and Consultant in Education Leadership

'We've had the most amazing JONK Learning to Learn Week. The children have come up with some wonderful ideas about how they see their learning, all talk about being in the pit when struggling in lessons, homework books have been replaced with family home learning journals, we have been using De Bono's hats, are planning maths calculation videos (the children love these!) for the website and in form time this afternoon every group are going to be having a philosophy session. Staff have been telling me how much they have enjoyed it and how it has reminded them why we do this job in the first place.'

David Oldham, Headteacher,
Mulbarton Junior School, Norfolk

'The whole JONK approach of giving children permission to learn from their mistakes and to own their own learning has had a significant impact on our outcomes. Moving forward we will be having a Learning to Learn Week in September. This is not a quick fix but rather a whole school approach to learning which if embraced by all staff will have a significant impact on your children.'

Bev Theobald, Headteacher
Mulbarton Infant School, Norfolk

'The JONK approach is inspirational to the point of transformational.'

Graeme Cushnie, Headteacher,
Ballaugh School, Isle of Man

'JONKing at Coastal Federation was one of the best things we've done to inspire our children- go for it!'

Teachers, Coastal Federation, Norfolk

'I just wanted to thank you for your JONK lecture today - myself and my peers were really inspired! We have all been talking about how excited we are to start our NQT year following your lecture, a welcome change as we are generally a bit overwhelmed (as well as being excited) at the prospect! Just wanted to say how useful it was and how much it was appreciated. I am sure we will all be buying your book!'

Student, University of Brighton

'I just wanted to drop you a little message to thank you for bringing in Marcelo this morning. To put it simply, he was utterly inspiring. His philosophy, ideas and approach to teaching has instilled in me a great deal of enthusiasm ahead of SBT2 and I cannot wait to get going again.'

Student, University of Brighton

The Joy of Not Knowing

A Philosophy of Education Transforming Teaching, Thinking, Learning and Leadership in Schools

Marcelo Staricoff

Querida Melissa,

It's a great pleasure to dedicate this book to you. I hope that you enjoy it enormously and that it helps to nurture many generations of students that love knowing how to know, what they wish to know, that they know they don't know!

Warmest best wishes,

Marcelo

#802
2022
#JONK
FEBRUARY

Routledge
Taylor & Francis Group

LONDON AND NEW YORK

First published 2021
by Routledge
2 Park Square, Milton Park, Abingdon, Oxon OX14 4RN

and by Routledge
52 Vanderbilt Avenue, New York, NY 10017

Routledge is an imprint of the Taylor & Francis Group, an informa business

British Library Cataloguing-in-Publication Data
A catalogue record for this book is available from the British Library

Library of Congress Cataloging-in-Publication Data
Names: Staricoff, Marcelo, author.
Title: The joy of not knowing: a philosophy of education transforming teaching, thinking, learning and leadership in schools / Marcelo Staricoff.
Description: Abingdon, Oxon ; New York, NY : Routledge, 2021. | Includes bibliographical references and index.
Identifiers: LCCN 2020038923 | ISBN 9780367172718 (hardback) | ISBN 9780367172725 (paperback) | ISBN 9780429055904 (ebook)
Subjects: LCSH: Education--Philosophy. | Inquiry-based learning. | Critical thinking. | Motivation in education. | School environment. | Educational leadership.
Classification: LCC LB14.7 .S726 2021 | DDC 370.1--dc23
LC record available at https://lccn.loc.gov/2020038923

ISBN: 978-0-367-17271-8 (hbk)
ISBN: 978-0-367-17272-5 (pbk)
ISBN: 978-0-429-05590-4 (ebk)

Typeset in Bembo
by SPi Global, India

To Emily and Thomas

Contents

Figures

Acknowledgements

I would like to thank Bruce Roberts, Commissioning Editor at Routledge, and Molly Selby for all their guidance, support and encouragement in the production of this book. I would like to thank John West-Burnham enormously for all his inspiration and guidance throughout my career and for his generosity in writing the Preface. Great thanks to Philippa Aldrich for her insight and invaluable recommendations that helped to shape the final version of the book. I would like to offer the most special thanks to Rosalia Staricoff, who throughout the writing process provided support and challenge over many hours of conversations which proved so instrumental to the development of this book.

There are multitudes of colleagues, pupils, families and friends I would like to thank enormously for all their moments of inspiration and wisdom that contributed so fundamentally to each stage of my career and to the coming together of this book. I owe them so much. I will always be incredibly grateful to Tony Tween, who as Headteacher of Christ Church Primary School offered me my first position and so many exciting opportunities. In particular, I would like to create a very special place in this book for Alan Rees (1952–2017), who, as my Headteacher at Westbury Park Primary School in Bristol, was my principal influence during my formative years as a teacher and who continued to be incredibly influential as a mentor and as a friend.

I would like to say a huge thank you to David Millington and Graham Pike for the way they both made every minute of working together so enjoyable and so full of the experimentation that constantly seemed to redefine the boundaries of possibility. I would like to thank Ruth Deaking-Crick for all the inspiration and insight that made participation in the Effective Lifelong Learning Inventory (ELLI) Project such an influence on my practice and Sally Jaeckle, who was so instrumental in the dialogues that shaped and rooted my practice in the wonders of the pedagogy and philosophy that make the Early Years so special.

I would like to extend a very warm and special thanks to the whole community of Hertford Infant and Nursery in School, in Brighton, for inducting me into Headship with so many magical and memorable moments. Many thanks to all the colleagues from the Infants Heads Group, the Partnership in Leadership and Learning (PILL) and the group of Heads that formed part of Cre8 for all the invaluable partnership working that helped to shape my practice and leadership. I would like to offer a very special thanks to Richard Bradford and William Deighan for all their inspiration and cross-phase collaborative working. Many thanks to Alison Peacock, whose friendship and professional guidance always were and remain such key components of my career.

I would like to say a huge thank you to Deborah Eyre and Lynne McClure for all their transformational leadership during the Flying High Project in Bristol and to Deborah Eyre for the subsequent opportunity to form part of the Think Tank that arose as part of the National Academy for Gifted and Talented Youth (NAGTY) and all her inspiration since. I will always be very grateful to Roger Sutcliffe, who introduced me to the wonders of philosophy, and to many memorable years working with colleagues on the board of SAPERE. I would like to say enormous thanks to Steve Williams and Howard Sharron for all their support and encouragement and for publishing my first book, *Start Thinking*.

I would like to give a very special mention for Denise Walker, Director of the Viscount Nelson Education Network CIC, and Clare Flintoff, Chief Executive Officer at ASSET Education, as well as all the colleagues and pupils across the member schools for providing the launch pad for so many of the aspects that form part of this book. Many thanks go to Sara Bragg, who was so influential as a colleague during my secondment at the University of Brighton and who facilitated the project grant that led to the work in this book being introduced to colleagues in Spain, and to Simon Thompson at the University of Sussex, who has now taken on this mantle.

Finally, I would like to thank Anna, Emily, Thomas, Gustavo and June enormously for all their encouragement, guidance, patience and support, without which this book would not have been possible.

Preface

In spite of all the work that has taken place in recent years on the nature of the curriculum and the importance of high-quality teaching, we are still some way from a professional consensus as to the nature of effective learning. Much has been written and the evidence base is growing and enjoying increasing confidence and influence. But we still have some way to go. This is not a search for an educational panacea that will solve all our problems about educational performance and securing equity but rather seeking credible models that have grown from practice in schools and have made a demonstrable difference to how teachers teach and how pupils learn. Historically, education has been beset by astrologers when what was needed was astronomers – offering coherent conceptual models and research-informed practice.

If it is true that 'The mind is not a vessel to be filled but a fire to be kindled', then *The Joy of Not Knowing* is a bonfire. Marcelo Staricoff has produced a resource that is radical and reassuring, challenging and supportive. JONK offers a deeply thought out, integrated and coherent model that focuses on securing optimal learning for every member of the school community but particularly every child. This is a highly inclusive strategy that supports academic success, personal development and building cultural capital. The various strategies are rooted in successful classroom practice and effective school leadership, and there are numerous examples that are reassuring and establish the credibility of the strategies described.

Every aspect of JONK grows out of Marcelo's professional practice and experience. This book is richly illuminated by examples of pupils' work, diagrams that explain the key concepts and a wide range of sources to support and validate key ideas. JONK can be seen as a manifesto for profound change or an invaluable resource offering a wide range of strategies to support thinking and learning. It will support teacher research, underpin school leadership and be an invaluable resource for professional development.

It is a significant resource that deserves wide circulation.

John West–Burnham

Foreword

In order to learn something new, we must not know it first
Marcelo Staricoff

This book is the culmination of all that I have learnt, of all the people who have inspired me and of all that has fascinated me throughout my career as a primary school teacher, headteacher, lecturer, author, consultant, Founding Fellow of the Chartered College of Teaching and, previous to the world of education, a research scientist. The book charts and disseminates how these experiences led to the evolution and creation of the Joy of Not Knowing™ (JONK™) philosophy of education and of school leadership, from its first experimental days in the classroom to its current form, which now embraces all aspects of leading, working and learning in schools (Staricoff, 2013, 2014, 2018a, 2018b).

I was tremendously fortunate that during my first year of teaching, I formed part of a two-year action research project.[1] The project, which was called Flying High (Staricoff, 2001), was originally set up to look at effective provision for what was then termed *more-able children* and funded through the sale of a section of runway at Bristol Airport! The project involved 12 local primary and secondary schools and was led by two national experts, Deborah Eyre[2] and Lynne McClure.[3] Forming part of this research project at such an early stage of my career proved to be very influential and instrumental in shaping my practice and philosophy of education. I started to realise the huge potential that education has not only to motivate learners with the curriculum but also to influence their *enjoyment* of the learning process. The evolution of the project introduced me to initiatives designed to develop students' ability to reason, to think analytically, critically, creatively and philosophically and to master the intricacy of language that drives curiosity and leads to such effective communication. The project gave me the inspiration, impetus and professional freedom to experiment with using these exciting ideas *with the whole class*, to inspire every child and to drive every aspect of the day. I was enthralled by this challenge. The children began to really enjoy *playing* with each idea, excited that we were all *playing* together. It quickly became apparent that we were developing a way of *being* in the classroom that was promoting *intrinsic* motivation, creative thoughts and an enthusiasm for *wanting* to learn.

A further opportunity to build on this work presented itself three years later, at my second school,[4] as part of a Beacon Project.[5] The initiatives this time focused on developing a whole-school ethos driven by values, thinking skills, entitlements, accelerated learning,[6] philosophy and lifelong learning. The choice of these focus areas was based on the idea of trying to emulate the practice and philosophy of education that underpins Early Years practice throughout the school. The project brought us into a collaborative partnership with the University of Bristol[7] to look at ways of incorporating the dispositions of effective lifelong learners within the daily routine of the classroom. The project allowed us to work closely with a number of other educational experts: Robert Fisher in terms of thinking skills and creativity, leading to a case study in his book *Unlocking Creativity* (Fisher and Williams, 2004); Roger Sutcliffe, Will Ord and Barry Hymer as colleagues on the Board of Philosophy for the children's organisation SAPERE; James Nottingham, who was leading an organisation set up to raise aspirations in society and education (NRAIS) in Northumberland, UK and who at the time introduced me to the concept of the Learning Pit,[8] which I have since reinterpreted to encompass the philosophy of JONK; John West-Burnham and his work on leadership and the personalisation of learning; Helen Wilson and David Coates, who were so instrumental in guiding me when engaging in action research focused on Primary Science; Deborah Eyre, who at the time was heading the National Academy of Gifted and Talented Youth (NAGTY) based at Warwick University and who invited me to form part of the NAGTY Think Tank which worked towards shaping national policy.

A telling observation of this whole-class, values-led, non-ability labelling, thinking skills, philosophical and lifelong learning approach (Staricoff, 2003) to teaching and learning was the passion and freedom with which the children began to frame their thoughts, theories, observations and ideas as questions. There seemed to be an endless richness of collective curiosity in the class. I knew this was working well when I started to realise that, with the majority of the questions they were posing, I didn't know the answer. I remember thinking that in *not knowing* the answer to their questions, it was helping to create a model where the children perceived the teacher as a *co-participant* in the learning. This culture led to another important realisation: everyone, including myself and the many visitors to the class, were starting to feel *safe* emotionally, socially and intellectually, especially when we found ourselves in situations of *not knowing* and *uncertainty*. Collectively, we learnt to embrace these moments of uncertainty and to use them as opportunities for discovery, learning and acquiring new knowledge. Up until this point, we had never realised how exciting *not knowing* could be, especially as we were *not knowing collectively* and at the same time developing a real enthusiasm for *wanting* to know.

The ability for curiosity and questioning to transform the way we view the world is wonderfully illustrated by the message contained within a letter that Scheff once wrote to the Editor of the *New York Times* (1988), in which he recounts how Isidor I. Rabi, a Nobel Laureate in physics, was once asked by his friend Arthur Sackler:

'Why did you become a scientist, rather than a doctor or lawyer or businessman, like the other immigrant kids in your neighbourhood?'

Rabi replied:

'My mother made me a scientist without ever intending it. Every other mother in Brooklyn would ask her child after school: "So? Did you learn anything today?" But not my mother. She always asked me a different question. "Izzy," she would say, "did you ask a good question today?"

That difference, asking good questions, made me become a scientist!'

The JONK approach encourages families to engage with their children in a very similar way, using the school day as an opportunity to formulate questions that inspire children to reflect upon their discoveries, observations, thoughts, reflections, wonder and newly found curiosities that day (F.1):

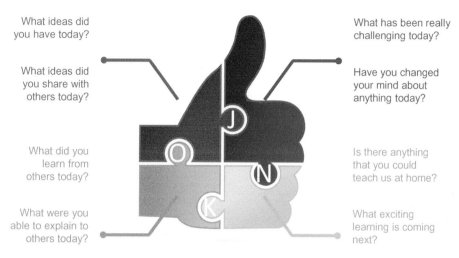

What ideas did you have today?

What ideas did you share with others today?

What did you learn from others today?

What were you able to explain to others today?

What has been really challenging today?

Have you changed your mind about anything today?

Is there anything that you could teach us at home?

What exciting learning is coming next?

FIGURE F.1 Ideas of Questions to Ask the Children After School

I am delighted that through this book, I now have the opportunity to share what I hope is a rich resource of inspiration, enabling you all to achieve things beyond what you envisaged or imagined possible. The freedom to experiment so broadly in the classroom during my formative years paved the way for what evolved, through senior leadership, headship and many other past and present collaborations, into what is now a whole-school philosophy of education and leadership (Staricoff, 2013, 2014, 2018a, 2018b) being applied nationally and internationally.

At the heart of the JONK philosophy and approach is the desire to create the conditions in schools that, when they act in combination, work towards maximising the influence that schools can exert on children's life chances and the ability to enable every child to thrive socially, emotionally and academically. It is believed that a child's life chances are influenced by three main factors, which Groves and West-Burnham (2020) refer to as 'the three spheres of influence'. Groves and West-Burnham state that 'successful learning of any type or subject is the result of the complex interaction of these three variables':

Personal genetic factors (50%)

Social and economic factors (20%–30%)

School (20%–30%)

It is so interesting that these 'life chances' determinant factors are so comparable to the three worlds that Nuthall (2007) describes as shaping the student's learning:

The student's own private world and experiences

The highly influential world of peers

The public world of the teacher

It was during my first headship[9] that I created the Joy of Not Knowing (JONK) phraseology to encompass the philosophy that underpinned the whole-school approach that we had established. After the fourth year of living within this JONK culture, the school observed a fourth year of year-on-year increases in standards, attendance, first-choice preferences of admissions and an *outstanding* judgement for its very first time.

It was a time of great creativity and collaboration, helping us to develop a wonderful partnership with the poet Roger Stevens, an association that eventually led to the publication of a book of poetry, *Once a Pond of Slime, Poems by and for the Under 5s'* (Bartlett and Johnson, 2012). I used the publication of that book as an opportunity to contribute to the work with a personal poem written to describe the ethos, philosophy and sentiments of the JONK approach.

As a native Spanish speaker, I wrote the original version in Spanish and translated it into English as illustrated in F.2.

Foreword

Un Canto Para Hertford

Aquí me pongo a cantar
Al compás de mi escuela
Con todos los chicos adentro
Aprendiendo tanto cada día
Me toca a mi ser el centro
De toda nuestra filosofía

Alegres y contentos
Los veo siempre a todos
Con tantas ganas de saber mas que antes
Y con tantas preguntas tan interesantes
No hay fin a la curiosidad
Que les surge a esta edad!

Los veo por todo tan interesados
Que es un placer increíble
Nunca se los ve cansados
O discutiendo o peleados
Pero si siempre tan entusiasmados
De tratar hasta lo imposible!

Que la escuela les este dando
Todo para el futuro
Pa'que nada en su vida sea duro
Es lo que siempre voy pensando
Para que puedan siempre disfrutar
De sus vidas, con alegría y mucho pa'cantar

by Marcelo Staricoff
Director.

A Song for Hertford

Here I begin to sing
To the beat of my school
With all the children here
Learning so much day by day
My destiny is to be
At the heart of our philosophy

Cheerful and happy
With a desire to know more than before
With so many interesting questions
There is no end to the curiosity
That emanates at this age!

So interested in everything
That is an incredible pleasure
You never see them tired
Or arguing or feuding
But always so enthusiastic
To attempt even the impossible!

I hope the school is giving them
Everything for the future
So that nothing in life is too hard
This is what I always wish for
So they can all enjoy their lives
With joy and much to sing about

By Marcelo Staricoff
Headteacher

FIGURE F.2 An Example of Using a Multilingual Thinking Approach in School

Above all, I hope that this book offers leaders, practitioners and students the inspiration to experiment in the pursuit of innovation, enjoyment and transformation and of building the motivational cultures of learning in each classroom and school which maximise what James, Renowden and West–Burnham (2013) so wonderfully refer to as 'the enormous potential of education to secure a richer quality of life for all'.

The Joy of Not Knowing™ and JONK™: Reg.: UK00003133651 and UK0000 3133650 respectively

Notes

1 Christ Church Primary School, Bristol, UK.
2 Deborah Eyre is now the Founder and Director of High-Performance Learning.
3 Lynne McClure is now Director of Cambridge Maths at the University of Cambridge.
4 Westbury Park Primary School, Bristol, UK.
5 Westbury Park Primary School was awarded Beacon Status facilitating funded collaboration, research and dissemination opportunities.
6 The Accelerated Learning in Primary Schools Approach (ALPS), Alastair Smith (1996).
7 The Effective Lifelong Learning Inventory Research Project (ELLI, Ruth Deaking-Crick, 2006).
8 James Nottingham is now the Founder and Director of Challenging Learning, Ref.: Nottingham, J. (2017).
9 Hertford Infant and Nursery School, Brighton, UK.

1 Introduction

It is because we are in a position of not knowing that we have the opportunity to learn
Marcelo Staricoff

The Joy of Not Knowing™ (JONK™) is an innovative philosophy of education that enables *all* individuals to flourish by creating the conditions that remove the worry and anxiety usually associated with *not knowing* or finding things difficult and by replacing them with a *love* for learning and an enthusiasm for *wanting* to learn and to know.

The JONK approach is intended to act as a *way of being* and a *way of life* for schools. This book has been designed to provide educators with an enjoyable and *practical* source of principles, strategies, systems and ideas that promote a lifelong love of learning, teaching, collaboration and leadership at all levels, including the students as leaders of their own learning and as instrumental voices of the school's strategic leadership teams. The ideas are all based on real-life scenarios, and the book uses a wide range of worked examples and case studies to illustrate how practitioners and leaders across the educational and social-economic landscape have interpreted, adapted and incorporated the range of aspects that make up the JONK approach.

The book ensures that each chapter is rich in practical and easy-to-implement ideas, explaining the theory and rationale behind each one and making each one exciting for all: student teachers, newly qualified teachers, early career teachers and experienced practitioners. The book also describes each of these ideas from the strategic perspective of senior leaders and headteachers and offers step-by-step guides to how they can be introduced, implemented, embedded and sustained as part of the whole-school planning and development infrastructure.

The aim is for the reader, at all stages of their career, to use the ideas in the book as an opportunity to *play professionally*, adapting, developing and personalising them according to personal contexts. The *professional and playful* approach that JONK promotes uses as its root the investigative, child-centred and inquiry-rich pedagogy of *Early Years education* and applies it in a way that inspires students of *all* ages and practitioners and leaders across all roles and phases of education.

The non-prescriptive nature of the JONK philosophy allows schools to create *bespoke* versions of each of the ideas presented, in line with their own educational ethos and philosophy and in a way that *builds on* existing practice and helps schools to achieve their next steps.

The JONK whole-school philosophy of education and leadership is defined by six interlocking *ethos- and principles-driven* domains illustrated in Figure 1.1:

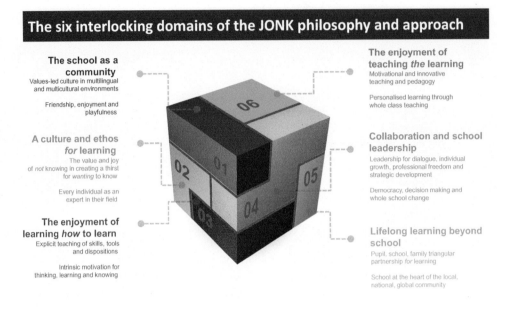

FIGURE 1.1 The Six Interlocking Domains of the JONK Philosophy and Approach

The six interlocking ethos- and principles-driven domains give rise to the JONK whole-school approach in practice. Figure 1.2 lists the components that facilitate each of the six domains to be incorporated as part of the school's infrastructure and that, when translated into practice, mirror the sentiments encompassed within Albert Einstein's quote, when he stated that 'I never teach my pupils. I only attempt to provide the conditions in which they can learn'. Within this quote, Einstein encompasses and summarises wonderfully the ethos of education, the purpose of educational establishments and the value that educators bring to the learner.

Figure 1.2 also acts as a colour-coded reference guide and road map that encompasses the whole of the JONK approach. The diagram demarcates for the reader the chapter in which each of the initiatives that underpin the six interlocking ethos and principles of the JONK approach is introduced and described.

The philosophy of the JONK whole-school approach is captured visually for the learner by the *JONK Models of Learning*. It is in the discussion of these models that children are provided with a very special sense of *learner emotional well-being*, as the models illustrate for them how the learning process evolves and how the school nurtures every child's expertise to enable them to thrive with every opportunity at school, beyond school and throughout their lives.

The JONK approach is founded on the belief that this learner emotional well-being is created when children *feel* equipped with all they need to succeed – emotionally, socially and academically. For this to be the case for every child, the JONK approach dedicates the first week of every academic year to a JONK Learning to Learn Week,

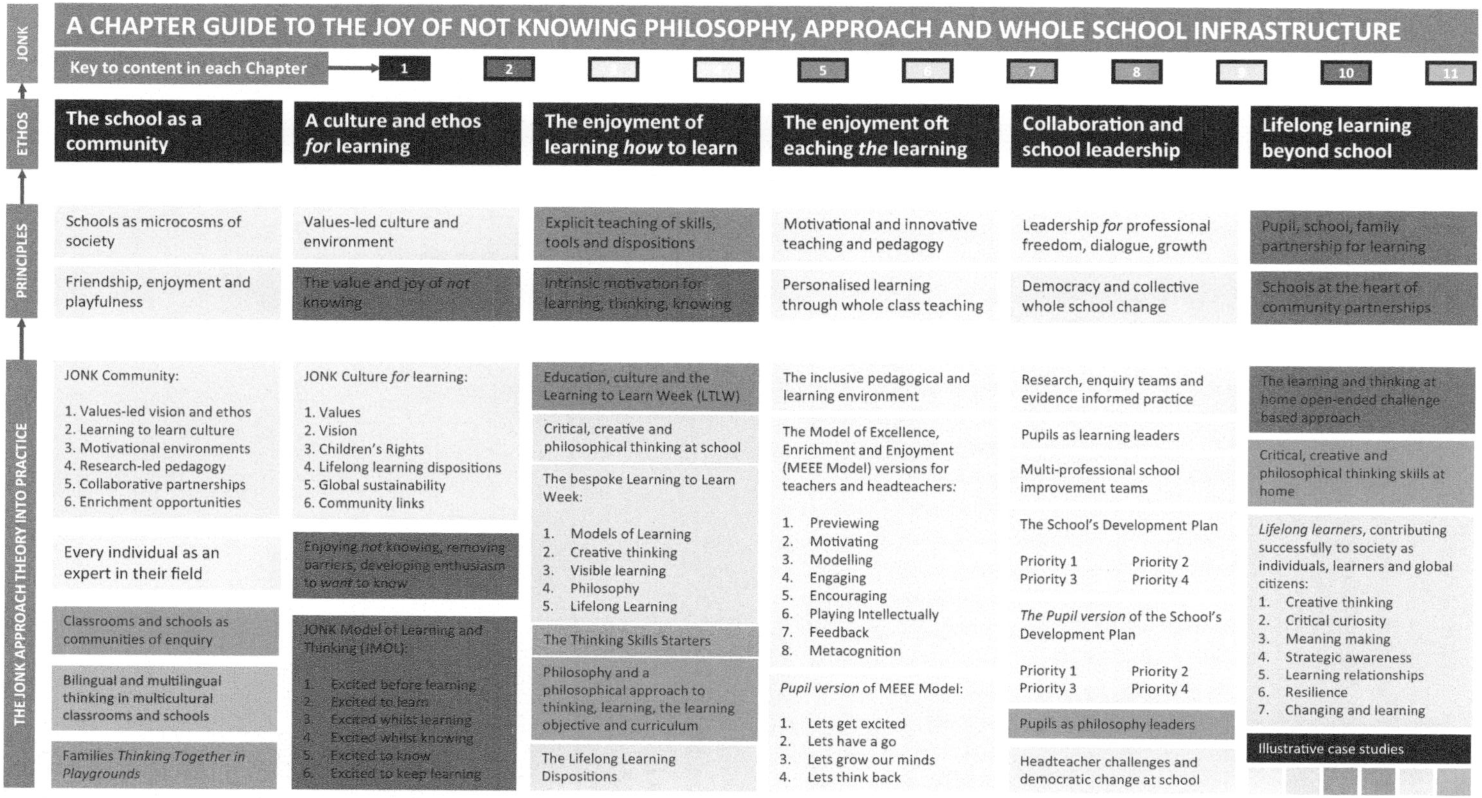

A CHAPTER GUIDE TO THE JOY OF NOT KNOWING PHILOSOPHY, APPROACH AND WHOLE SCHOOL INFRASTRUCTURE

Key to content in each Chapter: 1 2 5 7 8 10 11

THE JONK APPROACH THEORY INTO PRACTICE → PRINCIPLES → ETHOS → JONK

The school as a community

Schools as microcosms of society

Friendship, enjoyment and playfulness

JONK Community:
1. Values-led vision and ethos
2. Learning to learn culture
3. Motivational environments
4. Research-led pedagogy
5. Collaborative partnerships
6. Enrichment opportunities

Every individual as an expert in their field

Classrooms and schools as communities of enquiry

Bilingual and multilingual thinking in multicultural classrooms and schools

Families *Thinking Together in Playgrounds*

A culture and ethos for learning

Values-led culture and environment

The value and joy of not knowing

JONK Culture *for learning:*
1. Values
2. Vision
3. Children's Rights
4. Lifelong learning dispositions
5. Global sustainability
6. Community links

Enjoying not knowing, removing barriers, developing enthusiasm to want to know

JONK Model of Learning and Thinking (JMOLT):
1. Excited before learning
2. Excited to learn
3. Excited whilst learning
4. Excited whilst knowing
5. Excited to know
6. Excited to keep learning

The enjoyment of learning *how* to learn

Explicit teaching of skills, tools and dispositions

Intrinsic motivation for learning, thinking, knowing

Education, culture and the Learning to Learn Week (LTLW)

Critical, creative and philosophical thinking at school

The bespoke Learning to Learn Week:
1. Models of Learning
2. Creative thinking
3. Visible learning
4. Philosophy
5. Lifelong Learning

The Thinking Skills Starters

Philosophy and a philosophical approach to thinking, learning, the learning objective and curriculum

The Lifelong Learning Dispositions

The enjoyment oft *eaching the* learning

Motivational and innovative teaching and pedagogy

Personalised learning through whole class teaching

The inclusive pedagogical and learning environment

The Model of Excellence, Enrichment and Enjoyment (MEEE Model) versions for teachers and headteachers:
1. Previewing
2. Motivating
3. Modelling
4. Engaging
5. Encouraging
6. Playing Intellectually
7. Feedback
8. Metacognition

Pupil version of MEEE Model:
1. Lets get excited
2. Lets have a go
3. Lets grow our minds
4. Lets think back

Collaboration and school leadership

Leadership *for* professional freedom, dialogue, growth

Democracy and collective whole school change

Research, enquiry teams and evidence informed practice

Pupils as learning leaders

Multi-professional school improvement teams

The School's Development Plan

Priority 1 Priority 2
Priority 3 Priority 4

The Pupil version of the School's Development Plan

Priority 1 Priority 2
Priority 3 Priority 4

Pupils as philosophy leaders

Headteacher challenges and democratic change at school

Lifelong learning beyond school

Pupil, school, family partnership for learning

Schools at the heart of community partnerships

The learning and thinking at home open-ended challenge based approach

Critical, creative and philosophical thinking skills at home

Lifelong learners, contributing successfully to society as individuals, learners and global citizens:
1. Creative thinking
2. Critical curiosity
3. Meaning making
4. Strategic awareness
5. Learning relationships
6. Resilience
7. Changing and learning

Illustrative case studies

FIGURE 1.2 A Chapter by Chapter Guide to the Whole of the JONK Approach

which is used to *explicitly teach* the children *how* to learn successfully, *how* to establish a collaborative and inspirational culture *for* learning and *how* to contribute to this culture for the benefit of all, both within the classroom and throughout the school.

The JONK approach is designed to adapt to individual contexts by embracing and celebrating the uniqueness of every individual and of every school and by creating *values-led* and *personalised whole-school learning and social cultures* that enable every individual to thrive. Robinson and Aronica (2015) highlight the importance of establishing personalised learning cultures in schools as a way of achieving *transformation* in education. In their book entitled *Creative Schools*, they state that:

> We are in a position as never before to use our creative and technological resources to transform rather than reform education. We now have limitless opportunities to engage young people's imaginations and to provide forms of teaching and learning that are highly customised to them.

John West-Burnham, in his article entitled 'Leadership for Personalised Learning' (2010), also describes the benefits of establishing a personalised learning culture, describing it as:

> A strategy focusing all of a school's resources to ensure that the potential of each learner is realised by ensuring that the learning experience is appropriate to them personally and that they are able, with support, to decide what they learn, how they learn, when they learn and who they learn with.

JONK creates a personalised learning culture by establishing a wealth of values-led and challenge-rich initiatives that accompany each of the six principal domains as depicted in Figure 1.2. At the heart of this personalised approach is the belief that all children have the ability, capacity and potential to succeed when the learning is personalised in terms of motivation, provision and support. This ethos of high expectations and aspirations for all makes it possible for every opportunity and every challenge to be offered to all, bypassing the need to base provision on predetermined judgements of individual ability.

The benefits of a *challenge-for-all*, non-ability grouping-based approach to teaching and learning have been evidenced particularly eloquently by the works of Deborah Eyre (1997, 2001, 2011, 2016) and the Creating Learning Without Limits Project (2012):

In the Policy Exchange paper entitled 'Room at the Top, Inclusive Education for High Performance' (2011), Eyre argues that:

> More pupils than we previously thought have the potential to perform at the highest levels – that is to achieve advanced levels of cognitive performance – and that the way to secure this is to create a system that expects significantly more from more pupils. The consequence of such an approach will be to raise the performance of the whole system, more surely than through any specific structural or pedagogical reform.

In *Curriculum Provision for the Gifted and Talented in Ordinary Schools* (2001), Eyre and McClure support a challenge-rich approach for all, commenting that:

> Where teachers have focused on planning to create challenge for the most able/ gifted pupils, they often then choose to make the task available to a wider group

of children… In pedagogical terms the challenging tasks require more 'expert behaviour' or 'higher order thinking' and lead to higher levels of attainment but are also intellectually stimulating and likely to be highly motivating regardless of a child's ability level.

The Creating Learning Without Limits Project (2012) grew from the work of the Learning Without Limits Project (2004) and was a collaboration between the University of Cambridge and the team from the Wroxham School in Hertfordshire. Their premise was very inspirational as they set out to explore:

> The wider opportunities for enhancing the learning capacity of every child that become possible when a whole staff group works together to create an environment free from the limiting effects of ability labels and practice.

The key findings of the Learning Without Limits and Creating Learning Without Limits Projects led to the publication of a series of books (Hart 2004; Swann, Peacock, Hart and Drummond 2012; Peacock 2016) which the reader is referred to as part of the suggested reading list that supports the pedagogical principles described throughout this book.

The *democratic* way of life and culture *for* learning that the JONK approach thus establishes allows all individuals to become 'co-participants', 'co-contributors', 'co-creators' and 'co-enactors' of the school's strategic thinking. The JONK democratic view of the child and of the school's social and learning matrix has parallels to the philosophy that inspires the Reggio Emilia approach. Lorio (2016) states that:

> The Reggio Emilia schools are part of a public system recognising the fundamental rights of the child and the welfare of children and families as well as valuing democracy and coparticipation of educators, children, teachers, and community.

The whole-school JONK ethos establishes a values-led culture *for* learning and acts as the precursor of *effective understanding* and of the ability to assimilate *new knowledge*. The way that the application of these concepts can be maximised as part of daily practice is the central theme that defines the ethos and work of Project Zero, an organisation founded in 1967 by the philosopher Nelson Goodman at the Harvard Graduate School of Education. Project Zero refers to the conglomerate of these concepts as 'teaching for understanding'. The JONK teaching and pedagogical Model of Excellence, Enrichment and Enjoyment (MEEE) has been designed to ensure that 'teaching for understanding' forms an integral part of every aspect of the teaching and learning process.

The research carried out by Project Zero educationalists postulates that learning and understanding are *consequences* of thinking. A visual representation of this hypothesis is offered to the reader through the JONK Model of Learning and Thinking, which illustrates how learning and understanding are indeed the consequence of thinking and are part of an interrelationship that encompasses thinking, learning, understanding, knowing and *not knowing*. The importance of thinking in the learning process is a feature that runs throughout this book, and the reader is provided with a variety of strategies that have been specifically designed as part of the JONK approach to nurture and develop children's creative, critical, analytical and philosophical thinking across every area of the curriculum.

The values-driven, thought-provoking and discussion-based nature of the JONK approach develops learners who are intrinsically motivated to *want* to learn. Intrinsically motivated cohorts of learners (students and practitioners) constitute the JONK currency that provides schools with their 'collective thinking, learning and societal capital'. JONK defines *intrinsically motivated capital* as what is achieved *in addition* to what anyone may have expected or imagined possible. In other words, JONK is based on the idea that intrinsically motivated learners will use the learning opportunities offered to them in a playful way and thus take the learning *beyond* the limits of its original intention.

The JONK Learning to Learn Week instils a deep sense of intrinsic motivation in all learners from the *outset* of each academic year by explicitly teaching children *how* to enjoy thinking beyond their comfort zone, embrace uncertainty and challenge and thrive as inquisitive and independent lifelong learners. The JONK Learning to Learn Week also establishes a classroom culture where the teacher is not perceived solely as the expert who imparts knowledge, but more as the expert who motivates and creates *the conditions* that inspire them to *want* to learn and to *keep* learning beyond the boundaries of what was set.

The importance of this *co-participant of learning* view of the adult and child is very well described by David Wood in his book *How Children Think and Learn* (1998), in which he states that:

> When we help a child to solve a problem, we are providing conditions in which he can begin to perceive regularities and structure in his experience. Left alone, the child is overcome by uncertainty and does not know what to attend to or what to do.

It is fascinating that in this quote, Wood refers to the dangers of being overcome by uncertainty. The whole of the JONK approach was developed to stop this from ever being the case for learners and the approach achieves it by *always* making the learner feel *comfortable* with uncertainty as they realise that uncertainty is not only a prerequisite of *new* learning but also something that they are equipped to overcome, even if sometimes we are in situations where uncertainty seems to be the only certainty ahead. Sacchs reinforces the importance of feeling comfortable with uncertainty in his book *Unsafe Thinking* (2018), where he states that 'teaching ourselves to be comfortable with a bit of discomfort gives us a far better chance of changing habitual patterns and opening space for new possibilities'.

📖 SUGGESTED READING

It is very interesting, when considering each of the elements and principles that make up the JONK approach to education and school infrastructure, to cross-reference these to the research findings that accompany the all-encompassing Cambridge Primary Review (2010) and that were published in the book *Children, their World, their Education: Final Report and Recommendations of the Cambridge Review*.

This book uses the terms *students*, *pupils* and *children* interchangeably as all the ideas presented can be adapted to any age group. The same can be said for the use of *teacher* and *practitioner*; the intention is that all adults feel able to consider and apply each of the concepts within their own role.

The chapters are structured to include, at regular intervals, opportunities for reflection, dialogue, research and growth in the form of points for discussion, illustrative case studies and ideas for further reading.

 DISCUSSION OPPORTUNITIES

 CASE STUDIES

 SUGGESTED READING

Following this Introduction, Chapter 2 launches the book by introducing the principles and philosophies that underpin the JONK approach and offers a guide to how the JONK philosophy can be introduced to the class in a way that often transforms their perception of education, school and learning and of themselves as individuals. The chapter offers a series of JONK models that focus on the different stages of the learning process and on how children can use their metacognitive thinking skills to move from one stage to the next. The chapter also considers ways in which the concepts of thinking, learning, knowing and *not* knowing can be discussed with the class and ends by offering a model that encompasses the interrelationship of these four concepts as part of the overall process of learning.

Chapter 3 introduces the concept of schools as microcosms of society and demonstrates how a values-led approach to education helps schools to create whole-school cultures *for* learning which enables the community to appreciate the value of school and education and to live convivially whilst learning and thriving emotionally, socially and intellectually. The chapter describes the constituents that make up the JONK school culture for learning, which are represented by whole-school sets of values, children's rights, lifelong learning dispositions, global sustainability and community links. The chapter describes how the principle of the JONK Headteacher Challenge approach allows each of these characteristics to be sourced as sets of words for the school by engaging the whole school community in a process of democratic change.

Chapter 4 introduces the concept of 'the eight areas of influence' which make up the teaching, pedagogical and leadership JONK Model of Excellence, Enrichment and

Enjoyment (MEEE). Three different versions of the model are described for use by teachers, headteachers and pupils. All three MEEE models have been developed by using the principles that research and experience have shown to have the greatest impact on children's learning: *previewing, motivating, modelling, engaging, encouraging, challenge, feedback* and *metacognition*. The chapter illustrates how each of these areas can enrich and support the teaching and learning experience for all students, nurture the professional expertise of all staff and help to encompass, from a leadership perspective, every aspect of school life and help to establish a whole-school, intellectually playful, action research–driven, risk-taking, collaborative infrastructure. The chapter also introduces the concept that *all* staff are *experts* in their field and active participants in the school's *multi-professional teams* that drive each of the priorities of the school's development plan. Also introduced in this chapter is the concept of pupils as *learning leaders*, who are elected representatives from each class that work alongside the school's senior leadership team, providing student voice to the strategic decision making of the process. The chapter illustrates how the learning leaders contribute to school development by interpreting the school's development plan and creating their own *pupil version* of the plan.

Chapter 5 is dedicated to the principle that underpins the idea of schools launching each academic year with a bespoke JONK Learning to Learn Week (LTLW). The chapter explains how the LTLW can be established so as to be able to *explicitly teach* children *how* to succeed as individuals and learners and *how* to equip them with all the tools, strategies and dispositions that they need to succeed – emotionally, socially and academically. The chapter describes the principles and methodologies that enable schools to incorporate a personalised LTLW as part of their yearly cycle and introduces the five central themes that define the LTLW: models of learning, creative and critical thinking, visible thinking and learning, philosophy and a philosophical approach to the curriculum, and the lifelong learning dispositions. Although the LTLW principle was developed as a tool for schools, it can be equally valuable to adopt in higher and further education or within any establishment that has learning at the heart of its ethos.

Chapter 6 acts as the *practical backbone* of the JONK approach. It provides a comprehensive detailed and practical guide to how to introduce the class to each of the initiatives that make up each of the days and themes of the LTLW. The chapter begins with an invitation for teachers to start the LTLW and the academic year by engaging their class in a discussion about the meaning and purpose of education, which the chapter suggests can be driven by making a number of fascinating comparisons between the worlds of education and architecture. This conversation is followed by an exercise that makes it possible for the teacher and students to design their classroom in a way that maximises engagement in learning for everyone. Using an active learning approach, the students are then introduced to the principles and philosophies of the JONK approach demonstrating the value of feeling at ease with not knowing and ensuring that every child feels they are an *expert of learning*. The chapter then considers possible activities for each day of the LTLW, accompanied by a number of case studies that illustrate the versatility and impact of these initiatives in practice. The chapter concludes with ideas for reflecting on all aspects introduced during the LTLW and with the facility for every practitioner to be able to plan, design and incorporate a personalised LTLW as part of their yearly routine.

📖 SUGGESTED READING

Chapters 5 and 6 act as particularly useful reference points for *student teachers, newly qualified teachers and early career teachers.* These chapters contain a wealth of practical and easy-to-implement ideas that establish a motivational, challenging and inspirational learning environment in the classroom. The chapter entitled 'Gifted and Talented' (Eyre and Staricoff, 2014) in *Learning to Teach in the Primary School* (Cremin and Arthur, 2014) provides a very interesting guide that explains how each of the principles is introduced as part of the Learning to Learn Week and how they become incorporated as part of the daily teaching and learning routine of the classroom.

The book continues by dedicating chapters to discussing in detail the main principles introduced during the LTLW. The open-ended 'Thinking Skills Starters' take centre stage in Chapter 7. This chapter shows how the concept of the Thinking Skills Starters can have such a transformational impact on children's motivation, creative thinking and *perception of education and school.* The chapter describes how the daily routine that the Starters promote can be used to enrich all aspects of the curriculum, and through the idea of 'Thinking in Playgrounds', the same concept can be used to help the whole family enjoy *thinking together* before and after school.

In Chapter 8, the reader is introduced to the wonders of philosophy and to how a philosophical approach to teaching and learning across the curriculum nurtures and develops every student's natural inquisitiveness and thirst for discovery and knowledge. The chapter illustrates how philosophy can be used as an integral part of the daily routine to create learning environments that function as *collaborative communities of enquiry* and that foster a very special freedom to think critically, creatively and philosophically. The chapter introduces the reader to the transformational impact that presenting the learning objective as a *JONK philosophical question* has on children's engagement, imagination, curiosity and motivation and to how philosophical dialogue and debate in the classroom can enrich every lesson and play a key role in students' engagement and motivation. The chapter also describes how philosophy can be integrated as a subject and as part of the weekly timetable as a means of promoting questioning, creative and critical thinking, and debating skills and as a tool with which to reduce the *word gap* that children may encounter at school and which represents one of the principal determinants of children's life chances. The chapter also introduces the principle of electing pupils as Philosophy Leaders and discusses how these pupils contribute to the whole-school approach to philosophy at school.

Chapter 9 introduces the principles that underpin lifelong learning in schools and how schools are able to equip all students as effective lifelong learners by incorporating a set of *bespoke* lifelong learning dispositions. The reader is introduced to the findings of the Effective Lifelong Learning Inventory Research Project (ELLI, 2006), which established seven key dispositions common to effective lifelong learners: changing and learning, learning relationships, strategic awareness, resilience, creativity, curiosity and meaning making. The chapter describes how schools are able to acquire their own set of dispositions and how, through a process of action research, the dispositions can come alive and be adapted to inspire children of all ages across the school. The chapter offers a wide range of ideas to apply the dispositions as part of the daily routine, including their use as the basis of whole-class interactive displays and evaluation, metacognitive, and problem-solving tools and as a tool to support transition within school and to other schools.

The importance of maintaining learner motivation beyond the school day and building a strong child–school–family triangular partnership is the focus of Chapter 10. The chapter uses children's worked examples to demonstrate how the JONK open-ended, creative thinking skills approach can be applied to the setting of enjoyable, creative, challenging and thought-provoking home learning tasks to support and enrich all areas of the curriculum and to foster very special moments of the whole family's engagement in learning at home and engagement with the school.

The book concludes by introducing the reader to a concept that has become known as the JONK Bilingual and Multilingual Thinking (BMT) approach in *multicultural classrooms*. The chapter describes how a BMT approach to teaching and learning enables all students to benefit cognitively and socially from learning in a multilingual and multicultural environment that embraces the rich cultural heritage of every individual. The chapter describes how in Spanish the 'Joy of Not Knowing' approach has become known as '*El Placer de No Saber*', and the book concludes by illustrating how when a seven-year-old child in Spain was introduced to the JONK Model of Learning he created his own interpretation and called it his 'pit of happiness', illustrating so wonderfully the aim of the JONK approach: to consider the process of learning and of not knowing as something that is exciting and joyous!

2

Learning and the importance of developing a *joy* for *not* knowing

It is because we are able to enjoy and thrive when in a position of not knowing that we develop the mechanisms for being able to learn

Marcelo Staricoff

Not knowing is an integral and necessary *prerequisite* of learning. The JONK methodology described in this chapter introduces the concept that in order to learn something new, we must not know it first, and explains with the aid of a series of models how sharing this idea explicitly with children removes the anxiety that is usually triggered by feeling that we don't know. They then realise that it is *only because* we find ourselves in a position of *not* knowing that we have the *opportunity to* learn. The anxiety of *not* knowing is thus replaced by an enthusiasm for *wanting* to know.

Introducing the children to a *joy* of *not* knowing from an early age has a transformational impact on the way they are able to respond to, and then thrive in, situations when they feel uncertain, when they don't know, when they find things difficult, when they are faced with unfamiliar concepts and when they find themselves in a position that they perceive to be outside of their 'comfort zone'.

This teacher–pupil conversation illustrates how realising that we *don't* know is such a key component of helping us to learn and of making us *want* to learn.

'When we were just having a whole-class discussion and I was asking you some questions and you all knew the answers, how did you feel?'

The children very often say:

'It felt really good, we were really pleased we knew all the answers.'

The children are then challenged to think a little bit more deeply about this:

'Great, I am really glad you were pleased and felt really good, but can I ask you something: if you already knew the answers to all my questions, *were you actually learning anything new?*'

'No, we don't think we did learn anything new, as we already knew it' is a very common deduction that the children make.

This very simple realisation, which is the essence of the JONK approach, makes it possible for children to start to think about learning from a completely different perspective. It is not long before they start to *really* realise that in order to learn something new 'they must *not* know it first'. This represents the beginning of something very special: removing preconceived ideas, personal barriers and worries and replacing them with a lifelong love *for* learning, thinking and knowing.

The principles, theories, concepts and methodologies that underpin the JONK approach *and that make possible a joy of not knowing to act as the principal driver of the learning, thinking, knowing and teaching processes* are encapsulated within a series of models, which are described below and which can all be used as explanatory and motivational tools in the classroom.

The JONK Models of Learning described in the sections below introduce the reader to one JONK principle at a time. As a collective, the series of models allow:

- *the learner to navigate successfully* through each step of the learning process
- *the school to ensure that everything is in place* to enable the learner to navigate through each step of the learning process

The JONK Model of Learning (JMOL)

Using a model to illustrate the value of not knowing as a catalyst for wanting to know

In the JONK Model of Learning, the learner is presented with two choices. If the learner knows the answer to what has been proposed, they are allowed to jump across the Pit, moving from position 1 to 3 in Figure 2.1. However, if they don't know the answer or are uncertain or confused, they first of all enter the Pit, moving from position 1 to 2 in Figure 2.1, and when they have solved the problem and worked things out, they can climb out of the Pit, moving from position 2 to 3 in Figure 2.1:

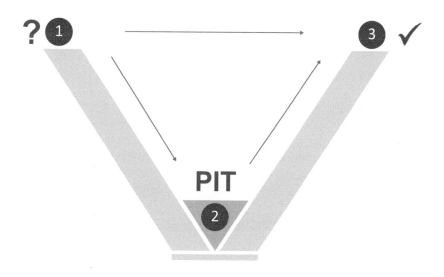

FIGURE 2.1 The JONK Model of Learning (JMOL)

The significance of these three positions

Position 1

The learner always starts on the upper left-hand side of the 'JMOL Pit', designated in the diagram by the question mark. The question mark is usually associated with the learning objective but actually refers to any problem we have to solve in life. If the learner knows the answer to the question, they are allowed to *jump* across the JMOL Pit, moving from position 1 to 3 in the diagram. However, if the learner *doesn't* know the answer or is uncertain, they go into the Pit, moving from position 1 to 2.

Position 2

In the JMOL Pit, the learner is reassured that the school equips them with all they need to succeed. This position is where the learning takes place, where the learner tries to work things out, ask questions, work with others, decide on what resources to use, choose from a variety of strategies, try again if needed, and take their time. Once the children reach a solution, they are able to climb out of the Pit, following the path indicated by position 2 to 3 in the diagram.

Position 3

This position represents a very interesting part of the model as it is the end point both for the learner who knew to start with and therefore was able to jump across the JMOL Pit as well as for the learner who didn't know to start with and therefore took the in-and-out route of the JMOL Pit. It is very interesting to discuss that although each route starts and finishes in the same place, the learners reach position 3 with a very significant difference. The learner who jumped across has reached position 3 without acquiring any new knowledge or learnt anything new, whereas the learner who went in and out of the JMOL Pit has reached this same position as a result of having acquired new knowledge and learnt something new. In other words, the only way to learn is to *not* know it first.

Analysing and discussing these three stages of the JMOL with the class help to crystallise the value that *not* knowing brings to the learning process and can also evoke some extraordinary creative thinking. A Year 4 child once challenged the idea that jumping across the JMOL Pit means that you are not learning anything new:

'Actually, I did learn something new when I jumped across the Pit', he said.

This was a very intriguing thought. How could he have learnt something if he already knew it?

He went on to elaborate his thinking very eloquently:

'Well', he said, 'it's very simple, what I learnt is that I already knew it!'

This thinking shows the value of discussing learning so openly and so explicitly with the class. The JMOL Pit discussion prompted the child to think very deeply and to become self-aware of *knowing* what he knew. In other words, he was thinking *metacognitively* – a skill that, when acquired, helps the learner to succeed at every stage of their learning process. These concepts are developed further as part of the JONK Model of Metacognition described later on in this chapter.

The JONK Model of Learning at School (JMOLS)

The infrastructure that helps the learner to move from a position of not knowing to one of knowing

Once the learner realises that in order to learn something new they have to enter rather than jump across the 'JMOL Pit' process, it is important to reassure them that the *school's pedagogical infrastructure* provides them with all they need to be able to succeed and to climb out of the Pit, as shown in Figure 2.2:

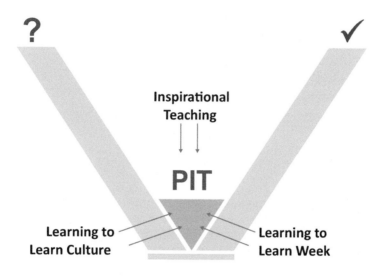

FIGURE 2.2 The JONK Model of Learning at School (JMOLS)

The Learning to Learn Culture

This refers to all that the school has in place in order for learners to be able to learn and succeed as individuals: the ethos and values that lead to establishing a classroom learning environment where all students are able to thrive. Developing a JONK Culture *for* Learning is the focus of Chapter 3.

Inspirational Teaching

This refers to the school's approach to the teaching and learning process that at all times enables learners to feel enthusiastic, motivated and inspired to *want* to learn. This is discussed in Chapter 4 as part of the teaching JONK Model of Excellence, Enrichment and Enjoyment.

The JONK Learning to Learn Week

This refers to the concept of devoting a week at the beginning of the academic year to teaching the children *how* to learn and equipping them with all the tools, skills and dispositions that will help them to access the curriculum and thrive as successful lifelong learners and creative, critical and philosophical thinkers. The principles and strategies that underpin the JONK Learning to Learn Week are the focus of Chapters 5 and 6.

The JONK Model *for* Personalised Learning (JMOPL)

Every learner is able to access their learning at their own pace

The JMOL caters to *all learners* at *all times*. In order to communicate this concept to the students, it is useful to imagine the JMOL Pit as a swimming pool, as shown in Figure 2.3:

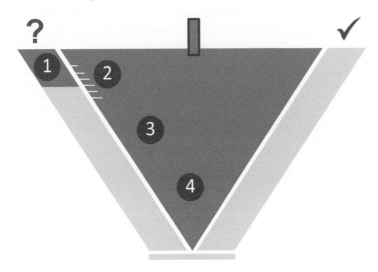

FIGURE 2.3 The JONK Model *for* Personalised Learning (JMOPL)

Position 1

In this situation, the learner is keen and enthusiastic to *want* to learn, but after the learning objective has been introduced, they feel that they need a little bit of support. This means that they can spend a little bit of time in the JMOL 'paddling pool' before entering the main pool. Chapter 5 describes how the metaphor of the 'paddling pool' becomes an integral part of the classroom layout.

Position 2

In this situation, the learner is confident to access their learning independently. However, they may be feeling a little bit cautious or slightly confused. These learners use the steps to enter the swimming pool, taking one step at a time, 'dipping their toes in', testing the temperature of the water, and gradually entering fully.

Position 3

In this situation, the learner is feeling confident, is familiar with the subject matter, and is able to work through their learning independently and successfully. These learners choose to jump into the swimming pool with great enthusiasm.

Position 4

In this situation, the learner is feeling *very* confident. They feel familiar with the subject matter and they know that they have a *range of strategies* to use to succeed with their learning. These learners jump from the diving board and into the pool.

The JONK Model of Learning *how* to Learn (JMOLL)

The six stages of learning that enable the learner to learn effectively

The learner up until now has developed an appreciation of the importance of developing a joy of *not* knowing and has been given the reassurance that they will be equipped with all they need to succeed and that they are able to launch into the learning process *at their own pace*.

This next stage of the JMOL process introduces the learner to the *six principal stages* that learners find themselves in when learning. The JMOLL also discusses the provision that the school makes at each of these stages to ensure that all learners are able to move successfully along the continuum that starts with *not knowing* and ends with *knowing*. These six stages are illustrated in Figure 2.4:

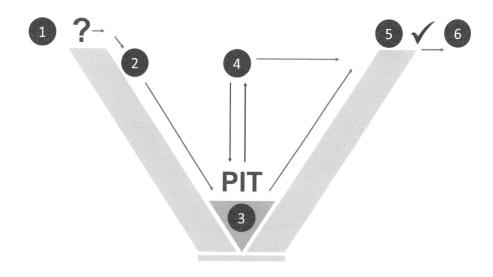

FIGURE 2.4 The JONK Model of Learning *how* to Learn (JMOLL)

Position 1

In this position, the learner feels *ready* to learn. At this position, the learner feels excited and *emotionally* able to engage in the learning process. This is where the school provides a welcoming atmosphere, an inspirational environment *for* learning and a means of supporting all learners socially, emotionally and academically.

Position 2

In this position, the learner feels *motivated to want to learn* as they perceive personal worth in engaging with the learning.

Position 3

In this position, the learner feels *intellectually motivated and challenged whilst they are learning*. The learner feels equipped with a toolkit that allows them to succeed.

Position 4

The learner accesses this position at regular intervals from position 3 to *reflect* on their learning progress and decide whether they can leave the Pit or whether they need to stay in a little bit longer.

Position 5

In this position, the learner has *succeeded* and climbed out of the JMOL Pit. This is where the learner is offered opportunities for intellectual challenge, extension and enrichment.

Position 6

This final stage of the process helps the learner to give *meaning* to what they have learnt and to investigate *how to apply* their new learning. This position also promotes the curiosity that leads to further questions and to the cycle starting again.

The JONK Model of Learning and Metacognition (JMOLM)

Metacognitive thinking enables the learner to move successfully across each of the six stages of learning

Once the learner becomes familiar with each of the six stages that make up the JMOL process, it is fundamental to introduce them to a range of *metacognitive thinking* strategies that will encourage *them to think metacognitively at each of these six stages so as to be able to decide* whether they are ready and able to progress from stage to stage, as represented by positions 1 to 6 in Figure 2.5. The play of words that this process introduces them to makes these particular considerations of *how* we learn very amusing and very memorable.

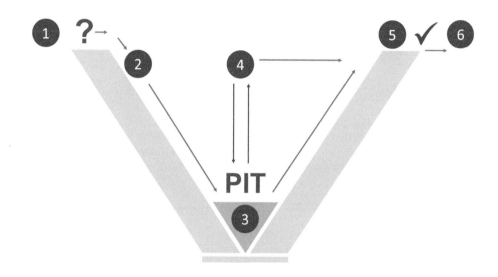

FIGURE 2.5 The JONK Model of Learning and Metacognition (JMOLM)

Position 1

In this position, the metacognitive learner considers the subject matter and reflects upon 'what they *know* they *know*' and very importantly also on 'what they *know that they don't know*'.

Position 2

In this position, the metacognitive learner considers whether they *want to know* what they know they don't know or whether, on this occasion, they may be *not interested* in knowing what they *know* they don't know.

Position 3

In this position, the metacognitive learner considers whether '*they now know how* to *know* what they want to know that they know they don't know' or whether they '*don't know how to know* what they want to know, that they know they don't know'.

Position 4

In this position, the metacognitive learner reflects on whether they now know what they wanted to know *well enough* or whether they need to *keep going* with getting to know what they *want* to know that they know they still don't know well enough.

Position 5

In this position, the metacognitive learner considers whether they have *mastered and can give meaning to what they now know* that they knew how to know when wanting to know it after realising that at the start they did not know it or whether they still need to explore and understand the concepts in greater depth.

Position 6

In this final position, the metacognitive learner considers whether they now know *how to use and apply* the new knowledge that they have acquired as a result of knowing how to know what they wanted to know that they knew they didn't know or whether they know that they have reached a solution but are not sure of how to give meaning to this new knowledge and develop the ability to apply it effectively in practice.

The JONK Model of Learning and Knowing (JMOLK)

Knowing is also important

Up until this point, the JONK MOL has been used to describe the importance of *not* knowing as part of the learning process. It is very interesting to use the model to discuss the *importance* of *knowing* and of sometimes being able to jump across the JMOL Pit, as depicted in Figure 2.6:

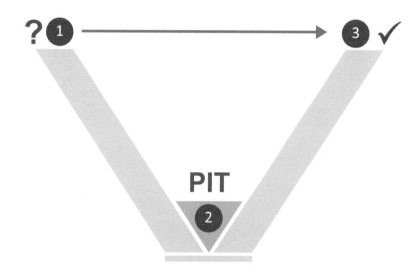

FIGURE 2.6 The JONK Model of Learning and Knowing (JMOLK)

The importance of knowing can be illustrated with the scenario of a broken arm that necessitates a visit to the local Accident and Emergency Department. The question is, which of the following scenarios is more desirable when the patient arrives and is greeted by the medical team?

a   'Welcome to our A&E Department and so sorry to see that you've broken your arm. Please don't worry. We all love not knowing in this hospital, we have no idea how to fix your arm, but we are really good at finding out, asking questions, trying things out. I am sure we will get there in the end if we all work collaboratively.'

b   'Welcome to our A&E Department and so sorry to see that you've broken your arm. Please don't worry, you are in the hands of experts who know exactly what to do, who have done thousands of these procedures before and who always make sure that the patient doesn't feel any pain at all.'

The JONK Model of Learning, Thinking and Knowing (JMOLTK)

Linking thinking, learning, knowing and not knowing

So far, the JONK MOL has offered us a number of ways of conceptualising the process of learning from the perspectives of knowing, *not* knowing and metacognitive thinking. It is very interesting to explore each of these concepts individually and to try to co-construct a definition for each with the class:

- What is thinking?
- What is learning?
- What is knowing?
- What is not knowing?

The collective thoughts, ideas and definitions make for a fabulous permanent display (in the classroom) that can be added to as the year progresses and as the students deepen their understanding of each of these terms.

 SUGGESTED READING

The discussion of these four principles provides the reader with a fabulous opportunity to delve into the work of Graham Nuthall and his very insightful book entitled *The Hidden Lives of Learners* (2007). It is so interesting that Nuthall postulates that '*students already know 40 to 50 percent of what the teacher is going to teach them, but this prior knowledge differs dramatically from one student to the next*'.

 DISCUSSION OPPORTUNITIES

Considering each of these four concepts in detail provides teachers with the oxpportunity to set the class a very interesting challenge:
Can the children think how *thinking, learning, knowing* and *not knowing* are inter-linked? Can they develop a model that connects all four of these concepts?

The JONK MOL can be divided into five zones to illustrate the inter-relationship between thinking, learning, knowing and not knowing, as shown in Figure 2.7:

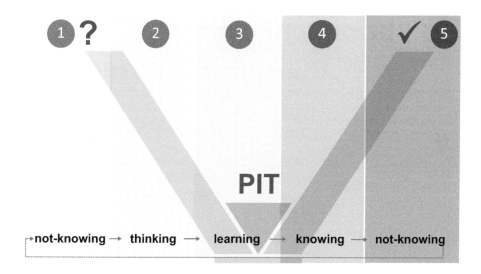

FIGURE 2.7 The JONK Model of Learning, Thinking and Knowing (JMOLTK)

In realising that we *don't know* (Zone 1), we have to *think* (Zone 2) about how we start the process of *getting to* know it. This is when we do our *learning* (Zone 3) which allows us to then *know* it (Zone 4). In *knowing* something new, our curiosity leads us to want to know more, something that we now know we *don't know* (Zone 5) and the cycle starts again.

In other words, as a child in Year 2 once said when we were discussing the inter-relationships between learning, thinking and knowing, '*thinking seems to be the opposite of knowing and learning is what takes us from one end to the other*'.

3

Developing a whole-school JONK culture *for* learning

Values in schools give value to school
Marcelo Staricoff

Schools are *microcosms* of society, existing within it and equipping children with all they need to contribute to it productively. Societies, defined by their sets of values, help to instil in all its members a sense of belonging and a common understanding of how to *be* and how to function within it, so that every member is able to contribute to its moral, social, educational, cultural and global capital for now and for successive generations.

Microcosms act as 'communities, places or situations that encapsulate in miniature the characteristics of something much larger'. The philosophy that underpins all aspects of the JONK approach enables schools to mimic and encapsulate in miniature the convivial and multicultural nature of society by establishing a values-led *way of life* and approach to education.

This chapter describes how this *values-led* approach creates a whole–school *culture for learning* which acts as the predominant factor that allows every individual within the school community to appreciate the *value* of school and education and to live convivially whilst learning and thriving emotionally, socially and intellectually.

The JONK approach identifies six key areas of influence which collectively make up the school's culture *for* learning (Figure 3.1).

FIGURE 3.1 The Six Key Areas of Influence of the JONK School Culture *for* Learning

This chapter introduces the reader to the importance for *each* of these six areas to be associated with its *own distinct set of words* as *each* area defines and refers to a *different* way of *being* as part of the school's overall culture *for* learning (Figure 3.2):

FIGURE 3.2 The Six Ways of *Being* as part of the JONK School Culture *for* Learning

The sections that follow illustrate how the JONK approach helps each school to acquire a unique set of *six* words that become associated with each of the six areas of influence and build the school's culture *for* learning. As a guide and reference point for discussion, Figure 3.3 includes examples of the type of terminology that schools use within each of the six areas:

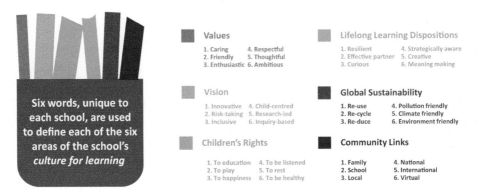

FIGURE 3.3 Exemplar Sets of Words that Define the JONK School Culture *for* Learning

In preparation for generating each set of words, it is very interesting to derive, as a whole school, a *consensus* of the *function that each set of words* will fulfil for each area in the context of each school's ethos and philosophy of education (Figure 3.4):

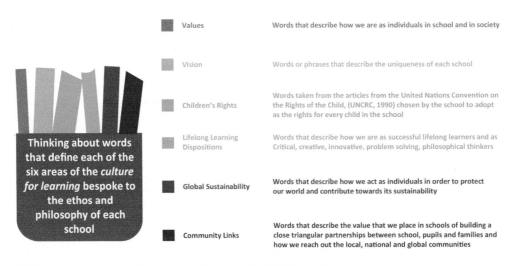

FIGURE 3.4 Defining the Six Key Areas of Influence of the JONK School Culture *for* Learning

The conglomerate of the words that become associated with each of the six areas of influence creates the culture for learning that acts as the school's *circulatory system that flows through every aspect of school life and nourishes it with all it needs*.

Schools, like 'living organisms', rely on a set of well-established and co-ordinated systems, each one carrying out a specific function that contributes to the well-being of the whole. The cells that make up each of the systems within a living organism obtain all they need to function from the constituent elements that make up its *circulatory system* which flows through the whole organism: plasma, red blood cells, lymphocytes, platelets, etc. Likewise, learners in JONK schools obtain all *they* need from the constituent elements that make up the school's *culture for learning* which flows through *every aspect of school life* (Figure 3.5):

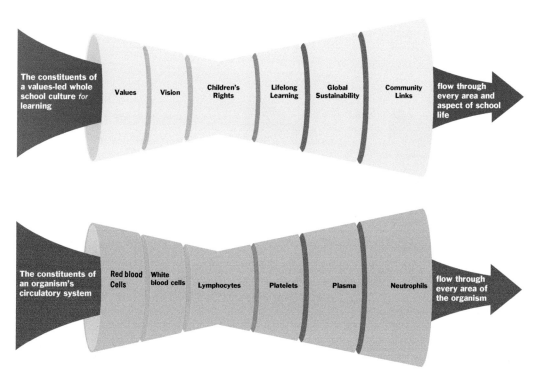

FIGURE 3.5 The Circulatory System of Schools and of Organisms

 DISCUSSION OPPORTUNITIES

An interesting exercise at this point for staff and pupils is to extend this analogy and come up with other examples of how a school is like a living organism. For example:

■ Could pupils' *intrinsic motivation* be the *heart* that pumps the school's culture *for* learning to all areas of school life?

■ Could the *pupils, staff, governors and families* be the *brain cells* that enable schools to evolve, create, adapt and innovate?

■ Could the *inspirational, creative and thought-provoking curriculum provision* be the *healthy diet* that provides every individual with all the nutrients they need to thrive?

■ Could the *classroom learning environment* be the *digestive system* that helps all the goodness from the *curricular diet* to be *absorbed*?

It is also very interesting to note that the six areas of influence themselves are intricately connected to and dependent on each other. Figure 3.6 demonstrates how the acquisition of a set of *values* allows the school's *vision* to become a reality. When the school's vision becomes a reality, every child can have their *rights* met. Once the children's *rights* are met, the conditions *for learning* are established, nurturing every individual as an *effective lifelong learner*. Being equipped as an effective lifelong learner instils a social, emotional and academic awareness that lets every individual contribute positively towards a more sustainable world as empathetic members of their local, national and international communities:

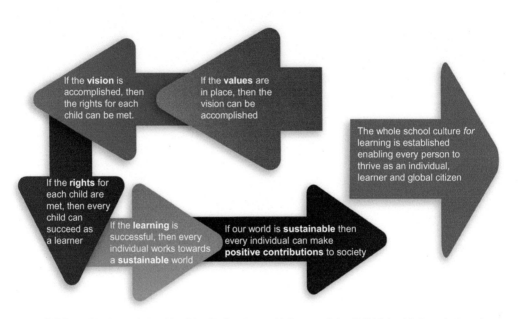

FIGURE 3.6 The Interrelationship of the Six Key Areas of Influence of the JONK School Culture *for* Learning

It is envisaged that the six areas are introduced *one area at a time* and as an integral part of the school's long-term strategic vision and goals. This process is illustrated by the example that led to the model shown in Figure 3.7. The school launched this gradual strategic process by first of all revisiting its *motto*, which was adapted from *I Can* to *I Can…We Can*. The sentiment of *togetherness* that emerged from this change paved the way for the introduction of a set of whole-school values, which in turn led to a set of principles for global sustainability, the philosophy underpinning Early Years pedagogy, the introduction of the lifelong learning dispositions and the creation of a varied team-working structure within the school and of links with the community.

This *sequential* and gradual building of the school's culture *for* learning, incorporating '*One New Initiative On aNother*', became known as the 'JONK *Onion* Model of School Leadership *for* Change (Staricoff, 2013):

FIGURE 3.7 The JONK Onion Model of School Leadership for Change

 DISCUSSION OPPORTUNITIES

Are you able to find reference to all six areas of influence within the layers of the Onion Model in Figure 3.7?

This gradual building of the school's culture *for* learning as part of the school's five-year strategic plan helped all pupils, staff and members of the school community to feel:

■ Valued as unique individuals and as experts of learning and of their own fields with so much to contribute for the benefit of all

■ Equipped emotionally, socially and academically to succeed in all aspects of life at school and beyond

■ Intrinsically motivated to *want* to learn and enthusiastic to *want* to know

■ Encouraged to take risks, experiment with their thinking and challenge themselves beyond what they imagine possible

■ A sense of purpose, co-existence and the ability to make meaningful connections that facilitates new learning to build on what they already know

■ That the school is not only a welcoming microcosm of society but also a microcosm *of their lives.*

 SUGGESTED READING

The school's culture for learning was the basis of a case study and action research project included within the book entitled *The EYFS: Assessing and Supporting Young Children's Learning* (Hutchin, 2012).

 DISCUSSION OPPORTUNITIES

At this point, it would be very interesting to discuss the potential *value* that a v*alues-led* approach to education brings to the school:

■ A values-led approach makes it possible for children to develop a seamless perception of their time at and outside of school.

■ A values-led culture communicates to everyone the *value* of being at school and of education from an early age.

■ A values-led approach equips all individuals with the dispositions and characteristics that enable them to succeed as constituent members of their families and their school, local, national and global communities.

The JONK Headteacher Challenge (JHC)

Acquiring and incorporating a set of words for each of the six key areas of influence of the JONK Culture for Learning

This section describes how the *JONK Headteacher Challenge* approach helps schools to acquire a bespoke set of words for each of the six key areas of influence of the school's culture for learning by engaging the participation of the whole school community in a series of *democratic* idea-generating and decision-making steps. The JONK Headteacher Challenge process can be used to introduce *any* initiative that will lead to whole-school change and that benefits from the involvement of the whole school community in the process of change. This process enables every member of the school community to:

1   Have a detailed understanding of what the school is trying to achieve

2   Have a conceptual understanding of how the new initiative builds on the school's existing ethos and infrastructure and the benefits that it will bring to every individual

3   Feel included and valued as part of a voluntary process

4   Feel free to submit and present thoughts and ideas in any way at all

5   Have the ability to discuss the new initiative that the school is planning with colleagues at school and as a family at home

6   Look forward to exercising their democratic vote as part of the final stage of the JHC process

Each JONK Headteacher Challenge process follows a generic step-by-step sequence, which is described below. The section that follows this generic description of events allows the reader to adapt the process for each of the six areas that make up the school's culture for learning.

Chapter 9 offers the reader a detailed exemplification of how to apply this process in practice using the lifelong learning dispositions as an example. The JONK Headteacher Challenge approach introduces the reader to the concept of the JONK Learning Leaders, who are elected representatives from each class and work with members of the senior leadership team on a variety of aspects related to school improvement and pupil-led whole-school initiatives. Examples of how the Learning Leaders engage in these roles are provided in Chapter 4 (developing pupil versions of the school development plan and model for teaching and learning) and Chapter 9 (acquiring a set of lifelong learning dispositions for the school).

The JONK Headteacher Challenge generic step-by-step process for enabling the introduction of change

STEP 1

The school decides that it wishes to introduce a new whole-school initiative, build on an existing characteristic or introduce an area as part of its ethos and culture for learning.

STEP 2

A JHC is designed in a way that helps the school to seek the thoughts, views and ideas from the whole school community as the process is launched.

STEP 3

The JHC is presented as an open-ended challenge for all to engage in on a voluntary basis, and the timescale for submitting contributions is set. This is usually set for a period of three or four weeks.

STEP 4

The contributions received by the school are grouped into six common 'themes', each group eventually contributing to one of the words that concludes the process. This 'grouping process' is ideally performed by the Learning Leaders but could also be an interesting exercise for staff and governors.

STEP 5

Once all the contributions have been grouped into main themes, the Learning Leaders choose the two or three words that they feel best represent all the contributions in that group. The final list of words chosen at this stage will represent the list that the community use to vote.

STEP 6

This is the step where the process takes on a very exciting dimension as the school starts to prepare for its own *General Election*. The final list of words is placed on a *ballot paper*, designed to mimic a real ballot paper as closely as possible.

STEP 7

Once the ballot papers have been produced, the school is ready to hold its *General Election*, which requires a number of considerations at the planning stage:

1   All stakeholders are notified of the General Election by sending home with each child a *Polling Card* that mimics a real polling card as closely as possible and that

contains all the information needed to enable everyone to vote, such as date, place, time and instructions of how to vote remotely if the person cannot get to school (email, website, text, etc.).

2   It is a great idea to extend the opportunity to vote as widely as possible to relatives (home or abroad), local authority representatives, local community, or anyone you think would welcome the opportunity to contribute.

3   In trying to mimic the democratic voting process as closely as possible, it is a great idea to source ballot boxes and convert a room in the school into the voting area with voting booths and volunteer returning officers. (This is a great role for governors and Learning Leaders.)

4   Though not always possible, if the school General Election can be timed to coincide with a Local Election or a real General Election, then the school election gains enormous value as the pupils will be experiencing at school exactly the same process that they will see their families experiencing when they accompany them to vote in the local or national elections.

STEP 8

The day of the 'General Election' becomes a very memorable day for all involved:

1   In order to maximise the opportunity for everyone to vote, arrange for the school to be open for voting from 7 am to 7 pm if at all possible.

2   On the day of the General Election, it is a good idea to have a book for comments. It is wonderful to hear and keep on record how much it means to certain families that they are able to vote with their children, including siblings who may not be at the school yet and those who have already left and are returning for the day.

STEP 9

Once the 'General Election' has been completed:

1   The ballot boxes are handed over to the Learning Leaders or a class (or classes) nominated to count the votes.

2   The counting of the votes can be a very interesting logistical and mathematical process for the school to undertake, especially if different classes are counting and needing to pool the results.

STEP 10

Once all the votes have been counted and ranked in order, the school is ready to announce the six words with the most votes, which become adopted by the school for that particular area of the school's culture *for* learning.

STEP 11

The resulting words that become associated with each area are incorporated into all aspects of school life.

The generic process described above for the JONK Headteacher Challenge process can be adapted for each of the six areas that make up the culture for learning, whilst taking into account the individual characteristics of each one. Tables 3.1 to 3.6 below are designed to offer schools the step-by-step process that generates a *distinct* set of words for each of the six areas.

Values	
Definition	These are specific words associated with how we are as individuals
Headteacher Challenge	Seek views of what all stakeholders would like these words to be for your school.
Analyse results	Group all the ideas submitted into 'common themes'.
Create ballot paper	Select 12 suggestions that are representative of all the themes generated to go on a ballot paper.
Hold General Election	The six words with the most votes following the election become adopted as the school values.

Vision	
Definition	These are specific words or phrases that define what the school believes in and aims for as a philosophy of education for the school
Headteacher Challenge	Seek views of what your stakeholders would like these words to be for your school.
Analyse results	Group all the ideas submitted into 'common themes'.
Create ballot paper	Select 12 suggestions that are representative of all the themes generated to go on a ballot paper.
Hold General Election	The six words with the most votes following the election become adopted within the school's vision statement.

Children's Rights	
Definition	These are the defined statements contained within the United Nations Children's Rights Respecting Charter
Headteacher Challenge	Seek views from all your stakeholders of which of these statements they feel are most important to uphold at your school.
Analyse results	List all the statements suggested in numerical order.
Create ballot paper	Place all of the suggestions received on a ballot paper.
Hold General Election	The six statements with the most votes following the election become adopted as the school's specific set of Children's Rights.
Responsibilities	For each right selected, generate the different responsibilities for the students and the staff to ensure that each right can be met at your school.

Lifelong Learning Dispositions	
Definition	**These are specific words associated with how we are as effective learners**
Headteacher Challenge 1	Seek views from all your stakeholders of what they think makes a successful lifelong learner by setting the HTC entitled 'A Recipe for a Lifelong Learner'.
Analyse results	Group all the ideas included within the 'Ingredients of the HTC' into six main themes.
Create ballot paper	Select 12 suggestions, two from each theme, and place these on a ballot paper.
Hold General Election	The six words with the most votes following the election become adopted as the school's lifelong learning dispositions.
Headteacher Challenge 2	Seek views from all your stakeholders of which animal they think best represents and can be associated with each of the six dispositions chosen.
Analyse results	Learning Leaders create a shortlist of ideas received for each animal, survey their class and then decide as Learning Leaders which animal should be associated with each disposition.
Headteacher Challenge 3	Seek views from all your stakeholders of what the six animals chosen to represent the dispositions could look like so that they are specific to your school.
Analyse results	Learning Leaders exhibit throughout the school all designs received and they choose three possible designs for each disposition.
Hold General Election	The three designs for each disposition are placed on a ballot paper, and the whole school votes for their preferred design of animal for each disposition.

Global Sustainability	
Definition	**These are specific words associated with how we act to ensure the future of our planet**
Headteacher Challenge	Seek views of what all your stakeholders would like these words to be for your school.
Analyse results	Group all the ideas submitted into 'common themes'.
Create ballot paper	Select 12 suggestions that are representative of all the themes generated to go on a ballot paper.
Hold General Election	The six words with the most votes following the election become adopted as the school eco-values.

Community Links	
Definition	**These are specific links that your school is committed to making with families, other schools and the school community, local community, national community and global community**
Headteacher Challenge	Seek ideas of what all your stakeholders would like in terms of the school forming meaningful and sustainable partnerships.
Analyse results	Collect all the ideas for each category.

Community Links	
Definition	**These are specific links that your school is committed to making with families, other schools and the school community, local community, national community and global community**
Create ballot paper	Select viable suggestions and incorporate these as part of the school's fabric and partnership work.
Making connections	Learning Leaders and Senior Leaders work together to establish partnerships and decide on how the whole school will contribute to each one.

As soon as a set of words is obtained for one of the six areas, it is very interesting to discuss as a whole staff the opportunities that exist to incorporate them within the everyday life of the school. Figure 3.8 offers a few suggestions that can act as springboards for discussion at school.

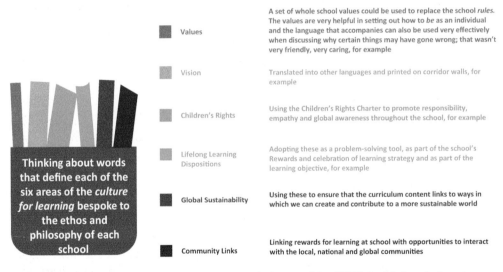

FIGURE 3.8 Practical Opportunities for the Six Key Areas of Influence of the JONK School Culture *for* Learning

The value of introducing a distinct set of words for each of the areas of the school's culture of learning is their potential to help the school to develop a common language and a common understanding of the characteristics that make it possible for everyone to thrive within the school's convivial community. These areas also act as catalysts for innovation and creative approaches to building effective communities and schools as microcosms of society. For example, the culture for learning that the Onion Model helped to establish in the school example described in Figure 3.7 led to the replacement of the school rules, as all that was needed to co-exist were the *ways of being* that the culture of learning instilled in everyone.

The *case study below* illustrates the *transformational* impact that a values-led culture *for* learning is able to have on all individuals and every aspect of school life.

CASE STUDY

The impact of establishing a JONK values-led whole-school culture *for* learning

Pupil's Comments

> Yr 5 was a special year for me and I know for the others too. ✓
> Before I came to year 5 I thought when you learn it's just ✓ about intelligence but ✓ now I know it's about love for ✓ learning, creativity, happiness and effort. ✓

FIGURE 3.9 End of Year Quote from a Child in Year 5

The quote that launches this case study (Figure 3.9) is a contribution from a child in Year 5 as part of her end-of-year report. With this quote, the child managed, in a very eloquent way, to encapsulate the essence, principles and philosophy of all that the JONK approach sets out to achieve. I knew the children in this Year 5 class very well as I had already taught them when they were in Year 2, when the school embarked on a thought-provoking, values-based, learner-focused strategic plan, rooted in the principles and philosophies of the JONK approach.

The school was aiming to create a learner-centred and learning-focused ethos by giving equal prominence to *how* we were teaching and *how* pupils were learning as well as *what* we were teaching and *what* children were learning. Fundamental to this ambition was the desire to raise standards by influencing the *culture* in which learning took place, the mindsets, confidence and self-esteem of the pupils and the perception of themselves as valued individuals, critical thinkers and lifelong learners. It was fascinating to see the strategies that had worked so well in the classroom (Staricoff, 2003) also working well as part of a whole-school strategic plan.

Change took time and focused on embedding one new initiative at a time. The school started by introducing a whole-school set of values and this paved the way for each of the next steps: the introduction of the concept of classrooms as 'communities of enquiry', inspiring everyone at all times, moving away from predetermined 'ability groups' for provision, the introduction of the open-ended thinking skills starters to welcome and motivate children at the beginning of the day, the adaptation of the learning objective as a question, and the introduction of interesting and open-ended challenges as integral components of every lesson and of the approach to home-learning tasks.

The transformation was gradual, but every day had a palpable and growing sense of progress and achievement. Staff and children soon began to feel a sense of *intrinsic* motivation and greater enjoyment and professional satisfaction. A sense of collective purpose was beginning to emerge which started to generate a wide range of ideas which could be incorporated into the infrastructure and strategic direction of the school. In retrospect, it seems that the more personalised, learner-focused, values-based, creative thinking approach was providing a motivational culture that was winning over hearts and minds as it was removing the fear of *not* knowing, of being uncertain, of findings things difficult. The children attributed their increased motivation to school and to learning to a number of very poignant factors. They felt that the learning process had become much more relevant to their lives, that they no longer felt worried when not knowing or finding things difficult. They reported that they were now feeling much more *intrinsically* motivated to *want* to learn and to see how much they could achieve. The culture created had a tremendous impact on standards, behaviour, attendance and the local and national profile of the school.

It is very interesting to note that Feuerstein (Sharron and Coulter, 2006) places children's ability to be open to new learning firmly in the *context* of their homes and families, stating that 'families interpret the world for them and in doing so instil the means for understanding and appreciating their own culture and for operating as intelligent beings within it'.

The initiatives that form the basis of change and that lie at the heart of the JONK approach also place the partnerships with the family at the heart of every child's experiences and of their development as a learner and unique individual.

4

Motivated learners, motivational teachers, collaborative leadership

Intrinsic motivation makes anything and everything possible
Marcelo Staricoff

Children enter the world of education at a time when they have an insatiable thirst for learning, for being inquisitive, for making friends, for wanting to discover how everything works and make sense of all they experience. When adults join the profession, they do so because they also have an insatiable thirst: for wanting to make a difference, for wishing to share their passions and expertise, for inspiring others to flourish as individuals, for ensuring that what they do as professionals will contribute to a better world. In inheriting all this enthusiasm and motivation, already pre-formed, from both children and adults, the world of education is in an extremely privileged position. The educational world therefore faces a fascinating challenge: how does an educational establishment shape its vision and infrastructure in a way that it is able to sustain, nurture and develop the intrinsic motivation that both children and adults 'arrive with'?

With this exciting challenge in mind, this chapter introduces practitioners, senior leaders and headteachers to the *JONK Model of Excellence, Enrichment and Enjoyment (MEEE)*, designed to inspire:

- motivated teachers to become motivational teachers
- motivated staff to become motivational collaborators
- motivated children to become motivated learners
- motivated families to become motivational partners in their children's learning
- motivated headteachers to become motivational leaders

The chapter introduces three adaptations of the MEEE Model:

- *Teacher-focused*: eight pedagogical areas that promote a whole-school approach to teaching, learning and researching and that maximise the impact of the school's philosophy of education for every child

- *Learner-focused*: the same eight areas interpreted from a child's point of view, which when used as part of the daily routine of the classroom encourage every child to *want* to engage with every step of the teaching and learning process

- *Headteacher-focused*: the same eight areas providing a guide and an infrastructure for whole-school leadership and management for the creation of systems that allow all staff to be part of the school development process (multi-professional teams) and all pupils to engage in a process that leads to them developing their own *child version of the school development plan*

The eight areas that comprise the MEEE Model (Figure 4.1) bring together all the evidence that personal experience, collaborative action research–led practice and analysis of the educational literature have shown to have the greatest motivational impact on children's motivation *for* learning, their enjoyment *whilst* learning and their curiosity to *keep* learning.

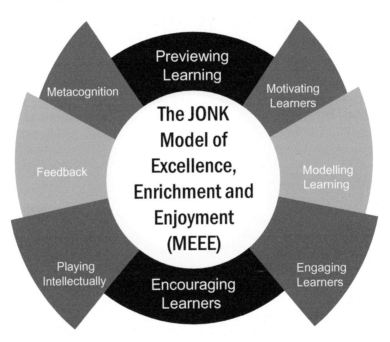

FIGURE 4.1 The JONK Model of Excellence, Enrichment and Enjoyment (MEEE)

 DISCUSSION OPPORTUNITIES

In terms of educational research literature, it is fascinating to analyse, as a whole staff team, the findings of John Hattie's research, published in his book *Visible Learning* (2008), which ranked the impact on children's learning of different initiatives. The Visible Learning research exercise involved the analysis of studies with over 300 million students. Corwin (2018) have produced a very useful summary guide (corwin.com/visiblelearning) showing the influences on students' achievement of over 250 initiatives as part of Visible Learning Plus™. Can the staff team map the initiatives that have been shown to have the highest impact on children's learning by Hattie's research within the eight sectors of the MEEE Model presented in Figure 4.1?

The Teacher-Focused JONK Model of Excellence, Enrichment and Enjoyment (MEEE) | Theory into practice | Illustrative case studies

As with all aspects of the non-prescriptive nature of the JONK approach, the MEEE Model is intended to act as a prompt and a stimulus for professional dialogue that helps all schools to create their own bespoke versions, incorporating individual contexts, philosophies of education, and current practices and priorities. A bespoke MEEE Model makes it possible for schools to create motivational whole-school approaches to teaching, learning and leadership by building on existing excellence. In designing a bespoke MEEE Model, schools may wish to set aside a number of professional development meetings and in-service training (INSET) days to ensure that the final model is informed by the views, insights and expertise of all staff.

The sections below describe the main principles, ideas and implications on practice that underpin each of the eight areas of the teachers' version of the JONK MEEE Model. The description of each area is supported by a case study that illustrates its impact in practice.

 DISCUSSION OPPORTUNITIES

The information and case studies in the sections below are intended to provide a helpful springboard for initiating discussions with colleagues. It is interesting to try to do a cross-referencing exercise between the aims and ideas described in each sector and the current routines that inform practice and policy in your school.

■ How can each of the sectors be adapted for the different age groups?

Previewing learning

Previewing the learning, as an integral part of the teaching and learning process, reduces the anxiety associated with *the unknown*. When the learning is previewed, children have the opportunity to familiarise themselves with it, discuss it at home, research it, try to give meaning to it and, very importantly, begin to *wonder* about it before it is introduced in class. Previewing develops a sense of curiosity for what's to come and allows children to approach new learning with already-formed questions and aware of any misconceptions or confusions they may have. Equally, if a child finds that they happen to have substantial experience, knowledge or interest in the learning that has been previewed, they are able to bring all of this with them. These could be artefacts or a family anecdote or a personal experience or a particular passion of theirs, all contributing to the enrichment of experiences for everyone and to the connection of school with their lives outside of school.

 SUGGESTED READING

A very interesting study on the benefits of previewing learning was conducted by Carpenter and Toftness (2017), entitled *The Effect of Prequestions on Learning from Video Presentations* and published in the *Journal of Applied Research in Memory and Cognition*. Their study concluded that asking students prequestions, which are questions that the students were asked to consider before they watched the video, resulted in a significant advantage over students who had not been asked to engage with these prequestions.

CASE STUDY | **MEEE MODEL**

Previewing learning

I often invite two volunteers to help me role-play and explain the principles and philosophy of the JONK Learning Pit. The scenario launches with both volunteers standing at the 'top' of the Learning Pit, at the 'Q' (for question) stage. Whilst they are both standing there and waiting for something to happen, I explain that this is the point we all find ourselves in whenever we have to do anything new in life; this could be the learning objective, achieving anything we need to do, solving any problem, finding our way to a new place – anything at all in life that we have to do starts here, at the Q stage. I then ask them how they are feeling. Invariably, they all say that they feel rather nervous, apprehensive, a little bit worried, on the spot. They attribute these uncomfortable feelings to *not knowing* what is going to happen. I then ask Person A a question: 'Where were you born?', for example. As Person A knows the answer, they are now allowed to 'jump' across the Pit. The key to why the previewing stage can have such an important impact on the learner is demonstrated by asking Person B how they are feeling now, having had a 'preview' of what may come next for them. Person B can be seen to be feeling substantially more relaxed even before they reply. On replying, Person B expresses a much more comfortable sense of being there, now that they know the question that was posed to Person A. In other words, Person B has had the privilege of having their learning previewed whereas Person A had their learning presented to them without any prior knowledge. This can be very easily transposed to the class and the everyday scenario of teaching and learning. If the learning has not been previewed in some way, the students are probably feeling like Person A as the teacher starts to explain and introduce the learning for that particular lesson, whereas a class that has had the learning previewed would most probably be feeling much more at ease emotionally, as illustrated by Person B. This example illustrates one of the main principles at the heart of the JONK approach: that the way the teaching and learning process is presented to the learner helps them to feel enthusiastic and motivated when *not knowing* (Person B) rather than apprehensive or worried about the *unknown* (Person A).

Motivating learners

The process of 'previewing' the learning automatically contributes to students' motivation to *want* to engage with the learning, as they are starting from a point where they are able to see the *value* of what they are about to learn. This intrinsic enthusiasm that every individual brings to the occasion can be built upon in the classroom to ensure that it translates into an intrinsic motivation to want to learn. The Thinking Skills Starters introduced in Chapter 6 as part of the second day of the Learning to Learn Week and developed in detail in Chapter 7 give teachers the opportunity to translate this enthusiasm into motivation as part of the daily routine of the classroom. Schools all adopt a range of techniques that act in similar ways, generally as part of an exciting launch into a new topic: 'stunning starts', working with an expert, bringing workshops into the school, going on recreational visits, exploring a theme through drama, watching a film, and many more.

The JONK MEEE Model also places great emphasis on the *learning objective* as a motivational tool. Co-constructing the learning objective with the children once the main ideas have been introduced gives children ownership and an understanding of what is going to be learnt. If this is *created as a question*, it allows all learners to use the question as a source of discussion and perceive the classroom discussion as a safe space to ask, take risks, speculate – a 'community of enquiry'. If the question starts with 'Can we…?' or 'How can we…?', it provides all learners and the teacher with a common sense of adventure, of wanting to solve a problem or take on an exciting challenge, which may or may not be possible for everyone to achieve in the course of the lesson, but everyone has the understanding that with the MEEE Model learners are able to take their time and learn concepts at their own pace.

 CASE STUDY | MEEE MODEL

Motivating learners

The concept of presenting the learning objective as a question to create a motivational learning environment in the classroom can be taken a step further. If the question is presented to the learners as a philosophical question, the collective motivation in the class rises exponentially. For example, when the plan is to teach children about any aspect of time – the concept of seconds, minutes, hours, days, telling the time, the 24-hour clock, digital time – the learning objective could be phrased as a statement, a question or a philosophical question:

- Statement: To be able to tell the time on an analogue clock
- Question: Can we learn how to tell the time using the hands on an analogue clock?
- Philosophically: Does time exist?

The philosophical approach generates a great amount of motivation and interest as it presents the learning in a way that children find amusing, unusual and interesting as it makes them think in a completely different way about something they already know. After introducing the lesson with the 'Does time exist?' question and having a great conversation with the class – concluding that time doesn't really exist, that it's a concept humans have created to help give our lives a point of reference, rather than something that we can touch or hold – I was approached by one of the children the next day. She explained that she had discussed the question with her family at home and could now prove to me that time does 'exist'. I was very intrigued by this and asked her to elaborate. Incredibly, she produced out of her pocket a wonderful bunch of the herb 'thyme'. It was extraordinary that a philosophical question in school to introduce a topic had led to the child developing an intrinsic motivation of wanting to discuss the focus of the learning at school with her family at home and that this, in turn, had led to such fabulous creative thinking, resourcefulness to source some thyme and an enthusiasm for sharing her original thinking at school.

Modelling learning

The modelling stage helps the teacher to shift the thinking that the learning objective promotes from w*hat* it is challenging us to achieve to *how* we may be able to achieve it and to *how* success with this particular objective may look and feel. It is fascinating to share with the class an 'excellent model' as an example of the objective they are striving to achieve. Discussing the reasons why this model is a particularly good example of the end product is very helpful and helps everyone in class to co-postulate and collectively agree on the 'success criteria or steps' needed to succeed with the task. Co-constructing the success criteria with the children gives them a sense of ownership and equips them with a very important pedagogical principle: that learning *is* possible if it is broken down into a series of coherent smaller steps. These steps may be different for different children, so having flexible success criteria is very helpful; some children may need smaller steps than others along the way. Viewing the learning as a sequence of small steps, all of which are achievable, provides the learner with a great sense of security and with a clear and *personalised* road map and timetable to their success. The MEEE Model enables the learner to perceive that learning is a continuous and evolving process that takes different amounts of time for each individual and where individuals are encouraged by the teachers to spend as much time as they need at each of the eight stages. The MEEE Model is a fluid structure that during the week accommodates all learners, progressing through it at their own pace, thus removing the anxiety and disappointment that can arise if a child feels they haven't *finished* at the end of the lesson.

The JONK approach introduces an extra dimension to the modelling sector by suggesting the idea of not only modelling and analysing an excellent example of what one is trying to achieve but also sharing with the students *a really 'bad' example* at the same time. Sharing an example that contains mistakes or inaccuracies or lacks thoroughness, depth or accuracy is very valuable indeed. The conversations that arise from analysing a not very 'good' example become very amusing and help children to self-identify, explain and justify their explanations in terms of what they have spotted being not quite right. Pedagogically, this also allows children to become self-aware of similar mistakes they may be making or trying to eradicate (for example, not using capital letters correctly or not applying place value correctly when setting out a sum).

 CASE STUDY | MEEE MODEL

Modelling learning

In walking around the school with the school improvement partner, we entered a Year 1 class. The children all seemed very enthusiastic and engaged and contributed lots of lovely ideas from the carpet. However, there was one child who unusually for them seemed rather distant and a little bit anxious and worried. When the children moved on to embark on their independent learning, we approached him and gently enquired if everything was all right. He explained very clearly that he had felt a little bit confused during the carpet session as the teacher had not yet made any mistakes. It was so interesting to hear this because it means that the routine of sharing not very good examples or of making deliberate mistakes for the children to spot starts to play an integral role in how children perceive learning and how much they look forward to the learning. For this child, the daily routine of spotting mistakes was a very motivational part of his day.

Engaging learners

Once the learning has been introduced, children have been motivated and strategic and curiosity-led discussions have taken place, practitioners then use their expertise to make it possible for the children to engage with the learning independently or collaboratively (or both). The JONK principle of always presenting, enthusing, inspiring and engaging the whole class at every step overcomes *the need for ability grouping*.

The ease with which a child will engage with any particular aspect of learning is determined by the *conditions of the moment* in which the learning is taking place, encompassing a complex and unpredictable set of parameters and factors: their previous knowledge, experience, motivation and skills as well as the child's emotional well-being and readiness to learn at that particular time. It may be a topic that, when presented in the way that today's presentation used, they suddenly understand in a much clearer way than on previous occasions. Equally, a child who would normally be expected to understand the concept presented and work independently may be feeling emotionally unable to engage. This could be for a multitude of reasons: personal or family circumstances, the learning environment or simply because they may have missed a crucial part of the introductory process through absence, lateness or a peripatetic class.

Inspiring *everyone* at *all* times with the same content and opportunities is supported *by a horseshoe-conference style seating plan of the classroom* with a table placed inside the horseshow as illustrated in Chapter 6. The central table acts as the place where support is offered by adults or peers for *any* individual who for whatever reason may need it at *that* particular time. The children perceive this table as a fluid resource that they can access at any one time from their usual seats round the horseshoe. Independent learners and post-support individuals always have the opportunity to *engage in the same concept and at a level of difficulty that they determine for themselves*. This gives all children a sense of responsibility and ownership in terms of how they navigate their learning through the steps to success.

The freedom to choose the level of complexity of engagement with a task and the fluidity of access to the support middle table ensures that learners do not feel *ability-labelled* or included within a 'less capable or less intelligent group', which can so often be the case with predetermined ability groupings and which can be so detrimental to children's motivation and self-esteem.

 SUGGESTED READING

As mentioned in Chapter 1, it is recommended that the reader at this stage refer to three interrelated works: *Learning Without Limits* (2004), *Creating Learning Without Limits* (2012) and *Assessment for Learning Without Limits* (2016).

 CASE STUDY | MEEE MODEL

Engaging learners

It is very interesting to discuss with children the different approaches that they take when deciding what level of difficulty they have chosen for particular tasks and then to discuss with them whether they always gravitate to the same level of challenge at first or whether it varies according to the task. When asked, children have explained that they really enjoy being able to choose their own level of difficulty and that *this takes a lot of worry away* as they know that there is always the opportunity to consolidate their understanding first before moving on to a greater challenge and that if there is something they are particularly competent with, then they don't need to waste time revisiting basic concepts, which could be quite de-motivating. Interestingly, many children choose to very quickly reassure themselves with an easier task first, before tackling the more complex task, even if both they and the teacher feel that they already know it.

Encouraging learners

This sector refers to the development of a learning environment that promotes experimentation, challenge and risk-taking, where learners are not worried about making mistakes, where they are able to continually reflect, discuss, edit, start again and feel free to take as many attempts as are needed to feel a sense of achievement and pride in their work.

An encouraging 'learning to learn environment' encourages all learners to *want to*:

i   engage with the learning

ii   keep going (resilience) even if there are difficulties along the way

iii   engage in further challenge

iv   use their curiosity, imagination, meaning-making skills and creative thinking to view answers and acquisition of new knowledge not as the end of the learning process but as the catalysts for the next step in learning, further exploration and discovery

Sharing with the children what the open-ended enrichment activity or challenge is at the outset of the lesson ensures that every child feels valued as they perceive that the teacher has equally high aspirations for them all. This also creates a motivational sense of looking forward to having the opportunity to engage with something really interesting once the main concepts have been mastered. The challenge can be placed on the board at the start of every lesson so that it is there for everyone to refer to when they get to that stage at different times.

 CASE STUDY | MEEE MODEL

Encouraging learners

The afternoon routine of performances described in Chapter 6 as part of the second day of the Learning to Learn Week provides us with an excellent example of how an encouraging learning to learn environment can have a motivational impact on a child. At the start of the year, a Year 5 child brought in a saxophone he had inherited from his father and asked to use Performance Time that day to play it to the class. Of course, we said yes. The ensuing 10 minutes were spent trying to open the case. The class were very intrigued and encouraged him to come back the next day and try again. The next day, he managed to open the case but spent the 10-minute slot trying to put the various components together. Again, the class encouraged him to come back. At the next 'performance', he was able to put the saxophone together, but when he tried to get a sound out, he found it very difficult. With the encouragement of all, he persevered, and within a few weeks, he was able to play a few notes; incredibly, by the end of the year, he had a joined a band! He always described how the level of encouragement he felt from the class not only allowed him to succeed with the saxophone but also contributed enormously to how he felt about all aspects of school and of learning.

Playing intellectually

Deborah Eyre introduced the concept of 'intellectual playfulness' as part of the Flying High Project (Bristol, 2001). From the outset, these two words seemed to encapsulate the potential that education has to transform learning at school. Early Years pedagogy uses play as the vehicle for learning. Intellectual playfulness is the concept that lets schools incorporate a 'playful approach' to learning across all year groups as the central principle that underpins the philosophy of education. It is fascinating to create a classroom learning environment that promotes *playing with concepts* as an integral part of the learning process. Playing with concepts runs throughout the JONK philosophy of education. For example, the Motivating Sector of the MEEE Model encourages a 'philosophical approach' to the learning objective. This encourages children to *play intellectually* with the concept that is about to be learnt, the self-choosing of difficulty to engage with allows them to play intellectually whilst they are engaged in the learning, and the extension and enrichment task allows them to play intellectually with the concepts they have just mastered.

The design of the extension and enrichment task is a fascinating component of the intellectual playful approach to learning. I learnt very early in my career that there is an enormous difference between (a) finishing a task and being asked to do a task that is rooted in MOTS (more of the same) and (b) finishing a task and being offered the opportunity to engage in a task that promotes HOTS (higher-order thinking skills), based on Bloom's taxonomy (1956). If children feel that once they have *mastered* a concept they will be given more of the same again, they become de-motivated and tend to view the answer as an end point that has no follow-up; they do not make links between the answer and other concepts that they may know and very interestingly start to time themselves so that they always finish at the end of the lesson so that there is no time to be given a MOTS activity.

'A Thinking Skills Approach to the Day' (Staricoff, 2003) describes how HOTS opportunities can be offered to children across all aspects of the curriculum and as part of the daily routine of the classroom, giving all children the opportunity to challenge themselves to:

i   Use and apply their new knowledge and understanding to solve a problem within a different context

ii   Find the same solution but in a different way. This involves going back into the Pit and trying to use a different strategy to get to the same answer. This is also a great strategy to help children check for themselves the validity of their original answer.

iii   Create a list of questions that have been prompted by having acquired new knowledge

iv   Act as teachers: the idea is that if a child can explain the concept to others, then it shows that they have developed a thorough understanding

v   Create a Mini-TED Talks video explaining the concept that can then be used as a teaching tool

The principle of intellectual playfulness also helps greatly with allowing children to distinguish clearly in their own minds the difference between '*having knowledge*' and '*being knowledgeable or understanding*'. Figure 4.2 can be used to illustrate this concept to children from an early age. The diagram shows knowledge as existing in isolation, whereas understanding or being knowledgeable is the result of being able to make connections that give meaning and purpose to the knowledge we possess.

FIGURE 4.2 The Difference Between Knowledge and Understanding

  CASE STUDY │ **MEEE MODEL**

Playing intellectually I

The first case study refers to a process that lets children use and apply their new knowledge in a different context, which in this case involves a real-life scenario. The Year 5 class had spent the week mastering the 'Grid' method as a way of being able to multiply two- and three-digit numbers. The Grid method is a very useful technique as it helps children to develop their concept of place value and it reduces a complex multiplication problem into a series of small manageable calculations. Towards the end of the week, the children were set a HOTS challenge: 'How much revenue does the Clifton Suspension Bridge make in a year?'

The school was very close to the bridge, which at the time charged cars 20p to get across. The challenge had the added incentive of being something that they, as part of the local community, could all relate to. As the children started to feel confident that they had mastered the Grid method, they began to think about this enrichment task. It was extraordinary to see how such a simple question could lead to such creative thinking. Self-formed groups started to think about how many cars they thought crossed in an hour, whether every hour of the day had the same traffic crossing, whether every day of the week had equal volume, each month and so on. The task became the focus for two consecutive Maths Investigation sessions and eventually led to each group being able to offer an amount. The fascinating thing was that to reach that amount, they all used the Grid method numerous times, combined with many other mathematical operations. We then contacted the Clifton Suspension Bridge Authority and asked them whether as a listed company they could disclose their annual profit. They told us their figure, which was incredibly close to the majority of the groups' findings.

The satisfaction was immense. Repeating this type of exercise while using a wide range of scenarios has always proved very enjoyable and each time has fostered an enormous amount of intellectual playfulness. These scenarios represent a further example of when children are 'learning' without realising that they are 'learning': from their point of view, they are playing, but from the teacher's point of view, they are playing 'intellectually' and 'purposefully'.

 CASE STUDY | **MEEE MODEL**

Playing intellectually II

The second case study illustrates the concept of giving the children the opportunity to act as 'teachers' and explain the concept they've just learnt to others. This is a very useful tool for teachers to have in their repertoire: it not only acts as a motivational means by which children can discover how well they have understood a particular concept but also has a great impact on their self-esteem and on how their peers perceive them. It is fascinating to see how much all children enjoy being offered this opportunity which can have such a positive impact for life. Taking this concept a step further in our technological age, it is very powerful to develop the concept of *Mini-TED Talks Videos*. The idea is to create a set of videos in which the children explain a concept as though they were the teacher. It is very useful to collect a whole-school set of Mini-TED Talks videos where, for example, children explain to their own year group how to add, take away, multiply and divide. These can be placed on the website so that children and families are able to access them at home and teachers are able to use them as intro- ductions to the lessons. For some children, it is much easier to understand, and invariably it becomes more enjoyable and engaging, when a concept is explained by a peer. This example again highlights the value of offering children the opportunity to engage in activities that pro- mote playfulness within an 'intellectual' context; reciprocal teaching is one of the initiatives with highest impact value within Hattie's research findings (Hattie, 2008).

 CASE STUDY | **MEEE MODEL**

Playing intellectually III

The children's quotes within the next case study summarise how incredibly exciting the process of intellectual playfulness can be. At the end of the science topic focusing on the properties of sound, we decided to challenge ourselves as a Year 5 class to try to actually measure the speed of sound! As the article describes, this was not something I had attempted before, although since then it has become a key element within the JONK repertoire of challenges. The experience was so wonderful that the children wrote it up as an article (Figure 4.3), published by CLEAPPS (2003), the Consortium of Local Education Authorities for the Provision of Science Services:

NEWSLETTER

Measuring the Speed of Sound

The article on sound & hearing in the last PST prompted a teacher and his class to investigate how they could measure the speed of sound. Here is an edited version of the article that they sent in. Congratulations to class 5S and Marcelo Staricoff of Westbury Park School in Bristol!

"We have just received the latest copy of the CLEAPSS newsletter and we were very interested to read your double-page spread on sound. We are a Year 5 class in Bristol, Westbury Park School, and have been studying sound since September.

We had quite an unusual lesson to finish the topic off! This is what happened...

Our teacher, Mr Staricoff [Mr S.], announced that he wanted to try out an idea, even though he had never tried it before, had no idea if it was possible to do, or knew what the outcome would be! As he was a scientist in a previous life we thought that it was worth listening to him for a bit longer.

To our amazement he announced his intention - for *us* to *measure* the speed of sound!!! All we knew about the speed of sound was that it travelled at about 340 metres per second. Trying to measure it seemed a bit optimistic, but who were we to argue; we were hooked and set about planning our investigation.

We quizzed Mr S. and managed to extract some hints of how we might tackle this seemingly impossible task. In small groups, we designed our own versions and created a poster of our ideas. We then presented our ideas to the rest of the class, which helped us to come up with an agreed plan of action, which we carried out...

★ Mr S. reset two stopwatches and started them at **exactly** the same time. He gave one each to children A and B.

★ We then measured the furthest distance we could in our school, using a trundle wheel. This was 114 metres. Children A and B were positioned, with their stopwatches still running, at either end of this measured distance.

★ Mr S. joined child A and blew a whistle loudly.

★ Child A and B both stopped their watches when they heard the sound.

★ We returned to the classroom feeling a huge sense of excitement and anticipation. Would there be a difference between the two times?

Our Results

To our total amazement we found that there was a difference between the two stopwatch readings!!! A quick subtraction showed that this was 1.04 seconds.

But what did all this mean? It was time to do some more maths...

As the speed of sound is thought to be around 340 metres per second, Mr S. asked us to calculate how long it would take for sound to travel 114 metres. We knew it would be about one third of a second, but in our groups we calculated it accurately.

340 metres in one second;
114 metres in ? seconds;

$? = \dfrac{114}{340}$

$? = 0.34$ of a second to two decimal places.

CLEAPSS School Science Service   number 25   Spring 2003   page 4

FIGURE 4.3 Measuring the Speed of Sound

Georgia

The expected time and our measured time were so close, only 0.7 of a second difference [1.04 - 0.34], we could hardly believe it! We were amazed; we had come so close to the real thing! We started to discuss the meaning of all we had done, but were not expecting Mr S's next question: **Why were we 0.7 of a second out?**

As a whole class, we came up with some ideas, in what turned out to be quite an interesting philosophical discussion.

❖ The stopwatches may not have been started at **exactly** the same time.

❖ The sound waves may have been blocked by buildings and trees in the way.

❖ The experiment relied on child A and B's hearing. We should repeat it with other children, which would also help to obtain an average and more scientifically valid data.

❖ The length of the whistle sound could be another variable to investigate.

❖ The real measurement of the speed of sound must have used very accurate instruments.

We really enjoyed ourselves and felt that we had experienced a little bit of real science. We went home very excited, with a great sense of achievement. We thor-

oughly recommend the whole thing and we would really like to hear how other schools' tests turn out! Are there any other ways of doing the measurement?"

From a teacher's point of view, it was probably the most rewarding science I have ever experienced. Working all together towards a common goal, overcoming problems as we went along and achieving a result that made so much sense was fantastic. The investigation has now become a regular topic of conversation amongst children, parents and our link scientist; as a school we have formed a link with a working scientist from the University of Bristol, organised through the Clifton Scientific Trust. We plan to invite him to share and contribute when we use different children to repeat our measurements. We also need to think of something equally exciting for our next topic 'Gases Around Us' - any ideas?

Mr Staricoff and pupils of 5S

We might quibble that, in presenting the results, it would have been better to calculate the actual speed of sound measured by the pupils (110 metres per second) - not quite as close to the 'real thing' as the pupils thought! Nevertheless, we are impressed by the work carried out.

We list below all the comments that class 5S pupils made about their investigation. We hope that the science activities in other schools also have such a positive effect! We'd love to hear about them.

▾ I never thought we could do such a thing, let alone do real science. [Jack]
▾ It was very exciting, much better than any old science lesson. [Joe]
▾ It was the best thing in school. [Alex]
▾ It was so interesting. I never thought it was possible. [Dudley]
▾ WOW! [Angel]
▾ I thought it was fun and amazing. [Alice]
▾ It was great doing it as a whole class. [Richard]
▾ It was absolutely amazing and we came quite close. This was real science. [James]
▾ I never thought we could measure something so big - science is really cool. [Chris]
▾ Everyone in the class was so excited when we worked out the result. [Lewis]
▾ I was surprised when I heard what we would do, but it turned out so well. [Rachel]
▾ I was excited when Mr S. announced it. [Lily]
▾ It was great fun to do. [Ella]
▾ It was great, it felt so good doing real science, great fun too. I really wanted to be a scientist, but now I want to even more. [Vinothan]
▾ It was such a fun day - I can't wait to try it again. [Sarah]
▾ I have always wanted to be a scientist and now I know what it is like, it is brilliant. [Louis]
▾ The experiment was absolutely amazing. I came home as a scientist. Thank you. [Larry]

▾ It was very interesting to do real science, at first I was very surprised. It was amazing we were less than a second out! [Michael]
▾ I thought it was a really good day; at home my Mum and Dad didn't believe me. [Georgia]
▾ I thought the calculations were amazing - it couldn't get better than this, it was so amazing. I felt really proud of our class. [Paloma]
▾ I can't wait until we do something as amazing as that again - I don't think we'll beat the excitement. [Bianca]
▾ I thought the day was great because we had a different experience and we did a proper experiment which they don't even do on TV. I never thought we would manage to measure the speed of sound, but we did. [Tom]
▾ We first thought Mr S. had brain damage, but at the end I went home and felt so proud of myself as a scientist - it was fun, the best day yet. [Kate]
▾ It was very exciting measuring the speed of sound because children hardly get the opportunity. [Matt]
▾ The afternoon was very different and I thought I was very lucky because most people wouldn't be able to do this. It was amazing. [Georgie]
▾ It was great fun. I thought it wouldn't work but it turned out so well. [Rosie]
▾ I never thought that we would be able to measure the speed of sound especially not at Primary school. [Rachael]
▾ I never thought we could measure it - the day could not have been better. I think I would like to be a real scientist. It was very exciting to be doing real science. [Natasha]

CLEAPSS School Science Service   number 25   spring 2003   page 5

FIGURE 4.3 (CONTINUED) Measuring the Speed of Sound

Feedback

Feedback also features prominently in Hattie's analysis (Hattie, 2008) of initiatives that have a significant impact on student achievement. Creating a classroom conversational culture and maximising the opportunities that arise to discuss the learning with the children, or for them to discuss it amongst themselves, are invaluable. The Learning Models (described in Chapter 6) that each child creates as part of the first day of the Learning to Learn Week are instrumental to the feedback process. It is invaluable for teachers to use the vocabulary that the child has used to describe their own model of learning when engaging in feedback conversations with each child. For example, one child explained that her model was that of a roundabout as she felt that throughout school she had been going round and round the same processes, encountering the same barriers and feeling quite frustrated that she was not able to make any progress. In feedback sessions, we began to use the language of the roundabout and then extended it to try to find 'exits' from it. This use of figurative language based on a model that she had created to explain how she perceived herself as a learner was very influential in her transformational progress that year and her sense of well-being, confidence and greater self-esteem.

It is also interesting to develop strategies that enable a teacher's verbal comments to be valued by the learner at the time they are made rather than these just being lost. In the course of the day, teachers and support staff speak with the children during numerous informal conversations that contribute to the overall feedback process. The child can be encouraged to record a summary of these conversations in their books using the acronym TC (Teacher's Comments) in the margin or next to their work.

It is also very powerful for teachers to pose questions as part of their marking strategy. This, however, needs to be accompanied with a system that routinely offers children the time necessary to respond to these questions in a meaningful way, encouraging them to share their thoughts, reflections, triumphs, difficulties and wishes, perceiving the teacher as their 'critical friend'.

 CASE STUDY | MEEE MODEL

Feedback with learners

It is very interesting to regard feedback as a continual conversation about thinking and learning with each child rather than a series of isolated events driven mainly by comments offered through the marking process. Feedback Books allow these conversations to materialise and are a great way of ensuring that the conversations are a central part of the pupil–school–home triangular partnership as illustrated in the example below (Figure 4.4):

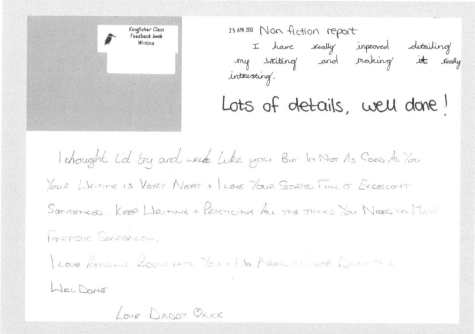

FIGURE 4.4 The Feedback Books and the Pupil–School–Family Partnership

These books also help to capture progress over time, providing a rich source of information for the teacher to use in order to be able to offer a *personalised* learning diet for each child.

Metacognition

Although the metacognitive sector is placed at the end of the MEEE Model cycle, the JONK approach encourages children to *use their metacognitive skills at all six stages defined by the JONK Model of learning and discussed in detail in Chapter 2*. In fact, using metacognition at the beginning of the learning process when in Position 1 of the model is very important for children as it allows them to reflect on what they already know as a way of being able to create meaningful connections with what they are learning next.

Once they've launched into their learning, the JONK Model of Learning invites them to *constantly fluctuate between the third and fourth positions*. In other words, children are encouraged to constantly reflect on how well their learning is progressing, enabling them to make informed choices about their next steps, applying alternative strategies, overcoming barriers, checking their results, improving, editing, and discussing their successes and mastery with others. At the final stages, which are depicted as Positions 5 and 6 in the JONK Model of Learning, the children are encouraged to reflect on the whole process they've just been through. They can use these reflections to drive their curiosity and make informed judgements about progress towards their current goals and the degree to which they feel the conclusions they've reached have allowed them to meet or surpass the expectations that were set at the outset. If these have not been met, the reflections serve to motivate them to keep trying to master the concept in greater depth.

It is interesting to give children the opportunity to engage in metacognitive reflections as part of their daily routine. Introducing the concept of a *TIL (today I learnt)* at the end of each piece of work or lesson works very well and this also provides the child with the opportunity to have a conversation with the teacher as part of the feedback process. They may say they enjoyed a piece of work but still feel unsure about a certain aspect of it. The teacher can then respond and plan accordingly.

The Thinking Page, which is introduced as part of the second day of the Learning to Learn Week in Chapter 6, also acts as an excellent tool for engaging in metacognition at all times during the day. It frees children up to write anything down and try anything out without worrying that it will be marked or judged.

 CASE STUDY | MEEE MODEL

Metacognitive learners

The story introduced in Chapter 2 about the child who jumped across the Pit as he knew the answer to a question but still considered that he had learnt something new is a perfect example of how the principles and vocabulary associated with the JONK approach encourage children to develop their ability to think metacognitively. When the child explained that jumping across the Pit helped him to 'learn that he *already knew it*', he illustrated how his metacognition was enabling him to be *self-aware* of *knowing what he knew*. The metacognitive sector of the MEEE Model invites children to be continuously aware of what *they know* as well as of what *they don't know*. The metacognitive skills that they build during the year allow children to create a thoughtful and meaningful reflective comment as part of their end-of-year report to parents and guardians, as was so well illustrated by the reflection from this Year 5 child (Figure 4.5), which also forms the basis of a case study presented at the end of Chapter 3:

> Yr 5 was a special year for me and I know for the others too.
> Before I came to year 5 I thought when you learn it's just about intelligence but now I know it's about, love for learning, creativity, happiness and effort.

FIGURE 4.5 Pupil Metacognitive Reflections on Their Learning

The Children's version of the Model of Excellence, Enrichment and Enjoyment | The C-MEEE

Once your school has developed and established a bespoke MEEE Model, it is interesting to discuss with the children the reasons for choosing each of the sections. It is fascinating to then work with the pupils and Learning Leaders to see whether they can transform the school's MEEE Model from a theoretical, adult-designed concept to one that they create and use in the classroom as part of the daily teaching and learning routine.

 DISCUSSION OPPORTUNITIES

At this point, it is very interesting to ask the Learning Leaders in your school or the children in your class to think of how they would word each of the sections of the school's MEEE Model so that they could be understood by every child in the school.
What ideas do the children have for making their version a helpful and interactive tool for learning in the classroom?

Figure 4.6 demonstrates how a group of Learning Leaders interpreted the sectors of the school's MEEE Model, discussed them with their peers and then worked

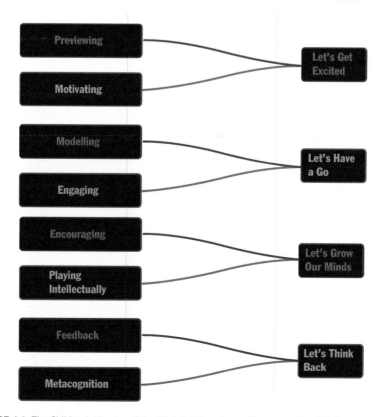

FIGURE 4.6 The Children's Version of the Model of Excellence, Engagement and Enjoyment

towards creating a child-friendly version of the MEEE Model, adapting the vocabulary and expressing the original eight areas as four statements that could be easily understood by every child.

The Learning Leaders then suggested the idea that every classroom could have a way of displaying these four areas prominently on or next to the whiteboards to indicate which section of the model the teaching was focusing on at any particular time. Some classrooms opted for 'Pizza Slices', adding one quarter at a time until the pizza was complete. For example, to show that the class were at the 'Having a Go' stage, the board would have the first two slices in the corner (Figure 4.7):

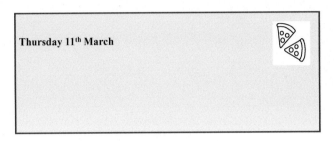

FIGURE 4.7 The Children's Version of the Model of Excellence, Engagement and Enjoyment in Practice

Others created a large display board using the model of a 'speedometer' (Figure 4.8).

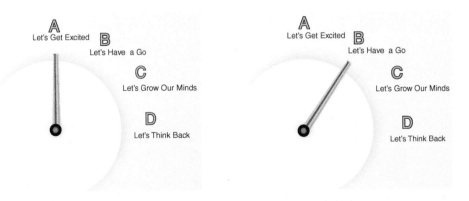

FIGURE 4.8 The Children's Version of the Model of Excellence, Engagement and Enjoyment in Practice

 DISCUSSION OPPORTUNITIES

How many other ideas can the children in your school come up with to ensure that the four areas of the children's MEEE Model are used as a helpful tool for learning in the classroom?

The Headteacher's version of the Model of Excellence, Enrichment and Enjoyment │ The HT-MEEE

There are many similarities between the stages that lead to teachers being able to inspire children with their learning and the global considerations that form the basis of a headteacher's role. Staff work collaboratively towards inspiring children with their learning and towards maximising the personal, social, emotional and educational benefits that schools offers them at different stages of their lives. In the same way, headteachers also work collaboratively to establish a culture in their schools which enables everyone to thrive as individuals, learners and professionals. If there are so many similarities between the aims and goals of the roles of teachers and headteachers, could the eight sectors of the teachers' version of the MEEE Model now be re-interpreted, as the children did to construct their own version, to provide headteachers with a useful framework for whole-school leadership and management? The HT-MEEE Model (Figure 4.9) was designed to do just that.

FIGURE 4.9 The Headteacher's Version of the Model of Excellence, Enrichment and Enjoyment

As with the teachers' MEEE and the children's MEEE Model, each of the sectors of the HT-MEEE Model is described in turn so as to promote the conversations and discussions that help each school to create their personalised and bespoke model.

Previewing learning

As it is important to 'preview' the learning for children, it is equally important to preview the strategic vision and the short-, medium- and long-term plans of the school with all relevant stakeholders. Previewing the plans for the school across all areas (pedagogy, improvements to the building, new partnerships, new collaborations or new opportunities) helps to create a sense of collaborative leadership and celebratory enthusiasm. This enthusiasm leads to everyone feeling that, in this school, anything and everything is possible. *How* it's possible for everyone to *feel* and *perceive* that everything is possible can be attributed to the respectful and inclusive working environment that a *values-led culture* helps to establish and to the *professional freedom* that is offered to all members of staff to experiment, take risks, research, collaborate and pursue their passions and dreams.

INSET days that include every member of staff and of the governing body provide an ideal platform on which to establish this ethos, using these opportunities to value and embrace everyone's thoughts, experiences and expertise as part of the school's strategic plans. Previewing the aims of the school and of each individual in this way leads to great discussion and a sense that democracy drives the decision-making process and that everyone has ownership of how the school moves forward and implements initiatives. Involving everyone means that each person is regarded as an expert in their field and that initiatives are considered through a wide spectrum of practical considerations before they are introduced: What is the feasibility of each idea being introduced? What are the current systems and mechanisms that the new initiative will build upon? How will each initiative look and feel for each year group? How can progression be planned for? How will changes be communicated? Are there any links between the new ideas and national educational priorities, the latest publications and frameworks and supporting evidence within the educational research fields?

Motivating learning

The children's MEEE Model combines the previewing and the motivation sectors brilliantly and refers to these two as 'Let's Get Excited'. This is because motivation starts with the previewing stage. Indeed, being aware of and having a say in what is coming in the next week, term, year, three years are very exciting for staff. This sector helps the headteacher to start to create the conditions that allow the ideas to take shape and be carefully planned for. Enabling all members of staff to be involved with how the school generates ideas and sees them to fruition is quite a challenge. To facilitate this process, the JONK approach has developed the concept of the *Multi-Professional Team* (MPT) approach to school improvement and to the School Development Plan (SDP).

MPTs are created on the first INSET day of the academic year. After the indicative aims that constitute the main priorities driving the new SDP are previewed with staff, every member of staff is invited to choose the one priority that they feel they can contribute to the most. Once every member of staff (and governor) has chosen their preferred priority for the year, the staff all form an MPT for each priority. It is a good idea for each MPT to include the member of the Senior Leadership Team who is also responsible for that priority. It is a great idea for headteachers to create a specific budget code so that each MPT is able to fulfil their action points. Although a basic equal sum can be allocated to launch each MPT, certain actions may require greater investment and these amounts may need to be adjusted as the year progresses. It is also very exciting to have a system that motivates MPTs to 'bid' for a sum from the central budget. This requires the team to create a proposal and usually involves engaging in an action research project, working with an expert, setting up a collaboration or buying a specific resource.

The first task for each MPT is to welcome every member of staff to the group by discussing why they have chosen to join this particular team, what their visions are for this priority, what knowledge and expertise they are able to offer and what barriers they foresee in ensuring that things come to fruition.

The second task is for the group to become aware of everyone's schedules, working days, working hours, preparation, planning and assessment times, duties and responsibilities. The success of the MPT relies on being able to meet, communicate and discuss progress of each action point at regular intervals. This can be achieved by securing the afternoons of every INSET day for MPTs to meet. MPTs may also arrange their own meetings throughout the year depending on everyone's availability.

The third task before starting to plan the priority is to decide on a communication and dissemination strategy. Does everyone have access to a computer? Is everyone able to receive communications following meetings if they were not able to attend? How will the group disseminate findings and progress to others, the SMT and advisors, beyond the school, etc.? How does the evidence from current educational literature and practice inform the goals for this priority? Is there a member who could be responsible for analysing and communicating the research evidence to the rest of the MPT?

The fourth task involves the MPT members drawing up the action plan for the priority and being clear about what success will look like for each action point, the people who are involved in facilitating the action to happen, the timeline for each action point happening and any resources that may be needed, including consumables and staff time. Will individuals need extra support, time out of class, extra hours, arranged visits, etc.?

The fifth stage involves developing a careful strategy that allows the impact to be measured. How will we know that the actions have made a difference? What will we measure? Will the measures be based on analysis of data, observations or questionnaires?

It is very important, in terms of motivation, for staff to perceive that even though they are working on their own MPT for the year, they will have plenty of opportunity to hear about the progress and excitement of all the MPTs. Equally, it is very useful for staff to perceive that even though there are individual MPTs, each focusing on a different area of school improvement, these are all based on whole-school values, principles and philosophies that bond and gel everyone and everything together. A great way of doing this to include two additional priorities, known as the *Universal Priorities* (UPs), as part of the SDP. These UPs provide headteachers with the opportunity to ensure that whole-school values and systems are in place to support the aims of each priority. Once the MPT system is set up, many wonderful things start to happen, particularly in the number of informal conversations that MPT members have in the corridors, staff rooms, whilst on duty, on trips and at all times!

The final task of the MPT process involves presenting the MPTs at the first Full Governors Board (FGB) Meeting of the academic year (Figure 4.10):

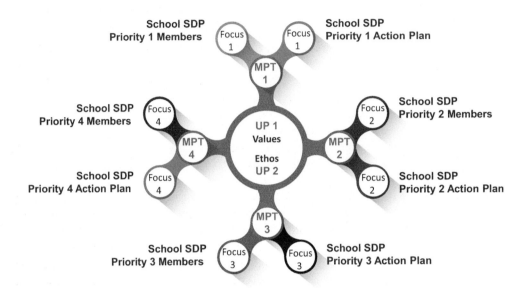

FIGURE 4.10 The Multi-Professional Teams and the School Development Plan

At this meeting, it is very useful to arrange for each governor to champion one of the MPTs. This is a great way of keeping the communication and monitoring of the SDP at the forefront of the FGB Meeting Agenda and also gives the FGB the opportunity to contribute to the actions planned if they have a particular interest or expertise in the areas being developed. It is very powerful for the governor linked to each MPT to feed-back to the rest of the FGB as a regular item on the FGB Meeting Agenda.

The MPT process establishes a culture in which all members of staff feel that they are leaders of their own learning, their own roles and the school improvement process. The next sector, the modelling stage, enables headteachers to also establish a whole-school culture where *all children also* feel and perceive that they are *leaders of their own learning and able to contribute to the school improvement process.*

Modelling learning

Modelling leads to Students Producing a Pupils' Version of the School's Development Plan

As with the teachers' version of the model that uses the modelling sector of the MEEE Model to share with the children an excellent example of what the learning is trying to achieve, headteachers can mirror this process and use the SDP as an example of an 'excellent model' that, rather than describing for the children what we are trying to achieve in the classroom, demonstrates to them what we are trying to achieve *as a school*. The idea of sharing the SDP with the children helps them to:

- *Understand what the school is trying to work on* and how it is thinking of helping the children to benefit from each of the focus areas

- *Have the opportunity to contribute their own views*, thoughts, ideas and suggestions for each of the focus areas

- *Discuss amongst themselves* whether their perception of what the school is thinking of focusing on matches their experience of being a pupil at the school

- *Create their own SDP* written as an interpretation of the school's SDP presented in a way that can be understood by and be meaningful to every child in the school

- *Feel that they have a democratic voice* in terms of how the school moves forward

Creating a children's version of the SDP is one of the principal roles of the Learning Leaders and one of the most exciting challenges for headteachers. In Chapter 3, we saw how the Learning Leaders, who are elected representatives from each class, enable the school to introduce whole-school change by forming an integral part of the *Headteacher's Challenge* process. In this section, we will look at the step-by-step process that headteachers and Learning Leaders can engage in that leads to the creation of a children's version of the SDP.

Headteacher and Learning Leaders Meeting 1

The headteacher (HT) meets with all the Learning Leaders (LLs) and welcomes them to their first official meeting and explains the main aim of the process: to produce a children's version of the School Development Plan (SDP). At this session, the HT explains that these meetings will be modelled on the formalities of formal meetings and these are explained to the LLs: agendas, minutes, the role of the HT as the chair, the protocols that allow every LL to contribute during the meeting, etc.

Headteacher and Learning Leaders Meeting 2

The headteacher (HT) welcomes the Learning Leaders (LLs) to their first formal meeting and presents them all with the Agenda for the Meeting. The HT explains to the LLs the concept of the SDP, what it is, how it is generated and how it is used during the year. The HT ends the session by saying that in the next day or so they will receive the Minutes of this Meeting (Figure 4.11) before previewing the focus for Session 2, which consists of the school's current SDP priorities.

MEETING (1) OF THE BOARD OF LEARNING LEADERS
Wednesday 18th September 2019 – 1pm to 2pm
Main Hall

AGENDA

TIME	AGENDA ITEM AND ACTIONS	LEAD PERSON(S)
1pm	**1. Welcome, Apologies and Declarations of Interest** - Apologies, Quorum and any Declarations of Interest	MS and JB
2.15pm	**2. Minutes of the Previous Meeting of the Board**	Chair
2.16pm	**3. Introduction** - The Role of the Learning Leaders - The first Project for the Learning Leaders	Chair
2.25pm	**4.The School Development Plan** - The 2019-2020 SDP - The Four Main Priorities	MS and JB
2.35pm	**5. The Children's Version of the SDP** - What it should be called - How it will be produced - How it will be shared and used at Wenhaston Primary	All
2.35pm	**6. The Name of the Children's Version of the SDP** - Ideas - Voting on the ideas to choose final name	All
2.45pm	**7. Learning Leaders Thinking for Areas of the School SDP** - Ideas for each currently specified area - Ideas for other areas of the school	All
2.55pm	**8. The Lifelong Learning Dispositions at Wenhaston Primary** - Ideas for each disposition - Ideas for animals for each disposition	All
	– Next Meeting to be held on Monday 18th October – 1pm to 2pm at Wenhaston Primary School	

FIGURE 4.11 Meeting (1) of the Board of Learning Leaders

**Minutes of the Meeting (1) of the Learning Leaders
held on Wednesday 18th September 2019 at 1.00pm – 2.00pm
Main Hall,**

Learning Leaders present:

(Acting Chair of Learning Leaders)	MS
(Class 1)	LC1
(Class 1)	EC1
(Class 2)	PC2
(Class 2)	LC2
(Class 3)	LM3
(Class 3)	LC3
(Class 4)	IC4
(Class 4)	DC4

In attendance: JB (Headteacher)   JB

Apologies: None received

1. **Quorum and Declaration of Interest**
   The Chair welcomed the Learning Leaders and the Headteacher to their first meeting and with all 8 Learning Leaders present the meeting was declared quorate. No conflicts of interest were declared.

2. **Minutes of the Learning Leaders**
   No previous minutes were available for approval as this is the first meeting of the Wenhaston Primary School Learning Leaders.

3. **Introduction by the Chair**
   MS welcomed all Learning Leaders to their first meeting and congratulate them on being elected as class representatives for the academic year 2019-2020. The Learning Leaders all introduced themselves to the group.

   MS explained that the Learning Leader would be working alongside JB and MS this academic year on a number of learning-to-learn based projects,which come under the initiatives being developed by the school in collaboration with JONKTL.

   MS explained that the initial goal for the board of the Learning Leaders was to work towards creating a children's version of the School Development Plan. Other responsibilities that will come under the remit of the role of the Learning Leader include working alongside JB when introducing new whole school initiatives related to learning, such as the lifelong learning dispositions and associated linked animals.

   MS explained that the Board of the Learning Leaders would be meeting half-termly

FIGURE 4.11 (CONTINUED) Meeting (1) of the Board of Learning Leaders

4. **The School Development Plan**

MS and JB introduced the Board to the principle and content of the current School Development Plan (SDP). The Board was informed that the four main priorities within the SDP 2019-2020 were;

    i.   Implementation of the new Pivotal Behaviour
    ii.   Arithmetic
    iii. Independent Writing and Comprehension
    iv. Awareness of the Bigger Picture

JB and MS explained the details that make up the action points of each one of these

5. **The Children's Version of the School Development Plan**

MS explained that the Board would now set about trying to write a children's version of the SDP (CSDP):

    i.   Understand as a group what the main four areas of the SDP 2019-2020 are trying to achieve
    ii.   Communicate the idea of the CSDP to their class
    iii. Gather from all children in their class ideas that the children feel would help the school achieve the four main priorities of the SDP 2019-2020
    iv. Bring the ideas gathered from the children in each class back to the next LL meeting
    v.   Discuss the ideas collected from each class as a Board
    vi. Decide on how all these ideas can be included as part of the CSDP
    vii. Write the CSDP

MS explained that once the CSDP has been written the Board will have the opportunity to communicate its contents by presenting it to:

    i.   Children and adults in their class
    ii.   Staff at a Staff Meeting
    iii. Families at a whole school assembly
    iv. Governors at a Full Governors Meeting

6. **The Name of the Children's Version of the Plan**

MS introduced the need to think of a name for the Children's Version of the SDP. The Board had the opportunity to discuss a possible name and each board member then contributed their ideas:

i.	School Interesting Plan	IC4
ii.	The School Getting Better at Learning Plan	EC1
iii.	The School Getting Better at Being Safe Plan	LC2
iv.	The Important School Stuff Plan	DC4
v.	The 'Be Learning' Plan (As with the others Be…)	LM3
vi.	The Nothing Worries Us Plan	LC1
vii.	The Kids Plan	LC3
viii.	The 'Learning Pit' Plan	IC4
ix.	The Top-Secret Plan	IC4
x.	The Octopus Plan (Eight Main Priorities)	DC4

The Board agreed that the best way to choose the name would be through a democratic vote in which all children and their families could participate in:

ACTION: JB to send to all families a document explaining the role of the Learning Leaders and what they are trying to achieve, namely the CSDP, and asking them to vote, as a family for their preferred name for the CSDP. The Board would like the children's names who had the ideas to be omitted from the voting process so that families are not influenced by which LL thought of the idea to be voted on.

FIGURE 4.11 (CONTINUED) Meeting (1) of the Board of Learning Leaders

7. **Learning Leaders Current Thinking on the SDP**
   The Board discussed the current priorities and offered some initial ideas for school improvement that may be worth discussing with their class:

   i.   Learning to ask more questions in Science
   ii.   Seeing if it is possible to have more outings and trips
   iii. Using PE as a way of learning in Maths and Literacy
   iv.   Maximizing the opportunities for learning in all subjects by using the outdoors
   v.   Behaviour Priority; helping each other at all times
   vi.   Arithmetic Priority: times tables with music
   vii. Writing Priority: nonsense sentences, humour, more opportunities for children to choose what to write about

8. **The Lifelong Learning Dispositions at Wenhaston Primary School**
   MS introduced to the Board the idea of establishing a set of lifelong learning dispositions for the whole school and linking each of the dispositions with an animal that children consider display those characteristics. The Board was very excited with the prospect of working towards this. As an example, we considered 'Resilience' and the Board offered some ideas, such as the Octopus, the Lion and the Shark (EC1 explaining that sharks never go to sleep).

Future Meetings

- Monday 18th October

Minutes approved by the Learning Leaders on

....

JB Headteacher

FIGURE 4.11 (CONTINUED) Meeting (1) of the Board of Learning Leaders

 DISCUSSION OPPORTUNITIES

The previewing of the next stage encourages the children to think, before the next session, what these priorities might be.

Headteacher and Learning Leaders Meeting 3

The Headteacher starts every meeting with the Learning Leaders by introducing them to the Agenda and leading them through the process of approving the Minutes of the previous meeting. The examples below demonstrate how fruitful it is and how interesting it becomes for the Learning Leaders to have the Agenda and the Minutes produced with all the ingredients of formal meetings. Producing such detailed documents also allows the Learning Leaders to share these with others – staff, governors, school partners, families and visitors to the website – in a very professional way. The Learning Leaders really enjoy taking copies of the Agenda and Minutes home to share with their families (Figure 4.11).

The headteacher then introduces the current SDP priorities and describes the reasoning that led to these priorities being chosen. The headteacher explains that their task in the next few weeks is to create their own Plan based on their interpretation of the plan and the ideas from all the children in their class. The Meeting then invites the children to think of a name for the Children's Version of the Plan. All the ideas are collected, and the final name can be chosen by a vote by the LLs, a vote by all the children or a vote by all the families.

 DISCUSSION OPPORTUNITIES

The Learning Leaders are then tasked with the process of explaining the SDP priorities to all the children in their class. Once the main priorities are introduced to the class, the class are invited to offer their thoughts and views of how each priority can best be achieved from their point of view.

Headteacher and Learning Leaders Meeting 4

At this meeting, the Learning Leaders have the opportunity to feed-back the thoughts and ideas they've gathered from their classes, and the rest of the meeting is devoted to starting to arrange all these ideas in a way that helps them to formulate their own plan.

Headteacher and Learning Leaders Meeting 5

The Learning Leaders are given all the time necessary, which may take several meetings, and the resources needed to be able to compile their plan and end up with a finished product that can be published, disseminated and used alongside the school's SDP.

Headteacher and Learning Leaders Meeting 6

Once the final version of the children's plan has been completed, the Learning Leaders are consulted on how best to disseminate their plan. In order to do this successfully, the LLs are offered the opportunity to present their plan:

- To their own class
- At whole-school assemblies
- As part of a staff meeting
- At a Governors' Meeting

Once disseminated, a copy of the plan is prominently displayed in each classroom and used as a working document and an interesting document to read.

Headteacher and Learning Leaders Meeting 7

Once the final version has been shared with everyone at school, the Learning Leaders decide how best to share their plan beyond the school. For example, a copy of the plan could go home for each family to enjoy or it could be placed on the school's website.

Headteacher and Learning Leaders Meeting 8

It is a great idea to develop a model or a diagram that incorporates both the staff and the pupils' version of the SDP. The diagram below (Figure 4.12) was inspired by a group of Learning Leaders in a primary school in Suffolk, UK, whose plan became known as the *Octopus Plan*, an idea that originated from a child in Reception who realised that when both the school and the pupils' versions of the plans are combined there are eight priorities in total!

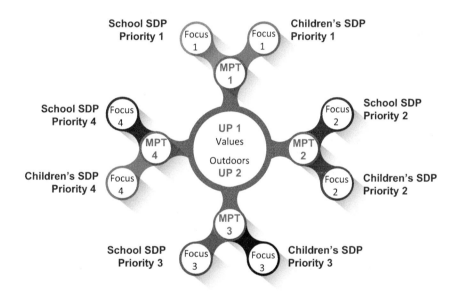

FIGURE 4.12 The Octopus Pupil Version of the School Development Plan

Headteacher and Learning Leaders Meeting 9

The final meeting achieves something very special indeed. The headteacher introduces the Learning Leaders to the concept of the Multi-Professional Team (MPT) and explains how every member of staff has chosen to join one of the priorities. The Learning Leaders are then invited to do the same. Each Learning Leader chooses the MPT that they would like to join this year and then is encouraged to develop ideas and become an 'expert' in that area. The amazing benefit of doing this is that they are then invited to *join the staff MPTs* when they meet! One of the most rewarding experiences and sights that I can recall is seeing the Learning Leaders run into school, with their families, on an INSET day, full of enthusiasm and excitement to join the staff MPT meeting. The feeling of seeing the Learning Leaders, from Reception to Year 6, work and contribute to their MPT Priority alongside all the staff members during the afternoons is very difficult to describe, but many staff and family members have commented that seeing the children like this '*makes everything worthwhile!*'.

Engagement

From a headteacher's perspective, the desire for all pupils to enjoy school and thrive whilst engaging with their learning is the same for all members of staff as they engage in their differing roles. The sectors of the HT-MEEE leading up to the engagement step have all been designed with this in mind. Prior to engaging with their everyday roles, the staff feel clear about the vision and ambitions of the school, they all feel fully included as part of the decision-making process that is helping the school plan and achieve its goals, and most importantly they feel they are working within a values- and trust-led culture that encourages, promotes and facilitates 'professional freedom'. The professional freedom offered is grounded in the firm belief that every member of staff is an expert in what they do and has access to the *resources, infrastructures and cultures that make it possible for them to fulfil their expertise.*

This JONK collaborative approach to leadership aims at setting up similar structures for staff as for children. In the JONK Model of Learning, the children develop an intrinsic enthusiasm to *want* to know and to engage with their learning because they know that the school has equipped them with all they need to succeed. The same value is afforded to staff, who feel enthused to engage with every aspect of their role in the knowledge that the school is also providing them with all *they* need to succeed, professionally and personally. Staff need to feel that, like the children, they have a 'middle table' (Chapter 6) where they can go to access all they need, working alongside other services and professionals. The goal with staff is the same as with the children: developing an infrastructure that promotes the well-being of all staff and the belief that for them, *in their roles, anything and everything are possible.*

Encouraging learners

The JONK Collaborative Leadership philosophy and approach create a culture that encourages all staff to feel free to take risks, follow their passions, experiment, discuss, reflect, collaborate within and beyond the school, accommodate personal interests and experiences, give everyone a voice and want to grow professionally. It is very exciting to plan for all-inclusive professional development staff meetings, INSET days and personalised programmes of professional development opportunities linked to the annual appraisal cycle of conversations and covering the school priorities, each person's professional role and their personal interests.

For many staff, the educational world can seem to be constantly changing with a feeling that they are always struggling to 'keep up' with the latest developments, strategies, demands, changes to routines, etc. As with the children, the JONK Collaborative Leadership approach, where, before implementation, the HT and the staff collectively consider the advantages and disadvantages and analyse proposals from a critical thinking perspective, removes barriers and enables the staff to focus on what, as experts, they know works well and leads to exciting outcomes whilst meeting regulatory processes.

Playing intellectually

From a headteacher's perspective, this sector is probably the most exciting one to see in action when walking round the school, when in meetings or when having professional dialogues with the staff. The JONK approach encourages all members of staff to view every day and every part of their role as an opportunity for professional growth through experimentation and action research:

- What do I really want to try today?

- What discussions have I had that have led me to want to try things out?

- What have I read that sounds really interesting to have a go at?

- What has a child or adult suggested that I think is really worth pursuing?

- What do I really *want* to accomplish with my role?

- How can I use the evidence of what I tried the other day to inform my future practice?

- How can I disseminate these findings and inspire others, in school, nationally, globally?

In order to make action research an integral part of the life of the school, the JONK approach developed the concept of *Enquiry Teams (ETs)*. ETs allow practitioners to discover new ways of doing things, interchange ideas, discuss the latest educational trends and perceive that they are working within a culture that allows them to flourish and grow professionally and that contributes enormously to their well-being, job satisfaction and retention rates.

The ETs are very similar to the Multi-Professional Teams and tend to be structured horizontally or vertically:

- Horizontally: All staff members across the same year group choose a topic, area or initiative to research.

- Vertically: Members from each year group combined to conduct research on a particular theme and discover how the same principle can be adapted to meet the needs of all age groups.

The Enquiry Teams work well if there is a focus for research for a whole term or sometimes for a whole year. The Enquiry Teams also make it possible for the headteacher to use the appraisal discussions and objectives to establish an action research theme for every member of staff as part of their role.

CASE STUDY | HORIZONTAL ENQUIRY TEAMS

The Learning to Learn Week

A Reception Team led an enquiry with the aim of investigating the best ways of introducing the concept of the Learning to Learn Week (LTLW) in the Early Years Foundation Stage. They dedicated the whole of the summer term to trying different initiatives out with the children who were now at their most receptive developmentally. They concluded that it would be best to launch their LTLW at the start of the spring term and use the whole term to introduce each initiative one at a time.

CASE STUDY | VERTICAL ENQUIRY TEAMS

The Lifelong Learning Dispositions

A whole staff team decided to dedicate a whole year to investigating how the concept of the lifelong learning dispositions could best be used with children in different year groups. The table below illustrates how this approach to action research can lead to an initiative being introduced across the whole school but manifested differently in each year group (Table 4.1):

	Evidence-Based Practice | Action Research | Enquiry Teams
EYFS	Taking one lifelong learning disposition and its associated animal at a time and devoting a set period of time to each (two weeks or a half-term, for example) to ensure that the concept of each one is fully understood before moving on to the next one. Some schools take the whole year to introduce all six and base a lot of their activities and opportunities on the disposition focus for that 'half-term'.
Y1	In Year 1, the children tend to really enjoy the dispositions from the perspective of the animals. They really enjoy having a physical representation of the animals in their classroom and love to go and get them whenever they engage in their learning. They also love to wear them as 'hats' and this makes them feel that they are being really curious, creative, resilient, etc.
Y2	In Year 2, the children tend to really enjoy using the dispositions to help them review their learning and check their understanding. Have they been really strategic in the way they worked out a problem? Could they have arrived at the same solution by using a different approach? Have they worked well as members of a group or independent learners? Are they curious for more?
Y3	In Year 3, the children tend to really enjoy using the dispositions to think carefully about the learning objective and about which dispositions they will need in order to succeed with their learning. They also enjoy using the dispositions to create and think through their steps for success or success criteria statements.

**Evidence-Based Practice	Action Research	Enquiry Teams**
Y4   A wonderful use of the dispositions in Year 4 involves using them as a means of building an inspirational, collegiate and supportive learning environment in the classroom. First the dispositions are placed on big charts on the wall. Then the students place the name of a friend they have spotted displaying one of the dispositions. This way, everyone can acknowledge and celebrate that person. Looking for these traits in others is a very special way of using the dispositions.
Y5   In Year 5, the dispositions represent an excellent problem-solving tool. The dispositions, by definition, tend to define what we need and how we need to be in order to succeed at anything in life. This led us to experiment with them as tools for problem solving (ELLI Project, 2006) and more specifically as branches of a Mind Map. Each disposition represents a different branch of a Mind Map, and the children use the prompts and their understanding of each disposition to structure their thinking and problem-solve. For example, if the children are conducting a science experiment, they place the title of the experiment in the middle of the Mind Map and use the disposition to plan, conduct and write up their observations by developing their thought process along each of the main branches of the Mind Map.
Y6   In Year 6, the dispositions have been found to be very effective in terms of transition. How do they need to develop each one with a specific focus on having a successful Year 6 and then making their transition to secondary school as smooth as possible? The dispositions have been great sources of primary–secondary transition projects and in helping with the language of learning that the Year 6 students use when they first meet their teachers and form tutors at secondary school.

Feedback

The JONK open-door policy and approach promote, at all times, a culture rich in formal and informal conversations, professional dialogue and opportunities to share successes, difficulties and barriers in a supportive way. Professional development is at the heart of the school's infrastructure, and as with the children, the professional dialogue and conversations allow all processes to become integral to the lifelong learning ethos of the school.

Equally important is the creation of an infrastructure that makes it possible for the headteacher to receive feedback from others, such as advisors, governors and peers. Regular critical-friend sessions with other headteachers are very valuable and work very well in the form of *Triads*. Visiting each other's schools on a regular basis and acting as a critical friend for each other are invaluable. So much can be learnt from visiting other schools as well from receiving feedback about one's own. The Triads are a great way of aligning visions, values and practices across collaborative partnerships and formal or informal affiliations.

Metacognition

The metacognitive stage for a headteacher is defined by the reflective and evaluative processes that allows the headteacher, governing body and Senior Leaders to make informed decisions based on the information gathered through a multitude of sources: the formal Self-Evaluation Plan (SEF), quantitative and qualitative data analysis exercises, questionnaires, evidence-based practice, the annual cycle of policy

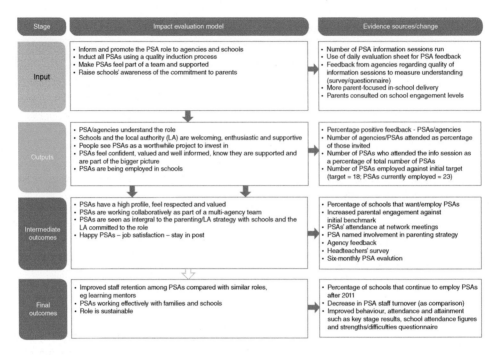

FIGURE 4.13 The Impact Evaluation Model in Practice

reviews, and a wide range of many other sources. In order to be able to plan for and obtain meaningful evidence from activities, initiatives, interventions or whole-school processes, it is very valuable to introduce the concept of the Impact Evaluation Model (Training and Development Agency for Schools, 2010). The Impact Evaluation Model takes schools through a step-by-step process (as illustrated in Figure 4.13) that enables schools to plan for an initiative and then ascertain the *impact* that it has had. The Impact Evaluation Model works extremely well when it is considered as a whole staff team as part of an INSET day.

The Teachers', Pupils' and Headteachers' versions of the MEEE Model combine to create a *whole-school* JONK Culture *for* Learning, Leadership and Management

This chapter has shown how schools are able to use the concept of the MEEE Model to:

- Help staff develop a set of bespoke areas that help drive the teaching and learning process and the school's philosophy of education

- Enable children to create their own version to help them navigate their way through their learning

- Provide headteachers with a structure for thinking about the considerations and strategic needs of a school

 SUGGESTED READING

In order to place this chapter in the global context of a whole school's infrastructure, it is very interesting to compare the principles introduced as part of the MEEE Model with the *nine intelligences* that MacGilchrist, Myers and Reed (1997) identify as characteristics of successful schools in their book entitled *The Intelligent School.* They define these intelligences as contextual, strategic, academic, reflective, pedagogical, collegial, emotional, spiritual and ethical.

5

The JONK 'Learning to Learn Week'

Principles and methodologies for implementation

The explicit teaching of how to learn is the most precious gift that schools can give
Marcelo Staricoff

The preceding chapters describe how the principles that underpin the JONK approach create the conditions that enable learners to develop a *joy* of *not* knowing and an intrinsic motivation for *wanting to know*.

Once learners become intrinsically motivated to *want* to know and learn, it is very important for them to feel that they know *how* to learn *what* they know they *want* to learn. Knowing *how* to learn therefore needs to be *taught*.

With this exciting challenge in mind, this chapter introduces practitioners, senior leaders and headteachers to the *JONK Learning to Learn Week (LTLW)* (Staricoff, 2014), which is designed to:

- Place the processes of thinking, learning and knowing at the heart of the teaching and learning process
- Create an inspirational and motivational learning to learn culture in the classroom
- Equip all learners with the tools, skills and dispositions of successful lifelong learners and creative and critical thinkers from the outset of the academic year
- Provide the practitioner with the opportunity to gain an in-depth knowledge of each child in the class as an individual, learner and creative thinker

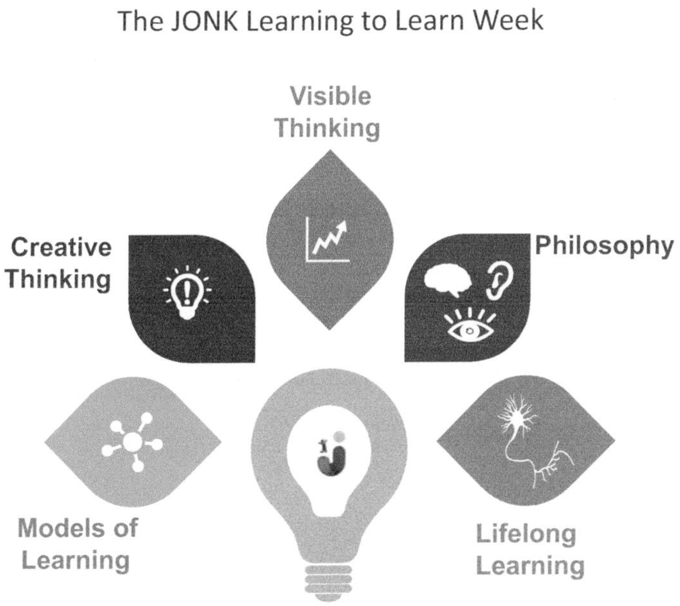

The JONK Learning to Learn Week

FIGURE 5.1 The JONK Learning to Learn Week

The JONK LTLW focuses of five principal areas of influence, as illustrated in Figure 5.1. Each of these areas of influence contains a series of strategies that are taught during the course of the LTLW. How to teach each of these strategies is the focus of Chapter 6.

Strategies for implementation

The most common approach for implementing the JONK LTLW is to use it as a way of launching the school's academic year, although as Figure 5.3 demonstrates, the non-prescriptive nature of the JONK approach allows for a number of alternative ideas. For example:

1   The concept of the LTLW can be extended to the start of each term or at specific points of the year. This gives practitioners the opportunity to introduce concepts gradually and strategically during the course of the year and in line with the learning trajectory of the class.

2   The introduction of the LTLW in the Early Years tends to be left to the beginning of the spring term, when all the children have had time to settle into their routines. Early Years practitioners may also want to extend the week to a 'Learning to Learn Month' (LTLM), giving more time for each initiative to be introduced and developed.

3   The last week of the school's academic year can also be devoted to a *Learnt to Learn Week (LTLW★)*, giving students the opportunity to reflect upon their year of learning and discuss the challenges of the year ahead. This schedule is illustrated in Figure 5.2:

The JONK 'Learning to Learn Weeks' (LTLW)

	Autumn Term				Spring Term			Summer Term			
	Sep	Oct	Nov	Dec	Jan	Feb	Mar	Apr	May	Jun	Jul
KS1 KS2	LTLW I				LTLW II			LTLW III			LTLW *
EYFS					LTLW / LTLM						LTLM *

LTLW I, II, III	Start of Term
LTLW	Start of Term EYFS
LTLM	Whole Month
LTLW *	*Learnt* to Learn Weeks

FIGURE 5.2 Scheduling of the JONK Learning to Learn Weeks

🗨 **DISCUSSION OPPORTUNITIES**

It is interesting to open up a conversation amongst the staff team and students to see whether the school would also like to adapt the phraseology of the 'Learning to Learn Week'. The options are endless and this is a process that can help staff and students to feel ownership of the concept of the LTLW that is being introduced:

■ The Learning to Learn and Think Week?

■ The Learning to Love Learning Week?

■ The Learning to Love School Week?

■ The Learning All We Need to Know Week?

Planning for a school-specific version of the JONK LTLW

The non-prescriptive nature of the JONK LTLW approach helps each school to develop their own bespoke versions of the JONK LTLW so as to embrace each school's unique ethos, vision, philosophy of education and emerging priorities within the school development plan.

Planning for year group- and class-specific versions of the JONK LTLW

The process of establishing a JONK LTLW in a school requires careful thought and an infrastructure that enables every member of staff to be able to plan for it. If the school is thinking of launching the academic year with a JONK LTLW, it is a great idea to devote the whole of the summer term of the previous academic year to getting ready for it. Devoting a whole term to the planning process can be very beneficial as it helps:

1   Every member of staff to become familiar with the principles and purposes of a JONK LTLW

2   Every member of staff to think about the types of initiatives that they would like to include from the 'pick and mix' menu and from their personal ideas that are relevant to the age group that they will be teaching in the following year

3   Every member of staff to use the summer term to engage in action research in their classrooms with their current cohort, experimenting with the ideas that they would like to include as part of the LTLW in September

4   Staff professional development meetings to be organised during the summer term that facilitate professional dialogue, the interchange of ideas, discussions based on the evidence emerging from the action-research projects, all enabling every member of staff to plan a bespoke LTLW that is specifically designed for their year group and that forms part of a whole school *progression map* of teaching the children *how* to learn across the school

A useful template to plan for a bespoke JONK LTLW

The template provided below (Figure 5.3) can be used as a tool to populate initial thoughts that would lead to a bespoke LTLW personalised for every practitioner and every year group, where initiatives to be introduced each day can be pencilled in the segments that emanate from each day.

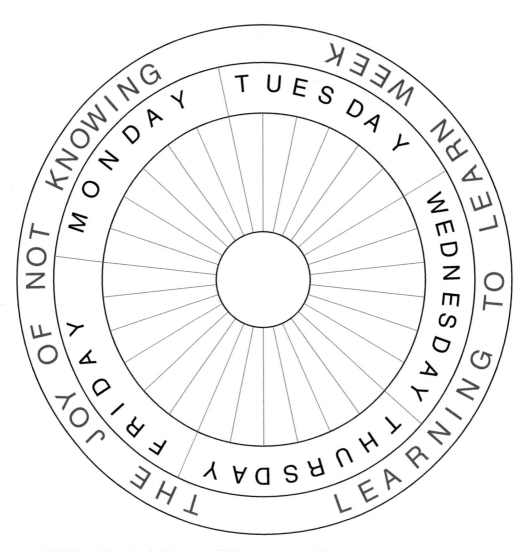

FIGURE 5.3 A Template for Planning a JONK Learning to Learn Week

6

The JONK 'Learning to Learn Week'

Theory into practice | A day-by-day guide of what to teach each day

We've had the most amazing learning to learn week. The children have come up with some wonderful ideas about how they see their learning, all talk about being in the pit when struggling in lessons, homework books have been replaced with family home-learning journals, we have been using de Bono's hats, are planning maths calculation videos (the children love these!) for the website and in form time this afternoon every group are going to be having a philosophy session. Staff have been telling me how much they have enjoyed it and how it has reminded them why we do this job in the first place.

Headteacher, Norfolk

This chapter takes the reader through a step-by-step process of how to launch the academic year by teaching each of the components that make up the five days and themes of the JONK Learning to Learn Week (LTLW), which are depicted in the diagrams that accompany Figure 6.1.

All of the ideas presented in this chapter are designed to act as prompts that enable practitioners to design their own versions of the LTLW personalised by age and year group. A blank version of the 'tube map' design is included at the end of this chapter for practitioners to populate once the final version of the LTLW has been designed.

The JONK Learning to Learn Week

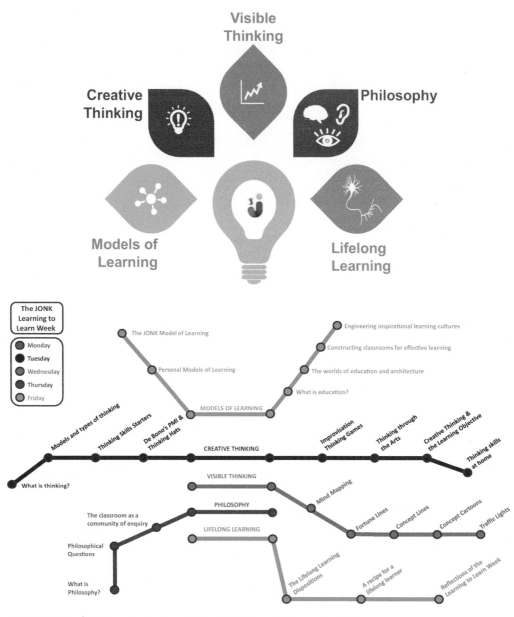

FIGURE 6.1 The JONK Learning to Learn Week and the Ideas to Cover on Each Day

Day 1: The models of learning day of the JONK Learning to Learn Week

What is education?

Schools as centres of excellence

The first day of the LTLW provides a wonderful opportunity to enthuse the children with a love of learning and an excitement of all that is to come. The idea is that by the end of the first day, the class will have built a consensus on the definition, purpose, value, benefits and relevance of learning, being at school and education.

The LTLW launches with a '*What is education?*' whole-class discussion. It is fascinating to immerse the children, from the outset of an academic year, in a conversation that helps them to tease out and reflect upon the purpose and value of education and of how schools work towards providing the very best educational experiences for all its students and staff.

Comparing the worlds of education and architecture

Teachers are architects of learning

Have you ever thought of greeting your new class with a discussion about architects and the world of architecture? Although this may sound a little bit unusual, I highly recommend it. Analogies, metaphors and models represent a well-documented way of giving meaning to a new concept by comparing it to something that the person is already familiar with.

The process that architects go through to create a successful end product, I believe, provides us with a very powerful analogy of how schools and education function. I have always been fascinated by how architects and the building profession manage to achieve what seems at first to be quite impossible. How is it possible to build a skyscraper, construct a suspension bridge or create a new underground system? Where does one start? There seem to be an infinite number of considerations that must be taken into account, planned for, time-lined, coordinated, communicated and resourced (as shown in Figure 6.2) before a project is able to get off the ground and go through the various stages that help it to come to fruition.

FIGURE 6.2 The Architect's Process

In order to ensure that the vision for a project is realised, architects start with an incredibly detailed plan in the form of a drawing, detailing exactly what they want to achieve. Architects then seek a wide range of skilled experts who work collaboratively over a period of time to achieve the final goal, continually evaluating their progress and reflecting on the aims of original plans. This is the same process for schools. As with architects, schools start with a very detailed strategic plan to realise their vision and then source skilled *experts* who work collaboratively over a period of time to achieve the final goals, evaluating progress and reflecting on the original plans along the way.

This analogy allows us to make a link in terms of the 'experts' that each profession uses as a means of ensuring that the vision is realised: architects source *expert* plasterers, bricklayers, plumbers and electricians; equally, schools source *expert* staff, children, families, governors and other service providers and stakeholders. It is fascinating for children to realise and take home with them at the end of the first day of their academic year the feeling that the school considers them one of the sets of 'experts' who make it possible for the school plans and visions to become a reality and that their role is to be the experts *of* learning.

Constructing a classroom for effective learning

Maximising learning interactions and participation

It is very interesting to continue to use the vocabulary of architecture to discuss with the children how best to construct their *classroom for effective learning*. What would be the best arrangement for the tables? How do factors such as the size and shape of the classroom, the number of children, health and safety considerations, fire exits, resource bases, reading corners, carpet areas, and light sources all affect this construction?

The JONK approach encourages the experimentation of innovative seating plans by co-constructing classroom spaces that maximise the effectiveness of learning for all. Great benefits are observed when the seating plan is based on a horseshoe or conference style design as shown in Figure 6.3:

FIGURE 6.3 An Example of a JONK Seating Plan

This design and configuration enable:

1   All children to *feel* equal as there is no predetermined seating arrangement that correlates with an assumption of a child's ability

2   All children to have a clear view of the practitioner and the board at all times

3   The learning to be presented to everyone at all times, making each person always *feel* included in the excitement that the teaching offers

4   Disruption of learning to be minimised as it reduces chats and distractions that can take place when students are seated in table groups

5   Everyone to focus on the person making the contributions

6   The centre table and space in the middle of the horseshoe to be used as a free-flowing and dynamic place of support that any child can access anytime they need a little reassurance or assistance. The design allows the practitioner or fellow student to engage in small group workshops with the children who have chosen to access support or reassurance.

7   The classroom to be very quickly adapted for group work, large space for drama, etc.

Engineering an inspirational culture *for* learning

An inclusive community of enquiry

Once the infrastructure and foundations for effective learning have been constructed, it is now a great opportunity to use the first day of the LTLW to establish the motivational and inspirational culture *for* learning for all. This is where each of the six areas that make up the values-led culture *for* learning described in Chapter 3 can be discussed. This enables every classroom to launch the year with a mutually agreed and co-constructed set of principles that transform the classroom into a 'welcoming and inclusive community of enquiry', where all views are equally valued and where everyone is encouraged to take risks with their thinking and to feel free to hypothesise, wonder, share ideas and value equally those of others. It is interesting at this stage to discuss and incorporate the principles that underpin the JONK multilingual thinking in multicultural classrooms approach, which are discussed in detail in Chapter 11.

> **SUGGESTED READING**
>
> At this point, it is fascinating to consider the seminal work of Lipman (2003). In his book *Thinking in Education*, Lipman describes the multifaceted value of developing communities of inquiry and, very interestingly in support of the section above, states that these communities allow students to '*draw on the experiences of each and make the resultant meanings available to all*'.

Introducing the class to principles and philosophy of JONK

Why and how feeling at ease with **not** knowing helps us to learn

Practitioners are now ready to use the JONK Model of Learning (MOL) introduced in Chapter 2 to inspire every child with a lifelong love of learning, thinking, knowing and *not* knowing. The concept of the JONK MOL can be introduced as an exercise that the children are able to experience by constructing a large JONK MOL on the floor of the classroom or school hall. The children can sit around the edge of the Pit as the process begins to unfurl (see Staricoff, 2014 for an illustration of this):

■   Two volunteers are asked to join the teacher and to stand at the top of the Pit.

■   Child A is asked a question to which they will definitely know the answer.

- When Child A replies with the 'right' answer, the teacher praises them and explains that as they knew the answer, they are allowed to jump across the Pit.
- Child A jumps across the Pit and lands on the other side.
- Child B is then asked a question to which they will not know the answer.
- Child B is given time to think about the question before they say 'I don't know'.
- The teacher gets really excited about Child B's reply and says to the class, with great enthusiasm, 'that's brilliant that Child B doesn't know! Why do you think that it is so good that Child B doesn't know the answer to my question?'
- They may or may not reply 'because they can then learn it!'
- The teacher then accompanies Child B into the heart of the Pit.
- Inside the Pit, the teacher asks Child B what resources, skills, tools, dispositions and strategies they possess and what the school equips them with that will enable them to have a go at exploring the answer to the question posed at the top of the Pit.
- This is a good opportunity to discuss strategies of effective learners, creative thinkers and problem solvers.
- Depending on the question posed, Child B may now ask a friend, research it on Google, try to work it out using a calculator, and so on.
- When they have come to a place where they feel they have been able to solve the problem and answer the question posed, they are allowed to climb out of the Pit and meet up again with Child A at the 'A'.
- The next question is the one that can have such a transformational impact on how children view the process of learning and how they feel about themselves as learners.
- The teacher asks the class, 'When I asked Child A a question and they knew the answer, did Child A learn anything?'
- The class magically reply 'No, Child A already knew it!'
- The teacher then asks the class, 'When I asked Child B a question and they didn't know the answer, did they learn anything?'
- The class then all shout out 'Yes!'
- This is the point at which the teacher points out that the only time when we are learning something new is when we don't know it to begin with, which is why it is *so brilliant to not know*!

The depth at which these concepts are shared with the children will depend very much on their age. It is important, at this stage, to discuss with the children that although today we have enjoyed thinking about how exciting it is to *not* know, there are many situations in life when it is actually vital and essential to know and to be able to 'jump across the Pit'.

Contributions from the class of situations in which it is vitally important *to know* can be very illuminating in helping children to distinguish between situations of knowing and of not knowing and of seeing the value of both (Chapter 2). The connection between *knowing* and *not knowing* can also be made by discussing the proposition that acquiring *new* knowledge *relies* on *building on what we already know*.

SUGGESTED READING

A very interesting article to refer to at this stage was published by Webb and Kirby (2019), who present '*an overview of three different models of education, relating to different educational purposes. Two emphasise conformity in knowledge acquisition – "mastering knowledge" and "discovering knowledge" – as well as a third, "not-knowing", that emphasises transformation in terms of what it is possible to know, to do and to be.*'

It is extraordinary how sharing the principle of the JONK Model of Learning with the children can have such a profound effect on the way they begin to perceive the process of learning and the way it encourages them to think, as they learn, about what *they know they know* and *what they know they don't know*. I will never forget the time when, after discussing the JONK Model of Learning with a Year 4 class, a child pointed out that when he jumped across the Pit, he *had* actually learnt something *new*; 'I've learnt', he said, 'that I already knew it'. This ability to think *metacognitively* is the basis of the JONK Model of Learning and Metacognition (JMOLM), introduced in Chapter 2.

Personal models of learning

Every child is an **expert of** learning

The first day ends with the most exciting and transformational activity of all. The day has so far helped the class to discuss learning in depth using a range of visual models. A great next step is to introduce them to the idea of thinking about how they view their own learning process to create their *own* model of learning. It is very helpful to share some examples with the children so that the remit becomes clear, enabling their ideas to begin to flow. For example, some children think of learning as climbing a stepladder or a staircase: they do it by taking one step a time. Or like building a wall, which they do one brick at a time (Figure 6.4).

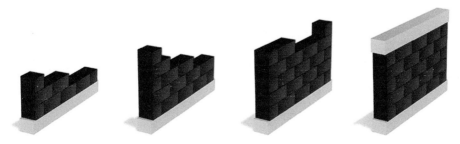

FIGURE 6.4 One Brick at a Time Learning Model

Some children view learning as climbing a mountain: They have to do it gradually. Sometimes it's easier, sometimes it's harder. They may have to camp halfway up overnight and need lots of *resources*, such as maps, nutrition and even another person who acts as the expert guide to help them reach the top (Figure 6.5).

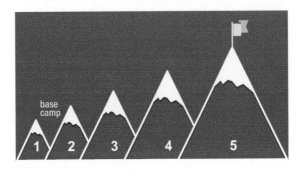

FIGURE 6.5 Climbing a Mountain Learning Model

Some children think of learning as taking part in archery: Sometimes they hit the sides, sometimes they don't hit the target at all, but sometimes they hit the bull's-eye! In this model, children also describe the 'effort' that it takes to load each arrow onto the bow, the concentration and focus they need when aiming. There are so many interesting parallels with the process of learning (Figure 6.6):

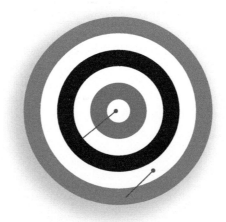

FIGURE 6.6 Aiming at a Target Learning Model

I really like the way this child described his learning. For him, learning feels like going into a maze (Figure 6.7): '*I'm not sure about the route out when I start, I often go down paths with dead ends, have to retrace my steps, but eventually, through lots of effort, I always find my way out*'. This model presents us with such a powerful analogy of how we all feel when we are learning something new.

FIGURE 6.7 Maze Learning Model

Children often describe their learning as being like a Formula 1 race driver: They have to manoeuvre around the circuit, use different gears and inevitably have a pit stop to re-fuel, change tyres, adapt to different weather conditions, etc. Or like an athlete on a running track, who is faced with hurdles to overcome and every time they jump a hurdle, that is when they are learning. Creating their own models of learning also encourages children to relate learning to something they are passionate about. This child used his passion for dinosaurs and his own interpretation of the JONK Pit MOL to create his 'prehistoric' to 'now' model of learning (Figure 6.8), where he is in *prehistoric times* before he learns and arrives at *human now time* when he has climbed out of the pit and learnt:

FIGURE 6.8 Dinosaurs Learning Model

This child used his passion for computers to create his model, which is wonderfully creative and original (Figure 6.9):

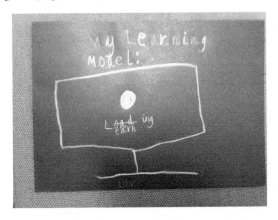

FIGURE 6.9 A Computer-Themed Personal Model of Learning

Once every child has had the opportunity to think about and create their own model, it is very powerful for them to illustrate it with an explanation of their thinking. The illustrated models make for a fantastic whole-class display and it means that they go home at the end of the first day feeling that their view of themselves as learners has been appreciated by the teacher and that *all children have been valued and celebrated equally as experts of learning.*

 DISCUSSION OPPORTUNITIES

The individual learning models represent a fabulous way for practitioners to communicate with each child about their learning throughout the year. Using the language of their learning model during feedback conversations is invaluable and allows these conversations to become metacognitively and pedagogically personalised for every child.

 CASE STUDY

The impact on well-being of the personal models of learning

One particularly powerful experience of this arose when a child described her learning at the start of Year 5 as consisting of a 'roundabout'. She explained that since starting school she felt as though she had just been going round and round in circles and not getting very far, which had led to her feeling frustrated and disillusioned as a learner. After she created her model, we used its terminology to find *exits* from the roundabout at every opportunity. By the end of the year, she was a transformed child, and she credited this transformation to the way the model had helped her to visualise her learning process, overcome barriers, develop a positive mindset and gain so much self-confidence.

Day 2: The creative thinking day of the JONK Learning to Learn Week

What is thinking?

Thinking for learning and learning to think

The first day (or Monday) of the LTLW introduced the JONK Model of Learning and described how the model can help practitioners to discuss the process of learning with their students and replace feelings of anxiety, uncertainty, worry and apprehension with enthusiasm, motivation, engagement, curiosity and intellectual playfulness. The second day (or Tuesday) of the LTLW also uses the JONK Model of Learning to focus on the importance that 'thinking' brings to each stage of the learning process. The second day is designed to place 'thinking' and 'learning' as *equal inter-related partners* in students' minds and as part of the daily routine of the classroom and school life.

The second day shifts the emphasis from learning to thinking and provides a wonderful opportunity to enthuse the children with a love of thinking in *all its forms* and with an appreciation of the value that thinking brings to their lives, in and out of school. The idea is that by the end of the second day, the discussions have enabled the class to build a consensus on the purpose, value, benefits and relevance of thinking creatively, of analysing concepts critically and of having the tools that help them to give *structure* to their thinking.

The day launches with a whole-class discussion about thinking: what it is, how it helps us, why it is important, how it can be defined, how it will help us to access the curriculum, how it links to the daily teaching and learning routine in the classroom, and how it plays such a key role in our lives. It is also really interesting to think of examples of great thinkers that they admire from history or their lives now.

What is thinking all about?

Is our ability to think creatively, critically and analytically something that differentiates us from other animals? Can animals think? How does our brain help us think? How do our brain cells work? What do they look like? Does thinking create new brain cells? Where is our thinking stored? How are we able to connect old thinking with new thinking? Should we always say what we think? Do adults and children think about the same things differently? Can we learn to change each other's minds after listening to each other's thinking? Can we demonstrate our thinking to others by using verbal language, written language and visual representations? Can machines think? Can we ever stop thinking? Do we think when we're asleep?

What are the different *types* of thinking?

This is a great question to discuss with the children and a fabulous way of starting to demystify and clarify the terminology that is usually associated with different types of thinking. What do we mean by creative thinking, critical thinking, analytical thinking, philosophical thinking, divergent thinking, concrete thinking and abstract thinking? Is it possible to develop our thinking *skills* in each one of these? Children really enjoy thinking about each one of these and find it fascinating that there are so many different ways of thinking.

Can we think about our thinking?

- What does thinking about our thinking mean?
- What does the word 'metacognition' mean?
- What does meta mean?
- What does cognition mean?

What is intelligence?

- How is intelligence linked to thinking?
- Are we all equally intelligent, just in different things and in different ways?
- Can we grow our intelligence?
- Are animals intelligent?
- Are computers and robots intelligent?
- Is artificial intelligence *intelligent*?
- Can artificial intelligence recognise feelings and emotions in our voices?

Welcoming the students to your class and to the new academic year by having these in-depth discussions about thinking is very powerful and 'previews' for them so many of the things that are to come, both as part of the Learning to Learn Week and as part of all that the JONK approach offers them during the course of the year.

Models, metaphors and analogies of thinking

The fastest car in the world

Earlier in this chapter, models, analogies and metaphors were used as a way of promoting a love of learning. In this section, they will be used to promote a love of thinking. In order to highlight the importance of developing the *skills* to think and to apply our thinking in a fruitful way, it is very useful to introduce the students to the model of *the fastest car in the world*. This model helps them to conceptualise the idea that *intelligence* is not very useful unless it is accompanied by our ability to *use it* in a purposeful way. It is interesting to ask the children to engage in a research exercise to try to find out which is the 'fastest car in the world'. At the time of publication, this accolade goes to the Hennessey Venom F5, which can reach speeds of 301 mph.

Once the class has determined which is the fastest car in the world, it is very interesting to equate our intelligence to the car's extremely powerful engine. In the case of the car, it would be incredibly dangerous to try to drive it if we didn't know *how* to drive it safely; equally, there is little benefit in a person's being incredibly intelligent if they don't possess the ability, or thinking skills, to use this intelligence purposefully. It is less about how much intelligence we have and more about how we use the intelligence that we all have. Viewed in this way, it enables all learners to feel *equally* valued as intelligent individuals. The LTLW is thus a great way of equipping each of them with all the skills of the best driver in the world!

The thinking skills starters

Daily open-ended thinking skills challenges for all to enjoy

> They make me feel so welcome and confident to create a new piece of knowledge. If I created a Mind Map of the Starters, it would be huge!
>
> R. (age 10)

When I started teaching, I was fascinated by that first interaction each morning with every child. I wanted them to look forward to coming to school, to enter the classroom, to the day that lay ahead for them. I wanted them to feel welcomed as they arrived, emotionally secure, part of the 'class family' and valued as individuals with so much to offer during the course of our days. I wanted to ensure that regardless of their experiences up to that point, either that morning or in their lives, they all felt equally special when in class.

I began to experiment with welcoming the children and their families with a little bit of structure, a routine that had purpose and that changed every day so that they would always have something to look forward to. For the families, I started to write the main learning objectives for the day on a whiteboard outside the classroom: they loved this and though a little bit time-consuming, it acted as a conversational prompt with families and as a way of linking learning at school with conversations about learning at home.

For the children, I started to have challenge-type exercises in the carpet area for anyone who was interested in having a go. I quickly realised that there was quite a thirst for engaging with these tasks, but the carpet area and one central place to write all the answers were beginning to get much too small for the interest they were generating. This is when I started to experiment with the idea of placing the puzzle-type exercise on the whiteboard so that all the children could access it. In giving each child their own Thinking Skills Book in which they could have a go at these challenges, I had started something that would become part of the daily routine of every class I taught since then and the publication of the book *Start Thinking* in the UK (Imaginative Minds, 2005) and Australia (Acer Press, 2006).

The Thinking Skills Starters have a multifaceted and transformational impact on children's perception of school, their intrinsic motivation, their creativity of thought, their enjoyment of thinking and their positive disposition towards all aspects of teaching, learning and thinking both in school and at home.

Chapter 7 is devoted to the Thinking Skills Starters – their philosophy, principles, strategies, ideas of how to implement them, and links with home – and is illustrated with numerous examples and anecdotes of the impact that the starters have had and are having across the country.

Chapter 7 also describes how the idea of the Starters extended to the playground so that families could engage with them before the start of the school, in an initiative that has become known as Thinking in Playgrounds (Staricoff, 2009).

Thinking pages

A freedom to experiment and take risks

One of the main benefits that I noticed with the Thinking Skills Starters initiative was the sense of freedom that the children experienced when having a go at them in their thinking skills books. The fact that these books make them feel so free to experiment with their thinking whilst engaging with the challenge is quite remarkable, presenting us with a fabulous opportunity to examine why this is the case and to ask whether the way the curriculum is taught can be adapted in certain aspects to achieve a similar feeling.

When asked, the children all explained that apart from the starters being fun and not feeling like 'formal' learning, they loved the fact that they knew that these books would never be 'marked' or 'judged' in any way. Could this feeling, this sense of freedom, be replicated in their everyday subject books? After many years of thinking about this, I think that the introduction of the concept of the 'Thinking Page' may be very powerful in being able to replicate this feeling and sense of freedom to experiment with their thinking in the course of the everyday lesson too. The idea involves devoting every left-hand page of their subject books to what is called a 'Thinking Page'. It is explained to the students that the Thinking Page is there for them to use in any way they like, experimenting with their thinking in any way that is helpful for them, and they are reassured that the Thinking Page, like the Thinking Skills Books, will not be judged or marked or commented on in any way unless they choose to.

The Thinking Page provides the student with the opportunity to have a go at things, not to worry if it's neat or not, if they need to cross things out or have several attempts at a spelling or a mathematical operation or at constructing a complex sentence. The Thinking Page allows the students to jot things down whilst the teacher is teaching. It is a great way of capturing their immediate thoughts without losing them or forgetting or feeling that they have to wait until there is a good moment to make a note of it.

In many instances, the Thinking Page is also a great substitute for the little whiteboards. They provide the students with the same ability to 'have a go', 'share' and 'show the class' but with the added advantage that it doesn't get rubbed out and lost for ever. The Thinking Pages provide a wonderful record of a child's understanding and of the depth and range of thinking strategies that they are using and the strategic resourcefulness with which they are tackling each learning objective or problem-solving exercise.

The Thinking Pages also provide students with a great place in which to write down comments that the teacher has made during feedback sessions, whilst walking around and looking at children's work, or that their peers have made during learning partner discussion and reflection of their learning discussions. It is a great way of ensuring that the teacher's continuous verbal feedback is recorded and not lost.

Students benefit enormously from the Thinking Pages and often describe how much freedom to experiment with their learning they give them and how they are much more willing to have a go at things, try things out without worrying and take greater risks with their thinking and learning. The main observation of seeing these in practice is how natural they seem to the children after being introduced to them and how much they enjoy using them.

 DISCUSSION OPPORTUNITIES

1   How could you introduce the concept of the Thinking Page?

2   Would you need to think about different age groups? Different subjects?

3   Do your staff or students have ideas for how it can be used in an adapted fashion?

4   Could they be every two pages, for example?

Structuring our thinking

Edward de Bono's PMIs and six thinking hats

I have always believed in and worked on the assumption that *all* children have a vast quantity of information, original thought, opinions and wisdom. I feel that as practitioners we find it very exciting to be able to offer them a range of strategies that allow them to make sense of it all, to be able to apply it systematically and to communicate it clearly. I refer to this enabling process as 'enabling children to be able to *structure* their thinking'.

There is no better source of inspiration for ways of 'structuring thinking' than the work of Dr Edward de Bono, who has dedicated his life to developing techniques designed at structuring thinking and developing the ability to think clearly, creatively and laterally.

 SUGGESTED READING

Edward de Bono has written extensively on the subject of thinking. I highly recommend one of his earlier books, *Letters to Thinkers* (1987), as a very enlightening, thought-provoking and inspirational addition to your library of books on thinking skills.

I will now describe two of de Bono's most useful techniques for the classroom – *PMIs* and the *Six Thinking Hats* – which allow students to structure their thinking and which are fun and easy to adopt as part of the everyday routine.

The PMI exercise | Plus, Minus and Interesting

PMI, which stands for 'Plus, Minus and Interesting', is a great tool to use in the classroom whenever one is trying to form an opinion or gather everyone's thoughts about a particular issue or subject matter. It allows the practitioner to quickly gather information from the whole class and use the collective thinking to make further decisions, plan next steps, ask further questions, or summarise thoughts about an initiative, topic or visit. Or if used before and after a topic is taught, to compare depth of thought and understanding of the topic, it can act as an insightful source of information for assessment.

If one asks students or adults to think about something that is about to be taught or discussed, hundreds of thoughts come into the person's mind, all as a conglomerate and emerging in one's mind in no particular order. PMIs transform these situations into ones of order and structure by asking us first of all to think, for *only* a minute, of all that is positive about the topic we are considering (P), then one minute solely on what may be the negatives (M) and finally one minute considering solely what we find interesting (I) about what we are considering. These could be, for example, questions, observations or connections.

The thoughts generated during each of these three minutes can be recorded by the students in any way at all: note form, pictures, diagrams or sentences. The process uses everyone's thinking and ideas as the basis for whole-class discussions to formulate hypotheses, reach conclusions, ask questions, discuss expertise and misconceptions, and make decisions about the next lines of inquiry and the trajectory of learning.

The six thinking hats │ Considering different perspectives

The six thinking hats are great fun to use in the classroom and are a fabulous tool for introducing children from a very early age to the concept that there are more ways than one to look at and consider a particular scenario, feel about a situation and try to find a solution. The thinking hats equip individuals for life with a multidimensional view and appreciation of the world. They promote an open mindset that helps individuals acknowledge and consider the ideas, thoughts, feelings and opinions of others whilst encouraging a self-exploration of alternative possibilities within one's own way of looking at things. H.L. Mencken (1880–1956), an American journalist, editor, essayist, linguist, lexicographer and critic, once stated that

> Moral certainty is always a sign of cultural inferiority. The more uncivilized the man, the surer he is that he knows precisely what is right and what is wrong. All human progress, even in morals, has been the work of men who have doubted the current moral values, not of men who have whooped them up and tried to enforce them. The truly civilized man is always sceptical and tolerant, in this field as in all others. His culture is based on 'I am not too sure'.

This quote is particularly powerful as it stresses very clearly the importance of valuing 'not being sure', of always leaving room for deeper consideration and possibly of entertaining alternative perspectives of what we believe at any particular time. The six thinking hats, by developing our ability to consider things from alternative perspectives, develop our ability to feel emotionally comfortable with being less certain and more unsure, the two traits that underpin the JONK philosophy and approach.

The six thinking hats are able to do this as they are designed to make us approach a problem by using six different ways of thinking about it. This is a very powerful tool, especially for those students who are convinced or have been used to thinking about certain scenarios in only one way. The premise of the six thinking hats is that each hat encourages the thinking, feeling about, visualisation and consideration of a problem or concept from a different perspective. The diagram below has been adapted from de

Bono's Group online portal (http://www.debonogroup.com/six_thinking_hats.php) and describes what each hat represents (Figure 6.10):

	The White Hat focuses on Information
	The Yellow Hat focuses on Positives
	The Black Hat focuses on being Judgmental
	The Red Hat focuses on Emotions
	The Green Hat focuses on Creativity
	The Blue Hat focuses on Thinking about all the hats

FIGURE 6.10 De Bono's Thinking Hats

Once the background and purpose of de Bono's Six Thinking Hats® have been introduced, it is very interesting to engage the children in fun exercises that help them to become familiar with the principle of and the type of skills needed when 'thinking about a problem using different perspectives'. Learning to consider life events from different perspectives is a very helpful skill to develop from an early age and contributes to the individual's ability to develop as a critical and creative thinker.

 SUGGESTED READING

Another excellent book from Edward de Bono (2004) is *How to Have a Beautiful Mind*, which devotes a separate chapter to each of the thinking hats. The book not only provides an excellent way of learning about each of the hats but also places the art of thinking within the context of everyday life and human relationships.

Improvisation thinking games

Using humour to build confidence and self-esteem

The Six Thinking Hats are fabulous for introducing humour into the daily life of the classroom. Indeed, Edward de Bono himself, in his book entitled *I am Right, You are Wrong* (2016), states that humour '*is the by far the most significant behaviour of the human mind*'. The idea here is to place children in scenarios that they volunteer to act out. The practitioner sets the children off with a particular scenario and then as the scenario is unfolding, they change the hats that the children are wearing:

1   Two children come up to the front, one is the waiter/waitress and the other one is the customer at the restaurant. The scenario is that they have come here for a very special meal and the food that has been ordered is taking a very long time to arrive. This works well if the customer is the one wearing the hats, and these are changed regularly as he/she is addressing the waiter/waitress with the problem they are facing.

2   The idea here is that the two volunteers take the role of a taxi driver and a passenger. The situation is that when the passenger arrives at their destination, they realise that they have no money or way of paying. The hats can be worn by both or just one of them: it works very well with all combinations.

Once the children become familiar with the properties and thoughts that each hat encourages them to have, it is exciting to start to introduce them within the daily teaching and learning routine. When the hats become second nature to them, it is fascinating to have a group of six children all considering the same problem, but each child is wearing a different hat. This allows different perspectives to be considered by the group and encourages the group to appreciate and benefit from the thoughts and ideas of others. If the hats that each child is wearing are exchanged between them during this process, then each child can consider the problem from a different point of view.

An alternative idea is to have big sheets of paper on the wall, each representing one of the hats, which the children can walk around, contributing their thoughts and feelings with post-it notes or by writing on the sheets as they go around. This is a very easy and non-threatening way of enabling the children to consider and think through a scenario, problem or task and of helping them structure their thinking and formulate their thoughts before discussing it as a class.

Thinking through the Arts

The image of the week

It is fascinating to introduce students to the concept of the 'Image of the Week' to promote their creative, critical and communication thinking skills. It works extremely well if, on a Monday, at a whole-school assembly, the students are introduced to a work of art (from an artist or from a child), which could be a photograph, a painting, a sculpture, a drawing or a mural. It could be linked to and have significance to a world event or a topic the school is about to focus on or it could be completely unconnected.

A little bit of background is offered to the students when the image is introduced, discussing the theme and the artist. The students then have a few moments to think about the work of art in assembly and contribute some thoughts. They can focus on how the work of art makes them feel, what it makes them think of or reminds them of, whether they like it or not and why, what they think the artist is trying to portray, or what it means to them. The image can be displayed as the home screen of interactive whiteboards so that the students can continue to think about the image during the week. It can also be placed as a 'display' in a corridor with post-it notes available for anyone who passes by to contribute their thoughts.

The 'Image of the Week' can also be placed on the school's website and in the school's newsletter to encourage critical and creative thinking through the arts at home. The website and blogs also provide excellent opportunities for the students to post their thoughts and share in the thoughts of others. Schools then decide on how the thinking that has been generated can best be shared and celebrated – in the end-of-the-week celebration assemblies, by creating a whole-school book, individually in each class, or by older children sharing their thoughts with younger children.

 **CASE STUDY**

Image of the Week

The Image of the Week initiative can be immensely powerful if one uses a work of art that has been produced by a child or parent: in terms of self-esteem, this opportunity is truly transformational! The image shown in Figure 6.11 was created by a Year 2 child as part of a Headteacher Challenge set to celebrate the number '100' on the hundredth day of the academic year.

The child went to the beach with his Mum, collected 100 things and created this sculpture. It was extraordinary to see how transformational it was for him – in terms of his confidence and self-esteem and of the inspiration he provided to lots of other children – that his 'image' was used as one of the school's Images of the Week (Staricoff, 2014).

An equally significant moment occurred when we used a painting from one of the parents, a local artist, as the Image of the Week. At the end of the week, the parent was able to come in and talk to the children about the art work, and the conversations, discussions and thoughts that ensued were extraordinary. It led to many children walking back to class, saying that they now wanted to be an artist when they grow up!

FIGURE 6.11 The Image of the Week Case Study

 **CASE STUDY**

Image of the Week and a national collaboration

The Image of the Week initiative, as well as promoting the arts in schools, has become the focus of a national community project: a collaboration between JONK and an arts charity, the Michael Aldrich Foundation. This project provides schools and other organisations in the community, such as care homes, with images of the works of art from the Aldrich Collection of contemporary art on a weekly basis for a period of three months.

The schools and organisations taking part have the opportunity to conclude the project by exhibiting the actual works of art within their setting, set up as a real Art Gallery. Each work of art is then curated using the comments that the students generated during the course of the project. The Art Gallery event is attended by the wider community and the friends and families of all those involved. This project provides a unique way of sharing the Aldrich Collection with a wider audience and allowing schools and other organisations in the community to readily access real works of art and make a direct connection with artists and makers.

Creative thinking and the lesson's learning objective

Engagement and motivation through curiosity and inquiry

It is very interesting to discuss with the class that the techniques introduced, designed to promote a love of critical and creative thinking, will become very useful when engaging with the curriculum and that these will be presented to them in a way that invites them to apply their creative and critical thinking skills as an inherent component of how all teaching and learning are approached. The details of how this is achieved across all areas of the curriculum make up the core component of the principles that constitute the JONK Model of Excellence, Enrichment and Enjoyment (MEEE) introduced in Chapter 4.

 DISCUSSION OPPORTUNITIES

At this point, it is interesting to give students a brief overview of the eight sections of the Model of Excellence, Enrichment and Enjoyment (MEEE) introduced in Chapter 4, highlighting how each section of the model promotes discussion opportunities for critical and creative thinking. A few examples (listed below) can be shared more specifically with the children at this stage so that they develop an enthusiasm for the way learning will be presented to them during the year:

1   The Learning Objective is a very useful example to use. The JONK approach postulates that the Learning Objective can be a more useful tool for creative and critical thinking if it is constructed and shared with the students *as a question* rather than as a statement.

2   If this question starts with 'Can we …?' rather than 'To be able to…', then students become used to the learning objective acting as a trigger for thinking and discussion, as a joint venture within a mutually supportive classroom learning environment.

3   If this question can be further developed and phrased as a philosophical question, then the depth of discussion that ensues and the level of engagement and motivation that results are extraordinary. Chapter 8 focuses on the impact of philosophy in the curriculum and has a number of examples of 'philosophical learning objectives'.

4   The concept of 'intellectual challenge' can also be shared with the students at this point, describing how they will have an opportunity to contribute their creative and critical thoughts when the learning objective is shared and through intellectual challenge whilst they are engaged in the learning and with specific follow-up activities when they have mastered their learning.

Creative and critical thinking at home

Start thinking at school, keep thinking at home

Chapter 10 describes how an open-ended, challenge-rich, thinking skills approach to 'Home Learning', which is the term JONK uses for 'homework', extends the creative and critical thinking culture from school to home. The approach is based on the principle of the open-ended nature of the Thinking Skill Starters. The idea being that the children *Start Thinking* (Staricoff, 2005) at school and *Keep Thinking* (Staricoff, in press, Imaginative Minds).

At this stage, the practitioner shares with the class the principles that underpin the JONK home-learning approach, which (as he or she describes) constitutes weekly, fortnightly or three-weekly open-ended challenges for them and their families to enjoy and which may be linked to the curriculum, world events or special celebrations or may be set as stand-alone activities.

Day 3: The visible thinking and learning day of the JONK Learning to Learn Week

What is visible thinking and learning?

Making thinking and learning visible and enjoyable for all

Among the most useful and valuable sets of thinking and learning tools that we can equip students with fall under the category of *visible* thinking and learning strategies. These are strategies that enable students to structure their thinking 'visually and 'diagrammatically'.

It is interesting, as children are introduced to more and more techniques during the LTLW, to discuss with them that all of the techniques form part of and contribute to their *'thinking and learning toolbox'*. As builders are able choose the right tool for each job from their toolbox, the idea is that children also feel that they have a toolbox from which they can at any time take the appropriate thinking and learning tool from their toolbox to access their learning.

Visible thinking and learning techniques help children to:

1   Circumvent the need for large amounts of writing

2   Make connections that they would not have made otherwise

3   Think without worrying that there is a right or wrong way of representing their thinking and expressing their understanding

4   Develop the ability to justify their thinking, provide opinions and explain their thinking to others

5   Feel free to create their own personalised visual design and interpretation of the learning being considered

6   Feel free to add to their visual representations at any time, as their thinking develops and they gain greater knowledge and understanding, freeing them from thinking that their initial representation has to be all-encompassing from the outset

Mind Mapping

Structuring thinking and making connections in our thinking

Teaching the children how to Mind Map has enormous benefits and becomes one of the most useful skills they acquire to structure their thinking at school and for life. Through Mind Mapping, the children are able to organise their thinking about topics, a piece of writing, a body of text, a problem to solve, a scientific investigation, a world event or anything at all.

The process of creating a Mind Map allows the student first of all to think about absolutely everything that they associate with the subject in question but without having to worry about the order or interrelationship of it all. The hierarchical nature of the branches of the Mind Maps allows them to order and classify these thoughts according to importance and by linking related concepts together. This process invariably leads students to make connections in their thinking that they would not have made otherwise, connections that may not always be prompted by other processes, such as taking notes or creating lists.

Mind Maps involve minimal writing and are icon-based, making them an ideal tool for all children. The applications are endless. When used before and after a topic, Mind Maps also provide the teacher with a very useful tool for assessment. Children use Mind Maps to describe themselves as they join a new class or to map all that they associate with an artist or a number. Children also use them for note taking, story planning, character sketching and science investigation write-ups. Mind Maps can be produced and added to whenever new ideas arise. They are visually very striking, and each child uses their creative flair to design a unique map even if the whole class are all focusing on the same subject matter.

The teaching of how to Mind Map is strategically linked to their first Home Learning Task (Chapter 10) where they are asked to produce a Mind Map of themselves whilst teaching a member of their family how to Mind Map. Teaching a skill to others is a fabulous way of ensuring that the student understands the concept. It can sometimes lead to some wonderfully unexpected benefits for their families too:

> When I started my nursing degree at University last year I was struggling with the written assignments. I could not get my head round planning my essays. Having learnt it with Mr Staricoff, my 10-year-old son explained what I needed to do was Mind Map my ideas. Suddenly what was a dark impenetrable mess of bits and pieces, became an organised plan from which a clear and concise essay emerged. He and I are very proud of ourselves.
>
> Year 5 Parent

 SUGGESTED READING

Mind Maps for Kids (Buzan, 2003) is an excellent book from the creator of Mind Maps, Tony Buzan, and contains excellent examples of different types of Mind Maps that can be used within a school setting and across the different areas of the curriculum. It is very useful to show the Mind Maps from this book to the children so that they see how creative every Mind Map can be.

It is important that a whole morning be put aside to the teaching of how to Mind Map. The instructions below are a very useful guide to offer the students a reference point for when they create their own at home. Once the principles and methodologies have been explained, it is a great idea to construct a Mind Map as a whole class to illustrate each step of the process.

A very good one to start with is a Mind Map of the school. Each child starts with a blank piece of A3 paper, which they use to create a column on the left-hand side. They write down in that column, in any order, all the things that come to mind and that they associate, in this instance, with school. This can range from pencils and rubbers to lessons, the purpose of school and education, the different parts of the building, members of staff, things they enjoy, their friends, events that take place at the school, numbers of children in each class and at the school, the timetable, anything and everything at all, all compiled as a long list within the column on the left-hand side of the page (Figure 6.12).

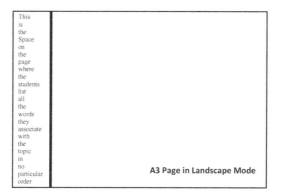

FIGURE 6.12 Making a List to Launch a Mind Map

Once the long list has been produced containing everything that the student associates with that particular subject matter, the 'making sense of all the information', the placing order to it all by structuring the thinking that has led to this list, begins to take shape with the use of the techniques that are part of the Mind Mapping process. The initial step, following the making of the list, involves each student creating an image that for them represents the subject matter being Mind Mapped. For example, if the Mind Map is about school, each student chooses their own way of representing 'school'. This could be in the form of a diagram, a letter, sets of words, or a photograph – anything at all. This is added to the centre of the page (Figure 6.13):

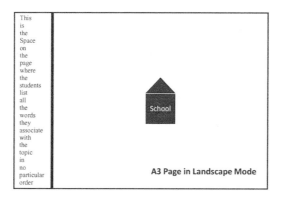

FIGURE 6.13 Adding a Central Image to Define the Subject of the Mind Map

The next step is very important as it is the step that gives the Mind Map its educational value. From the list that they have created on the left-hand side of the page, the student now needs to identify five or six key themes. These may be already listed as words or they may need to be configured as a result of looking at the words and thinking that 'all of these words have something in common'. These become the main branches of the Mind Map, out of which all the other information will be able to 'branch out'. These five or six key themes must be broad enough so that they let all the other words to be organised as subsections of these. In the example of a Mind Map about your school, the main branches may be:

1   Adults

2   Lessons

3   Buildings

4   Trips

5   Children

6   Families

The branches are then drawn coming out of the central image and this is where the main instructional point of Mind Maps needs to be made. In Mind Maps, unlike other types of concept maps, the *writing needs to go on top of the line*, not at the end. This is so that every line is able to keep 'growing'. The main branches should also be thicker and with bigger writing than with the other branches that develop from these. If possible, each main branch with its subsequent branches should have its own colour.

Once the main branches have been developed, the process repeats itself, but this time the student is looking at the list of words and thinking, what are the next most appropriate organisational sets of words that will help structure the thinking of each branch? For example, rather than listing all the members of staff out of the 'Adults' branch, one can organise this further and maybe start by thinking about:

1   Support staff

2   Admin staff

3   Teaching staff

4   Leadership staff

5   Specialists

6   Volunteers

From the Teaching Staff line, one could think about:

1   EYFS

2   KS1

3   KS2

Then from the EYFS line, it could divide further into:

1   Nursery class

2   Reception class

It is only at this stage that the named person or people may be added to the Map. This example illustrates how although on the left-hand side a student may have written the name of a teacher, the Mind Map has enabled the student to go through a very useful 'structuring of thinking' process that has allowed them to place each member of staff within the context of the whole school. If a similar process is followed, for example, with the branch dedicated to 'Children', this branch will eventually lead to Class A. The student has arrived at a piece of information with a direct link on a different branch, in this case being that the children in Class A are taught by the Teacher in Class A.

Whenever connections are made across different areas of the Mind Map, the student is able to show that they have made a connection by using an icon next to each of the words that the student wishes to link together (Figure 6.14).

DISCUSSION OPPORTUNITIES

Figure 6.14 illustrates how the student has made a connection in her thinking and then used an icon to demonstrate that she enjoys reading and writing at home and also at school. It is interesting to use this example with the class or the staff team to try to identify the other key features of Mind Mapping introduced above: the size of the writing on the main branches, the colour coding of the branches, the writing on the top of the line rather than at the end, the individual design of the map, and so on.

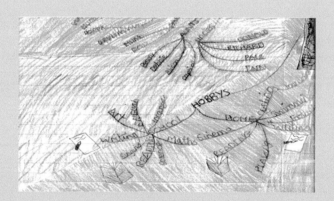

FIGURE 6.14 An Example of Using Icons to Show Connections in a Mind Map

In a Mind Map, each individual word that was on the original unstructured list is 'organised' within the map, and its position in the map is similar to a 'computer breadcrumb trail' where one starts with the hard drive, then the home drive, then the folder and then the document, and only then is the detail within the document seen.

The great value of Mind Maps is that the student is not constrained to the words they originally listed and wrote on the left-hand side. The actual process of generating the Mind Map will undoubtedly lead to new thoughts and new connections, which are added as the Map is being constructed. The way that Mind Maps are constructed promotes new thinking and also mimics the way our brain cells function and are structured. Tony Buzan's book entitled *Mind Mapping* contains a number of very interesting photographs of brain cells, which are very interesting to share with the students as they show how similar brain cell structure and Mind Maps are.

Once the student has included all the words on the left-hand side of the page within their Mind Map, it is a great idea to fold that column backwards so that all that shows is the actual Mind Map itself (Figure 6.15).

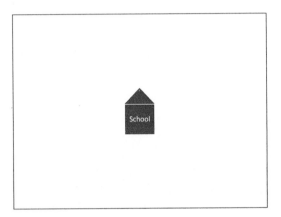

FIGURE 6.15 Folding the List Back to Leave a Clear Mind Map

Mind Maps also represent excellent sources for recording *works in progress* as they offer the opportunity to keep adding new information to them at any time. This is particularly useful if the students are asked to create a Mind Map at the beginning of a topic and are given the opportunity to return to it at any time during the topic to add newly acquired knowledge. Alternatively, they can be used at the beginning and at the end of a topic to demonstrate all that the student has learnt during the course of the topic.

A step-by-step guide to the art of Mind Mapping

It is very useful to generate a 'Guide to Mind Mapping' with the class and to give each student a copy of these guidelines to stick on the inside cover of their Home Learning Books. This helps them to complete their first Home Learning task and enables them to guide the adults at home through the process of Mind Mapping:

- Choose appropriate size/orientation of page.
- Create a central image that represents the whole.
- Write down all your ideas in no particular order.
- Decide on key issues/ideas (about seven).
- Create one branch for each key issue/idea using capital letters.
- Always write on top and at the end of lines so that the lines can keep growing.
- Make your branches grow and organise ideas from the list.
- Make your map personal and memorable.
- Use a different colour for each branch.
- Use word size to reflect importance.
- Use icons, diagrams and pictures to convey information and make connections.
- Add to it at any time.

Mind Maps can also be used as a *problem-solving* tool

Mind Maps are very versatile and can also be used as a way of thinking about a particular problem that is being considered or as a way of enabling students to summarise a particular piece of work. They work particularly well when used to write up a scientific investigation. The branches of a Mind Map are very useful: the student can use the different branches as a way of reflecting on the process, recording the method employed, the resources used, the results obtained, the conclusions reached and the new questions that have emerged after completing the investigation.

Fortune Lines

Analysing text and characters

Fortune Lines (White and Gunstone, 1992) are an extremely useful way of encouraging the students to become actively and emotionally engaged with text, both written and spoken. This could be a whole book, a chapter, an article, a poem or a video clip – anything at all that involves characters, either real or fictional. Fortune Lines allow students to analyse and interpret the 'fortune' of a character at any one time and to follow the 'fortune' of this character as time evolves. The student's thinking of how the character's fortune is evolving over time is represented as a line graph as shown below. Each character is depicted by a line of different colour, as shown in the example below (Figure 6.16):

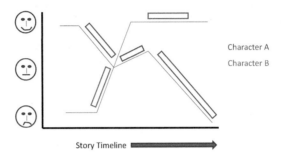

FIGURE 6.16 Graphical Representation of the Fortune of the Characters in a Story

The boxes that you can see on top of the lines are used by the student to annotate the significant events that lead to changes in the fortune, and hence the graphical representation, of that character within the graph, towards either a better or a less favourable 'fortune'. The boxes can contain sentences, they can be written in note form or they can be iconised. They are intended to act as an aide-mémoire for the student rather than something that will be marked or judged.

Fortune Lines are excellent interpretative and planning tools

Fortune Lines are very versatile. For example, the student can construct a Fortune Line Graph of the characters within a book that they have been focusing on in class. This serves as a way of illustrating their understanding of how the plot has unfolded and affected the fortunes of each character. This allows the student to visually summarise a large volume of text and to use the graphical representation to explain and justify their understanding and plan for what may happen next.

Fortune Lines enable all children to be actively involved as they are learning

There is nothing more wonderful than sharing a piece of text with the class and encouraging the students to construct a set of Fortune Lines to illustrate what is happening to each character in the text *whilst* it is being read and shared with them. In this way, students are constructing the graph live, listening to every detail and transferring their understanding as a linear representation of the changing fortunes of each character. This 'emotional' involvement with the text and the characters enables students to develop a great sense of curiosity for what is happening, inquisitiveness of why things are happening and a sense of wonder of what may happen next. Fortune Lines also provide an interesting alternative to the more traditional methods for note taking, such as using a bullet point list.

 SUGGESTED READING

At this stage, the reader is encouraged to explore a further set of fascinating work that is emerging as part of the University of Sussex Active Learning Network. The group, established by Dr Wendy Garnham, Tab Betts and Dr Paolo Oprandi, has created a global focus point for practitioners interested in an active learning process, which they define as when *learners engage in a series of activities which require them to produce observable evidence of their learning.*

Fortune Lines are excellent at promoting speaking and listening skills

In the example below (Figure 6.17), a 5-year-old child in Reception used a Fortune Line to interpret the story of Cinderella after it had been read to the class. The teacher was able to annotate the child's thoughts that accompanied the diagrammatic representation of the story.

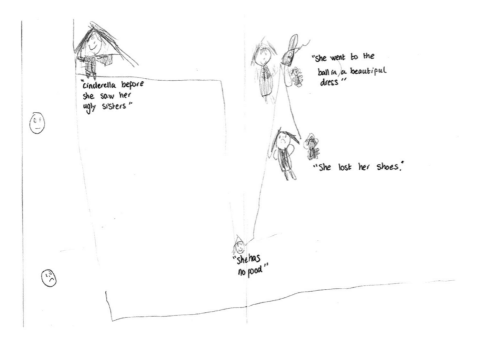

FIGURE 6.17 The Story of Cinderella as a Fortune Line

Fortune Lines can be combined with a 'Talk for Writing' approach

In the example below (Figure 6.18), the Year 2 child has drawn the Fortune Line 'live' as the teacher was sharing the story with the class. In this case, the story had been previewed with the class by using the 'talk for writing' process which had led to the chronological construction of the story using images from the book. The whole process made it possible for the child to annotate his thoughts beneath each of the images, thereby gaining an excellent understanding of the story.

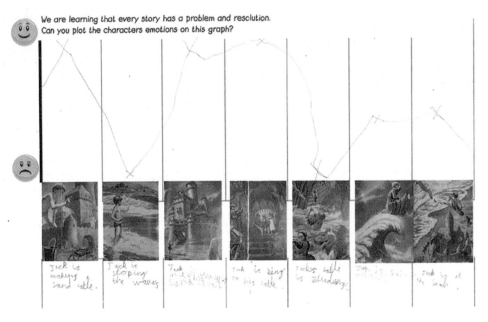

FIGURE 6.18 Fortune Lines Constructed 'Live' as the Story is being Read

Concept Lines

A continuum of thought and principles

Concept Lines are straight lines defined by containing 'opposite attributes' at either end. In this way, Concept Lines are able to create a 'continuum of thought' that stretches from one side to the other and from one concept to its opposite trait. The idea is that the student is able to indicate their thinking by placing a mark along this continuum. Without having to worry about there being a right or wrong answer, the student is encouraged to justify their reasoning by explaining why they have opted to place their thinking at a particular point on the Concept Line.

Concept Lines can be used across a whole range of areas. A common use is in the analysis of the characteristics of a character in a story. The student or whole class first decide on certain attributes for that character, one of which could be 'kind', for example. They then have to think of what the opposite for this may be. In this case, it could be said to be 'selfish'. The student draws the Concept Line with these two opposite attributes at either end and proceeds to place the character at what they think is the most appropriate point along the continuum. The versatility of the Concept Lines can allow the same lines to be populated with more than one character. This is a very useful way of visualising and comparing the relativeness of certain traits in different characters. It is also very useful to discuss that, with Concept Lines, it is not generally regarded as possible to be at the actual *ends* of the line. This is quite a philosophical concept. Can anyone ever be the most or least of a certain characteristic or attribute? The exception to this rule is when the Concept Lines are used mathematically and the line ranges from 0 to 1, for example. This can be very useful when learning about probability, whose range is 0 to 1 (0 indicating something that is impossible to occur and 1 something that is absolutely certain to occur).

Once a student has formulated their thinking, it is really interesting to involve the whole class in a critical thinking discussion scenario. It can be a great idea to recreate the Concept Line at the front of the class, using a skipping rope or something similar. The students stand and hold the line at either end, and they can have a whiteboard to indicate what they are representing. Another student is encouraged to come to the front of the class and place themselves along the line at a place that represents their thinking. The teacher can invite the class to see whether others agree or disagree. At this stage, a child may suggest that the student move more to the left or to the right. It is not necessary to reach a consensus at this stage, but it provides other students with a great way of appreciating the views, opinions and thoughts of others and, in the light of this, to maybe reconsider their own original thoughts. Creating a culture in the classroom where the students are open to changing their minds as a result of what others share is tremendously powerful and a great skill to have for life.

Concept Lines can also be used in combination with Fortune Lines

Concept Lines can be combined with Fortune Lines. When a whole story is examined as a Fortune Line, it is very useful to divide the Fortune Line Graph into sections. For example, one can draw vertical dotted lines to divide the Fortune Line Graph into Introduction, Build-Up, Conflict, Climax and Resolution. It is very interesting to place Concept Lines below each of these areas to map a character's attribute as the story evolves. Does a particular characteristic of a character change during the story?

For example, in the Fortune Line example above, Jack's bravery can be mapped using Concept Lines that consider how the character's fortune changes as the story progresses. In the example below (Figure 6.19), F represents *fear* and B represents *bravery*:

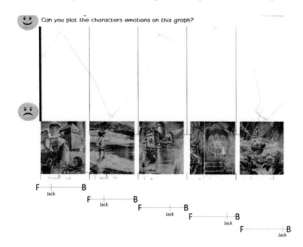

FIGURE 6.19 Combining the Use of Concept Lines and Fortune Lines

Concept Lines can also be used in combination with Mind Maps

The JONK approach and the explicit teaching of the learning and thinking strategies that are introduced as part of the Learning to Learn Week act to stimulate children's motivation and ability to think creatively. One of the most wonderful indications of how this can happen was illustrated by a child in Reception. The class were learning about Healthy Lifestyles and were using Mind Mapping as a strategy to structure their thinking about different types of *fruit* and their properties.

Completely unexpectedly and completely intuitively, this child chose to extend her thinking and make a connection between what was being taught and her personal life. She created a Concept Line to indicate how much she likes or dislikes each of the fruits on the Mind Map (Figure 6.20). We were truly amazed at the impact that introducing and *teaching* these concepts can have on children from such an early age: If the children have these strategies as part of their thinking repertoire and toolbox, they will intrinsically and independently incorporate them into their learning to further their understanding, challenge themselves, and make connections with their lives and the outside world.

FIGURE 6.20 Combining the Use of Concept Lines and Mind Maps

Concept Cartoons

Clarifying misconceptions, justifying opinions and considering alternatives

Concept Cartoons (Keogh and Naylor, 2000) are a fantastic way of presenting the students with the opportunity to think about a concept, which is usually represented visually in the form of a series of cartoons. As they set the students thinking about a theme or a concept through a set of statements that the different people in the cartoon are postulating, Concept Cartoons enable students to develop their critical, creative and philosophical thinking. However, out of all the statements stated, only one is correct. It is fascinating to use the Concept Cartoons as part of whole-class discussions, discussing each statement in turn and trying to work out the validity of each statement and challenging the students to offer reasons to support or negate each of the statements being considered.

In addition to representing an excellent source of discussion, Concept Cartoons are an excellent resource for assessment. If students are given a Concept Cartoon at the beginning of a topic and asked to comment on each statement independently using their knowledge and understanding of the topic at that time, they can be given the same cartoon at the end of the topic to critique. In this way, the teacher will be able to compare the reasoning, vocabulary and understanding shown by each student before and after the topic has been taught.

Traffic Lights

Everyone is engaged in learning and contributing together

Communicating with each other in class is a major component of learning and takes pride of place in the JONK approach. Introducing the children to the concept of 'traffic lights' encourages children to enjoy learning and thinking independently whilst contributing as a whole class and feeling directly engaged – something that the hands-up approach does not always facilitate.

Each student is given a set of three traffic light cards as part of the third day of the LTLW – one red, one yellow and one green – which they use to answer teacher-led questions. The idea is that the colours red, yellow and green could be made to represent anything at all, from feelings to opinions to specific scenarios. For example, red can be said to be solids, yellow liquids and green gases; the question can follow – what is steam? Is electricity any of these? And so on. In the example below (Figure 6.21), the teacher arbitrarily gives a numerical value to each card, which helps the teacher to ask interesting questions and for every individual to answer showing the teacher the appropriate card or cards. What is the biggest number? Which numbers are even? What number is two more than zero? What is the square root of four? By targeting questions of different complexity, the teacher is able to obtain an immediate baseline of understanding and a very useful indication of any misconceptions that may exist or gaps in knowledge that need to be addressed.

💬 **DISCUSSION OPPORTUNITIES**

Traffic Lights can be also used *during* the course of a lesson by students to communicate with their peers and adults in the class – placing a red card on their book to alert the teacher to a problem with their learning, yellow if they feel a peer on their table is able to help and green if they are ready for the enrichment task.

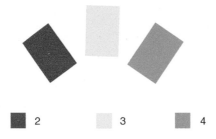

 2   3   4

FIGURE 6.21 Traffic Lights

Day 4: The philosophy day of the JONK Learning to Learn Week

What is philosophy?

A love **of** and **for** wisdom

The fourth day of the Learning to Learn Week provides practitioners with an excellent opportunity to introduce the children to the concept of philosophy and how a philosophical approach to learning at school enables the classroom to become an inclusive community *for* learning, critical thinking, wonder and inquiry.

It is very interesting to launch the day by analysing the etymology of the word *philosophy* itself. *Philosophy* stems from the Greek words *philo* and *sophos*, which mean *love* and *wisdom* respectively. This love for wisdom that philosophy instils makes it a fabulous tool for enjoying all aspects of the thinking and learning process. Children find it enjoyable because in philosophy it is impossible to be wrong … or right! Every view, thought, question and idea is equally valued and respected.

Philosophy trains everyone in being able to listen to each other, to appreciate and value each other's points of view, to discuss and pursue different lines of thoughts, to learn to see things form different points of view, to link learning to the outside world and very importantly to gain insights from others that can lead us to question our assumptions and even *change our minds*.

What is a philosophical question?

Questions without answers, more than one answer or impossible to answer

It is very interesting to discuss with the children that philosophy is all about discussing concepts and considering questions that *do not have an answer*, that have *more than one answer* or that are *impossible to answer*. Students find thinking about these three alternatives quite fascinating as they usually regard questions as concepts that have *answers*.

Generating examples of philosophical questions with the class

1 Can the class think of questions that do not have an answer?

- *Is there an end to space?*
- *Will time ever stop?*

2 Can the class think of questions that have lots of answers?

- *What is happiness?*
- *Is it ever right to do something wrong?*

3 Can the class think of questions that are impossible to answer … accurately? These are known as *Fermi Questions*, named after the physicist Enrico Fermi (1901–1954).

- *What is the population of the world?*
- *How many people holding hands does it take to go around the world?*

This introduction to philosophy also provides a great opportunity to discuss the concept of what *constitutes* a *question*. Can we define what a question is? What types of questions are there? Why do we ask questions? Why do very young children ask so many questions? What types of words do questions usually start with? Are there certain ways of asking questions that lead to more interesting responses than others? Why do people ask questions? What do we mean by curiosity? What do we mean by being inquisitive? Is wondering about the world around us and trying to work out how it works the reason why we ask questions? In which professions do people ask questions the most? Is the whole of scientific research and advancement as societies based on asking questions about things that we currently don't know but wish to discover? It is very interesting to note that Barrell (2003), in his book *Developing More Curious Minds*, places schools as places that can '*become cultures of inquiry wherein all our children learn to conceive and cherish questions and to act on these curiosities beyond kindergarten*'. Philosophy and a philosophical approach to the curriculum promote the asking of questions that emanate from our curiosity to be a central component of the teaching and learning process.

The classroom as a community of inquiry

Everyone contributing, enriching the experiences of the whole

Classrooms that are perceived by everyone as communities of enquiry enable every individual to feel free to ask questions, postulate ideas and take risks with their thinking. These classrooms develop a very respectful, inclusive and celebratory thinking and learning environment.

 DISCUSSION OPPORTUNITIES

What are the characteristics, values and behaviours that allow classrooms and schools to be perceived by everyone as welcoming 'communities of inquiry'?

At this stage, it is a good idea to use one or more of the philosophical questions that the students have come up with in the earlier exercise to engage in the first whole-class philosophical discussion, stressing and practising the main principles that need to be established as part of a philosophical discussion and way of life in the classroom:

- Listening to each other
- Only one person speaking at a time (the person holding an object chosen to signify who is talking to the rest of the group)
- Starting a new branch of thinking
- Building on what someone else has said
- Adult acting only as a facilitator
- Students choosing who the next person to contribute is
- Encouraging equity of participation
- Final words so that each person has a chance to summarise their thoughts at the end of the discussion even if they have not contributed during the discussion

The day concludes by explaining to the students that these types of whole-class discussions will form the basis for all learning and across all topics in the curriculum. This enables students to feel enthusiastic about all that is to come in the year ahead and to feel that the learning will take place in a very supportive and inclusive learning environment.

Day 5: The lifelong learning dispositions day of the JONK Learning to Learn Week

The lifelong learning dispositions

Successful learners and thinkers for life

We have now come to the fifth and final day of the Learning to Learn Week. This provides a great opportunity to introduce the students to the concept of 'effective lifelong learning' and to the dispositions and characteristics that are associated with *being* a successful learner for life.

The lifelong learning dispositions form part of the school's culture *for* learning, described in Chapter 3. Chapter 9 is dedicated to the theoretical and practical applications of the lifelong learning dispositions across all areas of the teaching and learning process and the routine of the classroom. This fifth day of the LTLW is designed to enable teachers to:

1   Discuss the concept that '*learning is a skill we all need for life*'

2   Develop a whole-class consensus of what is needed to become an effective and successful lifelong learner

3   Discuss the main features of the terms usually associated with lifelong learning: resilience, creativity, critical curiosity, strategic awareness, meaning making, learning relationships and changing and learning (Staricoff, 2006)

4   Make links between this consensus and the school's vision, ethos and values and culture *for* learning

5   Explain that the lifelong learning dispositions equip everyone with all they need to succeed as learners across all areas of the curriculum

6   Inspire all students to create their own *Recipe for a Lifelong Learner* (as described below)

7   Reflect on the *value* of all that has been introduced to help them learn *how* to learn during all five days of the LTLW

A recipe for a lifelong learner

The dispositions as ingredients

There is nothing more wonderful than devoting the fifth day of the Learning to Learn Week to discussing the concept of lifelong learning with the students, exploring with them how education and school equip them with all they need to thrive in the outside world and for each student to enjoy using their imagination to create their own recipe for a lifelong learner.

As with all recipes, the students start by thinking of the ingredients they will need. They think creatively of how much of each ingredient they will use in their recipe. They develop their step-by-step method to 'cook' the ingredients and they explain what the final product looks like and how it should be best 'served'. Chapter 8 describes how this task can be set as a Thinking Skills Starters challenge, and Chapter 9 offers an illustrated example of how this exercise can be performed as a whole as the first step of generating the dispositions for the school.

This exercise gives each student complete freedom to create their recipe as they wish, but what is so beneficial from this as a whole class is the list of ingredients that each student contributes. These ingredients will automatically contain all the attributes, characteristics, dispositions, traits and behaviours that we are seeking as practitioners to develop and instil in our students. This exercise helps the students to generate the dispositions themselves. When all the ideas for the *ingredients* are being pooled together, it is interesting to look for common themes and consider these in the context of all that the school already has in place to help children succeed as learners.

These recipes, like the personalised models of learning, also make for a fantastic display that the students are proud of and that brings the principles of the Learning to Learn Week to life as an integral component of the teaching and learning process.

Reflections on the Learning to Learn Week

Feeling equipped to succeed as an individual, learner and thinker and as a valued member of the classroom's and school's community of enquiry

It is very interesting to end the LTLW by asking the students some self-reflection questions:

1   *What do you think has been the value of the LTLW?*

2   *How do you think the LTLW will help you think and learn?*

3   *Is there anything else you would like us to include within an LTLW?*

The reflection process makes it possible for students to internalise all that the LTLW has given them and has equipped them to help them enjoy accessing and grappling with the demands of the year ahead. This time of reflection also provides the perfect opportunity to steer the conversation back to the more philosophical purpose of education and school which launched the week. As a class, it may be interesting to end the LTLW by co-constructing an agreed definition of the purpose of education:

1   *Prepares the student for a lifetime of success*

2   *Equips students with all the tools and dispositions that enable them to thrive in school and society and in all that they encounter throughout their lives*

  SUGGESTED READING

The end of the Learning to Learn Week, which launches the rest of the academic year, provides the reader with a great opportunity to place all the initiatives of the LTLW in perspective and explore the work of the Yurt Academy, an organisation founded by Alexandra Pearson and Bridget Rooth to explore and promote the *human intelligences of curiosity, creativity and connectedness*, which they regard as *the foundation of learning and growth and the pillars of individual and organisational development* that *strengthen* your *organisational resilience and engagement* and help build *agile, collaborative, innovative and stress-resistant teams*. In an interview for the Yurt Academy, I describe *curiosity as being the antidote to certainty*. Can you use this statement and the sentiment of the article (www.yurtacademy.com) as the basis of a discussion with students and staff? What is everyone's interpretation of this statement, and how can thinking about curiosity, certainty and uncertainty be integrated into the everyday teaching and learning process?

A useful template to design a bespoke JONK LTLW

The template provided below (Figure 6.22) can be used as a tool to populate the final choice that every teacher and every year group have chosen to include in their bespoke Learning to Learn Week, where each initiative takes its place as part of the stations on each day of the 'tube map'.

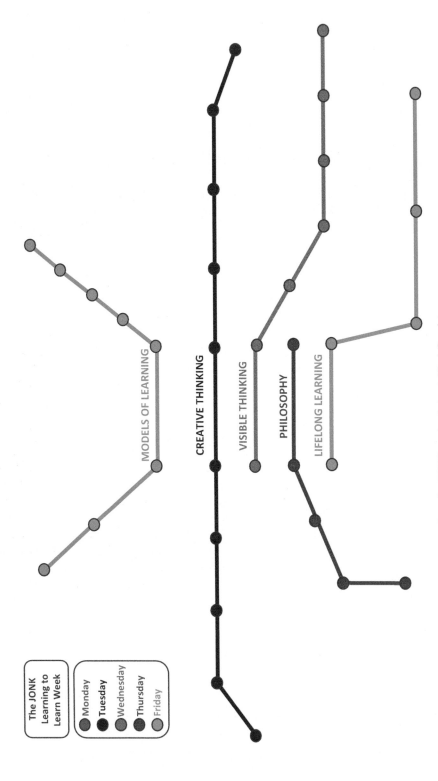

MODELS OF LEARNING

CREATIVE THINKING

VISIBLE THINKING

PHILOSOPHY

LIFELONG LEARNING

The JONK
Learning to
Learn Week

Monday
Tuesday
Wednesday
Thursday
Friday

FIGURE 6.22 A Template for Schools to Create a Bespoke JONK Learning to Learn Week Populate

7

The Thinking Skills Starters

They wake me up like an alarm clock, they make me feel wonderful, a magical start to the day

Child (age 10)

This chapter introduces the reader to the concept of the JONK Thinking Skills Starters (TSSs) (*Start Thinking*; Staricoff and Rees, 2005, 2006), which are open-ended challenges that greet the families as they arrive in the playground each morning (Staricoff, 2009) and the children as they enter their classrooms (Staricoff, 2003, 2004).

The concept of welcoming the children with an enjoyable, motivational and exciting creative thinking challenge was introduced to the reader in Chapter 6 as part of the second day of the Learning to Learn Week, a day that focuses on strategies that develop children's creative, analytical, philosophical and critical thinking skills.

Children often report that the Thinking Skills Starters are not just an enjoyable way to start their day but also an essential component that prepares them for the day ahead. The Starters also enable the teachers to start the day with a class in which every child has experienced success as a learner and creative thinker *before* formal learning is launched.

Whilst the children are immersed in the Starters, it is a great idea to play classical music in the background and to take the register, if at all possible, in a language other than that used as the principal language of instruction. Thinking creatively, within a learning environment rich in music and language, is a wonderful way to begin each day.

The Thinking Skills Starters approach offers:

1　Open-ended challenges for all children to enjoy and feel success with

2　Opportunities to promote creative thinking across all areas of the curriculum and of life

3　Children a dedicated Thinking Skills book, which becomes very special to them in terms of their ability to think freely and without worrying as they know that these are the only books that the teacher will not mark or judge in any way

4　Opportunities to keep engaging with the concepts in their own free time

5   Opportunities for all, adults and children to innovate and contribute suggestions that can be used as a Starter for the whole class – anything and everything can become a Starter.

The Starters can be used as stand-alone activities, as ways of celebrating a national or international event or as a way of previewing and pre-thinking a particular area of the curriculum, especially if that is the focus of the lessons that day. Once the Register has been taken, the next few minutes are dedicated to sharing the thinking and ideas that the Starter has inspired. These moments are always filled with the most wonderful examples of children's ability to think so imaginatively, creatively and innovatively when all the right conditions come together.

 DISCUSSION OPPORTUNITIES

At this stage, it is very useful to discuss with the staff how the principle of the Starters can best be introduced across the school so that all age groups can enjoy them. Some considerations for discussion are offered in the section below:

1   *In the Early Years*, the Starter could, for example, be placed on the carpet on a big piece of paper for the children to enjoy contributing to as a group, as shown in Figure 7.1:

FIGURE 7.1 The Thinking Skill Starters in the Early Years

2 *In Key Stage 1*, it may be more motivational for the children if they encounter them once or twice a week rather than every day. It works very well in Key Stage 1 if the Starter is pre-printed on a sticky label and stuck in the children's Thinking Skills books, ready for them to enjoy when they come in and open their books, as shown in Figure 7.2. The 'Odd One Outs' challenges are excellent ways of inspiring children to think creatively and justify their thinking:

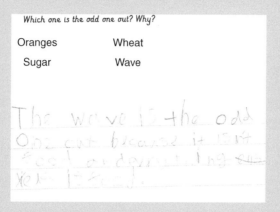

FIGURE 7.2 The Thinking Skills Starters in Key Stage 1

3 *In Key Stage 2*, the Starters tend to work very well when they are presented to the children as a daily routine and placed on the whiteboard for all to engage with as they come into the classroom in the morning. In the example below (Figure 7.3), the class is greeted with the challenge of *illustrating verbs by using the first letter of that verb* and with an example, which in this case is the diagram with a 'c' on an incline, representing the verb 'climb'. This Starter was used as a precursor to a lesson on verbs:

Thinking Skills

FIGURE 7.3 Starters in Key Stage 2

The Thinking Skills Starters initiative | Theory into practice

The book entitled *Start Thinking* (Staricoff and Rees, 2005, 2006) contains a large selection of challenges which are grouped into themed chapters: *mathematical, linguistic, scientific, creative, philosophical* and *favourites*. Each challenge is illustrated with a worked example (or examples) from children across the primary age range. Each challenge is also accompanied by a guide that shows the teacher how the Starter links to and supports the different areas of the curriculum. Two Starters are particularly geared towards helping teachers present the idea of Starters to the class for the first time:

Laughter is the best medicine

Things that make you happy or that make you laugh

This is a fantastic way of welcoming the children to their new class and the new academic year. This Starter gives children the opportunity to share special moments in their lives with the rest of the class and with the adults who will be with them for that year. For the children to feel that everyone knows, appreciates and values what makes them happy can be a very important part of how they feel throughout the year. This Starter is also a wonderful way of creating a sense of inclusion and well-being for each child and of placing humour at the heart of the classroom learning culture (Figure 7.4):

People tickling me	Some jokes
People telling me jokes	Being chased
My little sister	Being tickled
My Dad	Joe's hiccups
Finding funny things when we're spying in the playground	My sister Kate
	Mary Poppins
Standing on one finger in the baby pool	Terrible TV programmes
	My family
Xavier's made up song	My brother's emails
Talking in a made-up language	Mum's puddle fish impression

FIGURE 7.4 Things that Make Me Laugh

Anything and everything is possible

What could each one of these shapes represent?

This Starter, shown in Figure 7.5, represents a fantastic way of promoting creative thinking and providing children with the idea that their lives outside of school can always come to the fore and be valued in school. In the examples below (Figure 7.6), a child who was fascinated by space connected *the circle* to the sun and a planet, a child who loved maths immediately saw *the line* as a 'line of symmetry' and a child who was very artistic immediately connected the *four dots* to 'heads of people from above':

FIGURE 7.5 What Can These Shapes Be?

YEAR 5	YEAR 5	YEAR 5
Sun	String	The four on a dice
Egg	Ruler	Heads of people from above
Eye	Line of symmetry	Four coins on a table
Eardrum	Pen	Stars in a new galaxy
Hole	Javelin	Four peas left on a plate by a tidy person
Porthole	Charcoal	
Globe	Sausage	
Planet	Beginning of a mountain	

FIGURE 7.6 What Can These Shapes Be?

Using mathematics to promote creative thinking

There is so much one can do with mathematical-based Starters. They are a wonderful way of getting children to enjoy playing with mathematical concepts, to develop strategic thinking through maths, to make links between numbers and their everyday lives, to consolidate concepts covered in the curriculum and to enjoy playing with numbers – sometimes in ways that do not involve maths at all! Here is a very entertaining one to present to the children:

If 6 is the answer, what could the questions be?

This Starter invites children to think creatively and to make lots of links between number as a mathematical concept and how we use numbers without their having a specific mathematical operation linked to it. This child (Figure 7.7) has made many mathematical links but also used other aspects of his personal life to make connections with the number six. Realising that there are six letters in his name was fabulous!

The answer is six.

3+3   4+2   5+1   6+0   2+4   1+5
0+6

What is half of twelve?

What is a quarter of twenty-four?

How old was my sister a year and a half ago?

How many sides does a hexagon have?

How many letters are there in my first name?

What year will i be in next year?

FIGURE 7.7 Questions that have an Answer of 6

Magic triangles

Can you make the sum of every side equal?

This task – which involves using the numbers 1, 2, 3, 4, 5, 6 in the circles below (Figure 7.8) to make every side of the triangle add up to 9 – is entertaining and it is an excellent task for introducing children to thinking strategically.

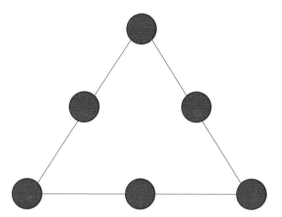

FIGURE 7.8 Magic Triangles

Once the children have completed the triangle to 9, they are asked to use the same numbers to make every side up to 12 (Figure 7.9). Before doing the triangle-to-12 version, the children are asked to consider the numbers at each apex of the triangle to 9. As the number in each apex is used twice in this exercise (compared with the numbers along the lines, which are used only once), can they think of how the triangle to 12 may look? This time, could they solve the problem strategically rather than through trial and error?

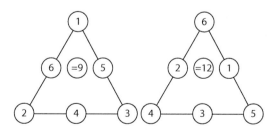

FIGURE 7.9 Magic Triangles to 9 and 12

The four fours challenge

Can you use four fours each time to make every number?

This is a superb challenge that introduces a great deal of playfulness to mathematics. The children are tasked with having to calculate every number using *four fours* each time and any mathematical operation that they wish. For this task, the children, across all ages, are introduced to concepts such as square root, squared, cubed, and power of zero (which makes any number equal one) and to factorials, which in the case of four is $4 \times 3 \times 2 \times 1 = 24$. Children very soon become addicted to this challenge as they begin to spot patterns that help them to generate more and more numbers. Incredibly, on one occasion, four 10-year-old children decided to get together after school, on the day that this task was presented to them, returning the next day having worked out every number up to 150 and having presented their answers so wonderfully on a large piece of card, as shown in Figure 7.10:

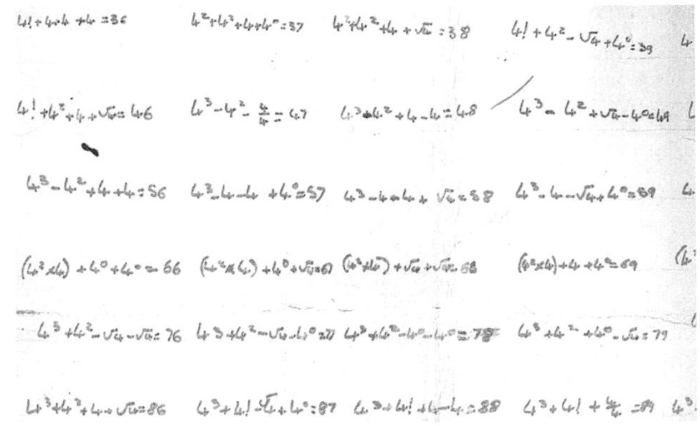

FIGURE 7.10 The Four Fours Challenge

The impact that the Four Fours Challenge had on children's enthusiasm for maths and on their creative thinking led to the publication of an article in the journal *Teaching Thinking* (Staricoff, 2004).

The Wonders of Pi

This challenge is fantastically creative and is usually set when the children are learning about shape or about the properties of circles. It is also an ideal Starter to set on the 14th of March, which is designated as International Pi Day – as when written in short as the month and day, it becomes 3.14! Once the children have been introduced to the mathematical concept of Pi, they are presented with the idea of *writing using the number sequence* of Pi.

Combining literacy with numeracy is very exciting indeed. The challenge is to write a sentence or phrase or even to make a list of words in which the number of letters in the words used follows the sequence of Pi. The first word of the sentence must use three letters, the second word must use one letter and so on. Figure 7.11 shows some examples from 10- and 11-year-old children:

YEAR 6

Can I have a large chocolate in France, Italy and Spain?

YEAR 5

Word pattern: Words begin with 'I'

Ink, I, Inch, I, Image, Important, In, Invent, Irish, Ice, index

YEAR 6

The 'B' note I sound strumming my guitar makes you happy.

FIGURE 7.11 Poetic Pi

This challenge, however, is not restricted to children. Teachers often become fascinated by it, too. This example from a teacher, linked so well to the world of education, is truly wonderful:

> *Why I need a sound education is simple. Where will folks discover challenge without knowledge?*

SUGGESTED READING

Writing in the sequence of Pi has even developed its own language, which is known as pilish. *Not A Wake* (2010) by Mike Keith is the first book ever written completely in pilish. The author writes the book using the first 10,000 numbers of the sequence of Pi!

Using literacy and language to promote creative thinking

Language and literacy-based Starters offer great versatility and are able to support learning across a wide variety of subject areas.

Word associations

Starters can often and very unexpectedly resonate so much with a child that they transform the way they feel about learning and about themselves as learners. This is wonderfully illustrated in the case study that accompanies this *word association challenge*. In this challenge, the children get the chance to play with the first word that comes into their mind and that they associate with the previous word. So, for example, if one starts with the combination:

Hat	Wear	then the next line could be
Wear	Clothes	and then
Clothes	Summer	and so on

 CASE STUDY

The Thinking Skills Starters and their impact on children's self-esteem, well-being and life chances

Prior to coming across this Starter, D was not a child who enjoyed literacy very much, finding it very difficult, especially when having a go at sustained pieces of work. As soon as he came across this Starter, something happened that meant that he could not stop. He wrote page after page after page at school and at home. It was extraordinary to see the transformation in him, in his confidence, in how others started to regard him now as a *literary expert* and in his love for learning and for school. He went on to have a very successful Year 6, transition to secondary school and currently adult life. Figure 7.12 shows a 'small sample' of what he produced:

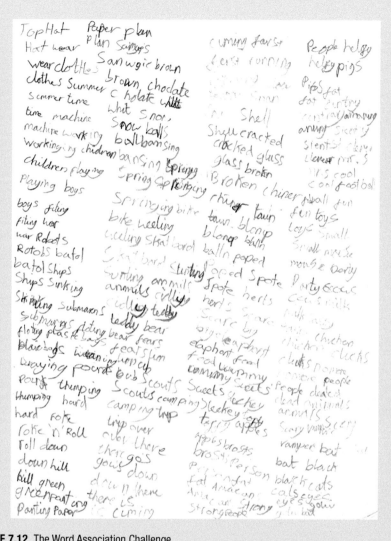

FIGURE 7.12 The Word Association Challenge

A-Z lists

Creating an A-Z list can be adapted to many different situations, and the children really enjoy the fact that they don't necessarily have to find an answer to each of the letters in the allocated time since when the sharing takes place the alphabet set will be completed by the different contributions from everyone in the class. These tend to be set at the beginning of a topic or when there is an interesting event taking place in the world. For example, when the Olympics are on, it is a great idea to do an A-Z of Olympic Sports.

In the example below (Figure 7.13), the Year 1 class created an A-Z of 'School'. It is very interesting to note that the P is associated with philosophy!

YEAR 1: SCHOOL

A: Assembly

B: Books,

C: Concentrating, capacity

D: Drawing

E: End of the year, experiment

F: Fun, football

G: Garden shop (home corner)

H: Home corner

I: ICT

J: Jumping

K: Kicking a football

L: Literacy

M: Music

N: Numeracy

O: One hundred blocks

P: Philosophy, planning, PE, playtime

Q: Quiet

R: Reading

S: Sweets, symmetry, sports day, science

T: Terrific work, TV

U: Umbrella mending (materials topic)

V: Victorians

W: Work

X: Xavier second in running race

Y: Yummy food at the class party

Z: Zach winning all his races

FIGURE 7.13 An A-Z of School

Using philosophy to promote creative thinking

Philosophical Starters instil a unique love of creative thinking and of developing the ability to considering things from different angles, perspectives and points of view. They also have the ability to connect school with the outside world, current affairs, and global events and celebrations. Why do they think certain things happen (wars, for example)? What would they do if they were able to dictate policy (if they were Prime Minister, for example)? How would they improve the people's lives (in different eras, in our country, in different countries)? What are the advantages and disadvantages of various scenarios (childhood vs. adulthood, for example)? What would they do if they found some money or won the lottery? These Starters can also be used to develop the art of questioning. For example, can they think of questions that have no answer or more than one answer?

The two examples below demonstrate how the Starters can promote children's love of thinking creatively and 'philosophically':

Can you create a recipe for a perfect world?

The priorities for our world are ever changing and it is fantastic to give children the opportunity to think of the ingredients and how much of each ingredient that they consider as essential to produce a 'Perfect World'. This Starter links very well with the school values and children's rights. Interestingly, it also promotes a great deal of mathematical thinking (weight, amounts and percentages) (Figure 7.14):

YEAR 4

A recipe for a perfect world

300g of Love

600g of peace

A handful of sunshine

100g of friendship

200g of sunshine

100% no war

100% no murder

FIGURE 7.14 A Recipe for a Perfect World

What questions would you ask a spoon?

The creativity of thought that arises from this one tends to be extraordinary and leads to a very humorous sharing session. This Starter can be adapted to ask questions of anything else at all. Promoting questioning and developing well-constructed questions are very valuable skills to develop and practice for children of all ages (Figure 7.15).

YEAR 4

Do you get dizzy when we stir you?

Do you speak a different language?

What is your name?

Did it hurt when you were cut into shape?

What tree did you come from?

Does it hurt when people dip you in hot soup?

FIGURE 7.15 Questions for a Spoon

Using science to promote creative thinking

The science-based Starters are instrumental in highlighting and bringing to the fore the importance of science and scientists in our lives. As a prelude to these Starters, it is very interesting to ask the children whether they can think of anything in the world that does not have, in some way, a link to science!

What are the most valuable scientific discoveries?

This Starter enables children to appreciate the role that science plays in society and it makes it possible for an equal emphasis to be placed on the scientific contributions, current and past, of both male and female scientists. This Starter is also very powerful in motivating children to research scientific discoveries and aspire to contribute to our world in similarly innovative ways (Figure 7.16).

> YEAR 5
>
> Abacus (500BC) Crossbow (1050) Lighthouse (280BC) Cooker (1679) Wheelbarrow (230 BC) Pencil (1565)
>
> Magnifying glass (1250) Watch (1504) Telescope (1668) Submarine (1620) Rocket (1100) Printing Press (1454)

FIGURE 7.16 Scientific Discoveries

What are the differences and similarities between blood and ketchup?

The concept of 'differences and similarities' works extremely well as a thinking tool and can be applied across all subjects and at any time. This Starter provides an excellent way of introducing this way of thinking using a question that always prompts lots of laughter when first asked. This Starter allows children to think scientifically about everyday scenarios and it provides a great platform for discussing a wide range of scientific principles: the physiology of the human body, for example, or the properties of solids, liquids and gases (Figure 7.17):

> YEAR 5

SIMILARITIES	DIFFERENCES
Both are red	Blood is thinner
Both have sugar in them	Blood is darker
Both are used by people	Blood is made in the body and ketchup in a factory
Both are man-made (but in different ways)	You can't eat blood
They can both be inside your body	Ketchup is made out of tomatoes, blood isn't.
	You need blood to live, but not ketchup.
	You don't bleed ketchup.

FIGURE 7.17 Blood and Ketchup

Using imagination to promote creative thinking

These Starters tap into children's imagination and promote creative thinking in a way that is full of fun and that enables their interests to come to the fore and be celebrated at school: inventing new flavours of ice cream, new designs for existing products, new words for existing songs – the list is endless.

Can you invent your own words and explain what they mean?

This example lets children to use all their creative thinking, their perception of the world and their sense of humour to invent their own words. It is in the explanation of what each word means that the humour is at its best (Figure 7.18):

New word	Definition
Ovaralities	Similarities that are obvious
Crockle	The sound of an old lady
Doft	Soft soil
Buggle	To juggle with bugs

New word	Definition
Aquse	Underwater house
Femit player	Female cricket player
Bodzine	Magazine about the human body
Kidologist	Someone who studies kids

FIGURE 7.18 Inventing Words

What would the flags of the countries in your new planet look like?

This Starter combines creative thinking with artistic flare. It can also lead to very interesting philosophical discussions around the concept of countries, boundaries, territories, historical conquests, invasions and wars. Could we live in a world that is not so divided? (Figure 7.19).

FIGURE 7.19 Inventing Flags

How many things with wheels can you think of?

List-based Starters are a great way of promoting creative and innovative thinking (Figure 7.20):

YEAR 1		YEAR 6		
Unicylce	Roller coaster	Tractor	Cart	Roller
Car	Roller skates	Skater	Camper Van	Skate boards
Bicycle	Tricycle	Hospital bed	Trike	Unicylce
		Combine harvester	Penny farthing bike	Cameras
		Swirly chains	wheel chair	Ferris wheel
		Legoland cars	motor bike	London eye

FIGURE 7.20 Things with Wheels

The JONK Thinking *Together* in Playgrounds initiative

The Thinking Together in Playgrounds (Staricoff, 2009) approach was created to extend the inspiration and benefits that the Thinking Skills Starters initiative offers, from the classroom to all the families and all generations *in the playground*. The journey to school becomes filled with anticipation for families if they know there is an interesting challenge waiting for them on the playground as they arrive. The approach involves setting up a large blackboard in a convenient corner of the school's playground: the blackboard contains a daily Thinking Skills Starter as a way of greeting the families in the morning. A bucket of chalk is placed by the blackboard, and as soon as the gates are open, the magic starts to unfold.

The versatility of opportunity that the Thinking Together in Playgrounds initiative offers is fascinating. It promotes a very special cross-generational intra- and inter-family thinking and socialising community at the start of the school day and it allows the school to become a hub of connectivity to the world. As Chapter 1 describes, the blackboard initiative provides a further example of how schools can become *microcosms* of society. For example, I will never forget the morning after the Chilean miners had all been rescued from the underground mine that they had been trapped in for several days and that at the time had captured the attention of the whole world. The Starter on the blackboard that morning read: '*Messages for the Chilean Miners*'. The contributions and drawings from the children and their families were so moving that we collated them and actually sent them to the miners. On another occasion, to celebrate *World Languages Day*, the Starter on the blackboard invited families to write words or phrases in their mother tongue or in any other language they were familiar with. Again, this challenge provided a very meaningful moment for the families and enabled the school to celebrate its internationally rich culture in a fun and enjoyable way. The concept of *schools as multilingual and multicultural communities of learning* is central to the ethos that underpins the *JONK Culture for Learning* and that takes centre stage as the concluding chapter of this book.

It is also very interesting to note the transformational *impact* of the blackboard from the perspective of the families themselves:

- JS, the wife of FS, who built the blackboard, said 'I think it's a good idea. Lots of children express themselves with things they wouldn't say to other people. I am very impressed with it.

- SF, the mother of five-year-old R, is an enthusiastic supporter. 'It's really good,' she says. 'The kids rush over to see what's written on there. The best one was during International Week, when the children were encouraged to think of as many countries as possible and where they had relatives in different parts of the world.'

- AC, a mother of pupils aged four and five, agrees. 'I think it's a brilliant idea. When the kids come to school, they are always interested in what's on there, and some of the things are quite mature for little kids. It makes me think too.'

■ LE, mother of B, six, says: 'When they had the biggest number question on there, someone wrote "infinity". That was good. It opens their world.' EK, aged seven, is the girl who wrote 'infinity'. Her mum, PI, loves the board. 'Infinity is something we had talked about before but it's really good to get them thinking about things at that time in the morning when you may be in a rush. It puts you in a good frame of mind.

The blackboard offers families the opportunity to enjoy a very special moment before school starts, when they are able to learn and think together, free from distractions, whilst nurturing a very special child–school–family triangular partnership, which, as the photograph below so wonderfully illustrates (Figure 7.21), also includes the *siblings* who are not yet at school!

FIGURE 7.21 The JONK Thinking in Playgrounds Blackboard

Pupils views and thoughts about the Thinking Skills Starters in School

The chapter concludes by providing the children themselves a voice that expresses so clearly and insightfully the *impact* of the Starters, as shown in Figure 7.22:

 IMPACT CASE STUDY

What the children say about the Thinking Skills Starters

- 'They are fun and make me feel happy and ready for the rest of the day.'
- 'They are a really good influence on your thinking.'
- 'They are really good fun and challenging and they make me as ready as I can be.'
- 'When I come in, I try to relax with the music that's on and get my brain working for the other lessons.'
- 'They make me feel welcome and confident to create a new piece of knowledge. If I created a Mind Map of the starters, it would be huge!'
- 'They make me feel relaxed for the rest of the day and they switch my brain on. They never stop!'
- 'They wake me up like an alarm clock. They make me feel wonderful – a magical start to the day.'
- 'They help me a lot with my learning. I love the way they are so challenging.'
- 'They are really challenging, and they give me a lot of confidence for my work. They stretch your brain in all sorts of ways and they make you feel good about what you've done.'
- 'When I get my book out, I try to think things that are in my imagination.'
- 'They wind me up like a clockwork mouse, so I buzz through the rest of the day.
- 'It's a fun way to start the day and after your brain feels like it's just woken up and it's fun because it's challenging.'
- 'They are brilliant for focusing my concentration and they prepare me for the rest of the day ahead. They make me feel like my brain has switched on.'
- 'The best bit is that you can go on and on with them. I really enjoy doing them very much.'
- 'They are fun and they make me warm up for other lessons at school.'
- 'They make me feel revved up for the day. I want to skip time to get to the next one. We are allowed to bring our own ones in!'
- 'They can never stop. They get right into my brain!'
- 'They make me feel calm if I'm cross. They make me feel good and happy.'
- 'Monday morning makes me feel happy because it is a new week to learn more thinking skills.'

- 'They make me think about what I have to do, they are great fun. I like it when we share our ideas with everybody else.'
- 'They make me think, warm me up, they make me feel happy.'
- 'They get my brain going and thinking. I can't wait for tomorrow's!'
- 'They warm up my brain, like in games – after I've done them, they make me feel I can achieve a lot more than I could before.'
- 'They wake me up and keep my brain active.'
- 'They make me feel ready to start to work hard and do my best.'

These quotes from the children illustrate the value that the Starters have on being able to influence their perception and enjoyment of thinking, learning, school and education.

8

Philosophy and a philosophical approach to learning

Life is a gap between endless time
Marcelo Staricoff

This chapter introduces the reader to the wonders of philosophy and how a philosophical approach to teaching and learning enables practitioners to nurture students' natural inquisitiveness and thirst for knowledge and discovery.

Chapter 6 demonstrates how the fourth day of the Learning to Learn Week is dedicated to introducing the class to the concept of philosophy. The chapter describes that the word *philosophy* originates from the Greek roots *philo* (meaning *love*) and *sophos* (meaning *wisdom*). The JONK approach makes use of this implicit and natural association between philosophy and education to introduce the concept of *teaching philosophically*, where *philosophical values, dialogue and thinking are explicitly taught* as an integral component of the teaching and learning process.

Incorporating an explicitly taught *philosophical dimension* to the teaching and learning process inspires learners not only with a *love of wisdom* but also with an intrinsic *love for wisdom*, which in turn leads to a love *for learning, for curiosity, for wondering, for asking why, for innovation with their thinking, for enjoying considering the seemingly impossible, for making meaningful connections between their lives and their learning, for thinking without worrying about right or wrong answers, for discussing, debating and learning to respect the thoughts, feelings and views of others, for sharing opinions openly, for wanting to listen to others and view concepts from original perspectives, broadening horizons, developing open minds, enjoying not knowing and uncertainty.*

The use of philosophy within the JONK approach represents a way of *being,* co-existing and interacting – providing us with all the foundations that we need to enjoy thinking and learning freely. From a *strategic leadership* point of view, it is really interesting to consider this unique role that philosophy plays in the life of a school by referring back to the analogy of schools *as* living organisms, introduced in Chapter 2. In Chapter 3, this analogy was used to draw a comparison between an organism's circulatory system, which flows through all areas of the organism to provide the cells with all they need to function, and the school's culture *for* learning, which also was said to flow through every aspect of school life to provide the school with all *it* needs to function.

The analogy now makes us think how these functions in organisms and schools are *expressed*. This is where the role of DNA comes into play. Cells in living organisms contain sets of chromosomes made up of DNA, which is made up of a series of *genes* arranged as an interconnected double helix. Versions of each gene (inherited as one from the mother and one from the father) reside on each strand of the DNA, and their function is based on their acting as a *pair* to give that organism all its genetically controlled characteristics.

Let us now consider how the genes within the two strands of the *school's* DNA act to give schools all *their* characteristics. For this, we need to imagine that one strand of the school's DNA contains all the *genes* that are responsible for expressing every aspect of the school's infrastructure whilst the other strand, its *philosophy* strand, allows for each of these genes and thus aspects of school life to be expressed *philosophically* to impact on all that makes up the characteristics of the school (Figure 8.1).

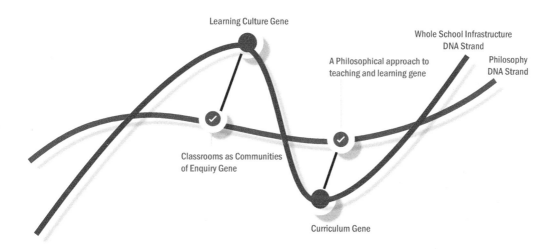

FIGURE 8.1 Philosophical Expression of the School's DNA

This DNA analogy can also be used to help us think about children and their *innate* way of being. If we consider how babies and very young children use their *innate curiosity* to learn and to discover how the world works, it would *appear* that they *also* contain *the philosophy strand* within their DNA; from birth, children have an unquenchable desire to be inquisitive about the world they live in, about all they see, feel, touch, taste, experience. In these formative years, *learning* and *being* become one. The *philosophy* of the JONK approach to education harvests this innate enthusiasm for learning, nurtures it in the Early Years setting and keeps it ignited throughout their time at school and for life.

From a practitioner's point of view, establishing a philosophical approach to teaching and learning and to co-existence in the classroom supports every aspect of the JONK *values-led culture for learning* introduced in Chapter 3 and supports Johnson's (2020) assertion, described in his book *The People's Republic of Neverland*, that '*the values of playfulness and dialogue, are naturally and manifestly essential to the fundamental well-being of the human animal*'.

Philosophy also plays a key role in enabling children to develop an appreciation of and respect for each other and for creating the conditions that enable them to feel free to think, hypothesise, share opinions and benefit from the richness that each individual brings to the *community of inquiry*. When these communities are established, children feel equipped with all they need to think, learn, co-exist and manage situations of uncertainty or difficulty (Staricoff, 2006).

In addition, establishing a philosophical approach to teaching and learning across the curriculum (Staricoff, 2007) provides an extremely useful vehicle with which to develop children's creative and critical thinking skills. There has never been a more important time than now for the need to equip children with the *ability to think critically*, to question and interrogate the information they encounter, to analyse information, to develop the insight that allows them to differentiate between what is 'true' and what may be 'fake', to make value judgements in terms of what is important, and to decide to what extent it is prudent to become personally involved in a particular discussion or scenario being played out on social media, for example. The ability to think creatively and critically that makes it possible for individuals to make considered, well-informed and rational decisions is an invaluable skill at school but also for life.

 SUGGESTED READING

At this stage, the reader is encouraged to explore the fascinating work that is emerging as part of the University of Sussex *Transform-in Education* initiative (www.transformineducation.org). In an article published in *Education Today* (2018), the founders of Transform-in Education – Dr Perpetua Kirby and Dr Rebecca Webb – define the initiative '*as being designed to support teaching staff and pupils to have time and space within the day to break with convention which the campaign's founders believe is necessary to ensure a creative and critical society where everyone is better able to respond to life situations where the answer is not always clear*' (Kirby and Webb, 2018).

The world that children are growing up in is very different from the world a lot of teachers and parents grew up in. It is not so long ago that there was no email, no computers, no internet, no social media, no Spotify, no iPhones, no cable TV, no ability to watch programmes outside of their scheduled time, no digital photography and no ability to alter images digitally. Technology and social media now make it very difficult to decipher whether what we are seeing or reading is real and to what extent, if at all, the reality has been changed. How do we know whether a photograph, for example, has been altered in any way? When a story goes viral on social media, how do we know it's true? If a statement is written as 'fact' on Wikipedia, how accurate is this? What would the impact be on our well-being if we believed, without thinking critically or inquisitively, everything that we see, read and receive on our social media timelines? It seems that this and ensuing generations will need to be able to make 'moral' judgements and decisions with every aspect of their daily routines. Furthermore, the frequency with which these decisions are having to be made is phenomenal. Not much can be taken at face value nowadays.

 SUGGESTED READING

Equally valuable at this point is to refer to the work of Simenon Honoré and Michael Porter. In their book entitled *Education for Humanity*, the authors describe that in educating our students for *humanity*, '*intellectual rigour and clarity of thought need to go hand in hand with creativity and experimentation*'. They describe how an essential part of this process is equipping students with the ability to distinguish whether something is true or not. They explain that this issue '*has been with us for all human history and one that has become especially urgent now as the growth of the internet means that we are exposed now to a wide range of opinions and unsubstantiated claims which often pose as facts*'. The philosophical approach to the curriculum presented in this chapter acts to fulfil the response that the authors argue is required from the educational system, namely '*intellectual rigour: learning to test evidence, evaluate arguments, paying attention to the use of language and the sub-text of an argument*'.

Philosophy as an integral part of the teaching and learning process

The principal value of incorporating a philosophical approach to all aspects of the teaching and learning process is that it very quickly realigns two major misconceptions that children tend to have and that often present as limiting factors to their engagement, enjoyment and achievement:

1   **That questions always have and need an answer**

    Philosophy is fabulous as it is introduced to the children as being all about questions that do not have an answer, that have more than one answer or that are impossible to answer.

2   **That the teacher or supporting adult always *knows* the answer**

    Philosophy provides an excellent vehicle with which to engage the class in dialogue and discussion that enable children to perceive the teacher not so much as the expert who has all the knowledge that they impart, but much more as being the experts at presenting the learning in a way that is motivational and open-ended and that can be discussed, explored, investigated, questioned and played with intellectually.

The principle of *teaching philosophically* is very enticing, but how can this be achieved so that it becomes part of the everyday routine and *lived culture* of the classroom? The sections below explore the opportunities that exist to use each of the stages that define the Teaching Model of Excellence, Enrichment and Enjoyment (MEEE), which was introduced in Chapter 4, to *teach philosophically* (Figure 8.2):

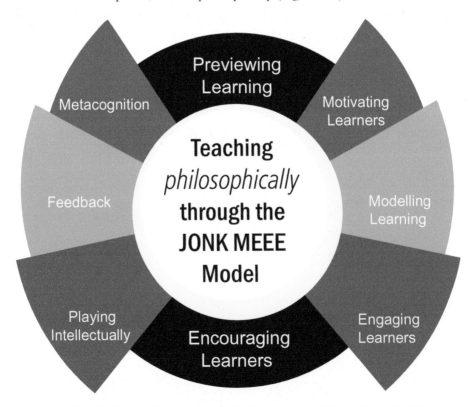

FIGURE 8.2 The JONK Model of Excellence, Enrichment and Enjoyment from a Philosophical Perspective

Previewing learning

Philosophical questions, posed as a way of previewing the learning, allow children and their families to engage enthusiastically with the learning *before* learning or a school community event takes place. The Thinking Skills Starters and the Thinking in Playgrounds initiatives, which are the focus of Chapter 7, provide excellent means of achieving this.

For example, in Chapter 4, we saw how by asking the children the philosophical question of whether time exists (as part of the preview process to learning about time), it encouraged a child to discuss the question at home and then bring in, the next day, some 'thyme' for the lesson. In Chapter 7, we saw the impact that the Thinking Together in Playgrounds Blackboard had on the communities' global and social awareness of an event that had occurred that day in Chile: the rescue of the miners who had been trapped in a coal mine. Using the blackboard in this way can be adapted to preview and encourage philosophical thinking on a range of topics or upcoming school events. For example, the day before the school takes part in a national charity fundraising event, such as Sport Relief or Macmillan Coffee Mornings, the question of the blackboard could read 'How would you spend the money that will be raised tomorrow as part of our fundraising event?'

Using the Thinking Skills Starters as a philosophical vehicle for previewing learning encouraged a child in a Reception class to one day ask the teacher a very interesting question:

CHILD 'You know how you always ask us lots of philosophical questions?'
TEACHER 'Yes, there's nothing I enjoy more than starting the day hearing all your ideas.'
CHILD 'Well, we have lots of philosophical questions, too. Could we have a book to write them in please?'
TEACHER 'Of course, that would be great. What shall we call these books?'
CHILD (without any hesitation): '"Why Books"!'

This child launched something very significant in the school, and by the end of the week, every child in the class had also requested to have their own 'Why Book' (Figure 8.3). These books become very special indeed and it is a joy to see the excitement with which children enter the classroom and go to find their Why Books and start populating them with the philosophical questions that they have arrived with

FIGURE 8.3 Why Books from Children in the Early Years

that day (Figure 8.4). Families would often share these first few minutes of the day, thinking philosophically together in the classroom.

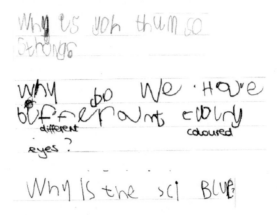

FIGURE 8.4 Examples of Why Books from Children in the Early Years

Children regard the process of writing in the Why Books as a natural way of start-ing their day and of being able to express and communicate their thoughts. It is *writ-ing for purpose* at its very best; children feel intrinsically motivated to write. The Why Books are also an excellent source for children to *preview their own* learning and can contribute to teachers' planning, informed by children's interests and inquisitiveness. The questions in the Why Books are used by teachers as the basis for whole-class phil-osophical discussions and give practitioners a great insight to be able to plan and tap into children's curiosity and their understanding of the world. The Why Books can also be used to record children's thinking during these whole-class discussions, using sticky labels in the books containing the child's thoughts (Figure 8.5). Throughout the year, the collection of these thoughts and the progression of the depth of language used provide an excellent source for making formative assessment judgements and identifying significant cognitive achievements made by the child.

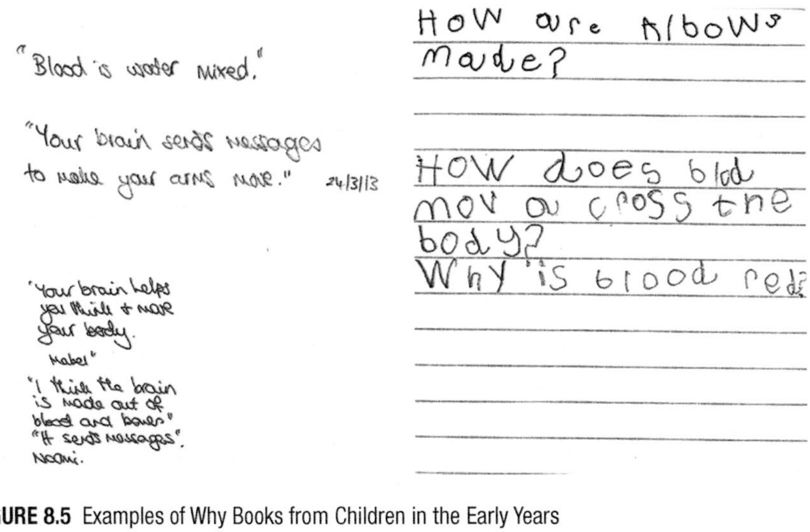

FIGURE 8.5 Examples of Why Books from Children in the Early Years

A further advantage of the Why Books is that they help children to formulate an understanding of what 'a question actually is' and how they are formulated and then used.

Motivating learners

In Chapter 4, we saw how a philosophical approach to the learning objective can have such a motivational impact on children, class discussions and their enthusiasm for *wanting* to engage with the learning. The JONK approach applies the concept of launching the learning through a philosophically constructed learning objective to all areas of the curriculum (Staricoff, 2007).

Chapter 4 looked at learning about time and using a learning objective such as 'Does time exist?' as a way of previewing the learning objective for the day. Let's now take another example, the teaching of the properties of 2D shapes, to illustrate the impact on motivation that a philosophical learning objective offers. The example below considers three different scenarios for constructing a learning objective for the teaching of 2D shapes:

 DISCUSSION OPPORTUNITIES

Scenario 1: The Learning Objective is formulated as a statement:
LO: To be able to learn about the properties of 2D shapes

As a statement, the learning objective has a danger of triggering negative thoughts, such as 'I'm not sure I *am able to* do this', which can preclude children from engaging with the learning at all.

 DISCUSSION OPPORTUNITIES

Scenario 2: The Learning Objective is formulated as a question:
LO: Can we investigate the properties of 2D shapes?

Formulating the Learning Objective as a question rather than as a statement is very beneficial as from the outset it promotes whole-class discussion, speculation and wonder about learning. If the Learning Objective is expressed as a 'Can we …?' question, it reassures every pupil that the class is embarking on the journey as a supportive collective and very interestingly it leaves open the possibility that, for some, this may not be possible to achieve. It makes it acceptable to take longer and seek further support. From a child's point of view, this scenario tends to make them feel much more curious and engages the class in mutually supportive, insightful and enabling discussions that reassure everyone.

DISCUSSION OPPORTUNITIES

Scenario 3: The Learning Objective is formulated as a 'philosophical' question:
LO: Do 2D shapes exist?

When the learning objective is posed as a philosophical question, it places the teacher *as an equal partner of learning* and gives the teacher the opportunity to motivate learners through inquiry-based whole-class discussions. These discussions help learners to give meaning to what they are learning, to view everyday concepts from different perspectives and to analyse concepts in depth. The discussions also provide the teacher with very useful moments for ascertaining understanding and identifying misconceptions and for the learner to ascertain their understanding by thinking metacognitively in view of the thoughts and ideas being discussed. The philosophical learning objectives invariably bring a lot of humour into the proceedings, and as is the case with time and 2D shapes, children find it fascinating to wonder why they are about to learn about something that doesn't exist!

The DNA analogy introduced at the beginning of this chapter can also be used to illustrate how philosophy helps to 'express' the learning objective and the discussion of the content of lesson *philosophically* across all areas of the curriculum.

Figure 8.6 shows the section of the school's DNA strand that contains the lesson *genes* responsible for the *expression* of the learning objective and the content of the lesson. It can be seen from the diagram that the *gene* that is responsible for communicating the learning objective is not expressed in *isolation* but in *combination* with its interconnected *gene* on the other strand of the school's DNA molecule, its *philosophy* strand that contains the 'I wonder *why*' gene, the 'I wonder *how*' gene and the 'I wonder *what if*' gene.

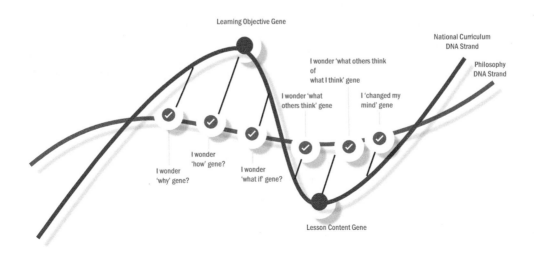

FIGURE 8.6 The Curriculum through a Philosophical Perspective

Similarly, the expression of *the lesson content gene* is influenced by the interrelated genes on the philosophy strand: the '*I wonder what others think*' gene, the '*I wonder what others think and what others think of what I think*' gene and the '*I've now changed my mind*' gene.

This model can be extended to investigate the influence that a philosophical approach is able to have on every area of school life.

Modelling learning

Philosophically driven discussions of what is about to be learnt provide a great platform for modelling the expected outcomes of the learning objective. In Chapter 4, this section discussed the principle of sharing with the children, both a high- and a poor-quality example of the 'end product'. Thinking about both of these scenarios philosophically can be very interesting and can lead to lots of 'why' questions being considered: Why did the original author choose certain words or phrases? Why are the mistakes observed in the poor example so common in our writing? Why did history take this course? Why is a character portrayed in a certain way? The more philosophical approach to modelling outcomes also serves to discuss expectations in occasions where the end product is not based on a right or wrong answer, inspiring children with the freedom to create and innovate.

Engaging learners

Posing philosophical questions as the children engage with their learning acts as a motivational force, enabling questioning and wonder to become integral parts of their active learning process.

For example, if the class are reading and analysing the story of *Little Red Riding Hood*, it is very interesting to ask them to consider questions such as *What do you consider to be Little Red Riding Hood's best qualities?* In Science, when studying the properties of solids, liquids and gases, the children can be challenged with a philosophical question such as *Is there anything that is not a liquid, solid or gas?* In History, the children could be inspired to wonder about a conversation they may wish to have with someone from the past or challenged to consider how the course of history could have changed if certain moments had or had not happened.

Picture books are also a great conduit for philosophical engagement with the learning. There are many books that have been written through a philosophical lens. A particular favourite is *Ug: Boy Genius of the Stone Age* (Briggs, 2002), about a boy who loves to engage his family in philosophical thought as he attempts to make the *Stone Age* a better place for all!

Encouraging learners and playing intellectually

The great advantage of philosophy is that it is so multi-disciplinary, so versatile and so thought-provoking. Philosophy trains children to think critically and innovatively and it enables them to use questions, seek evidence and explore the thoughts of others so as to deepen their own understanding. Philosophy encourages children to *want* to play *intellectually* with concepts and the curriculum and to perceive that getting to an answer is merely the beginning of lots more questions. A philosophical approach encourages learners to engage with these two sectors of the MEEE model as a natural sequence of events in the classroom.

As well as establishing a philosophical launch to the day and the learning, it is very exciting to include *philosophy as a distinct lesson* and as part of the timetable. Engaging in regular philosophical dialogue as a whole class equips children with a multitude of attitudes, dispositions and transferrable skills. Introducing philosophy as a subject per se makes it possible for philosophical discussions to be perceived as an integral part of the school routine rather than as something that is *extra* or unconnected to the learning and the curriculum.

These sessions work particularly well if they take place on a Friday. If children really look forward to the sessions all week, they use the learning and discussions during the week to suggest topics for discussion. If the discussions need more time, they can often be extended into the afternoon. The Friday debates also mean that children launch their weekends at home full of the excitement, enthusiasm and motivation that these sessions have provided. They tend to use the weekend to elaborate their philosophical thinking at home with their families.

It is very useful to have a range of texts that provide prompts for launching philosophical discussions with the class. This chapter itself begins with a quote – 'Life is a gap between endless time' – that fits into the realm of philosophy that deals with the *big questions*, those questions that do not have an answer but are fascinating to ponder. What is the meaning of life, for example? The quote that opens this chapter could form the basis of an interesting conversation when considering this.

The Philosophy Files (Law, 2000) is a great resource for these big questions. The stories in the book never fail to inspire children and practitioners with a love of philosophy. The author has a wonderful way of enticing the reader with an initial 'big question', which is set out as a story that children find very easy to understand and relate to. The characters in the story develop the philosophical problem from different points of view, offering the reader convenient stopping points for discussion, reflection and considering whether they agree or disagree with what each character is postulating. Each story continues to develop the reader's thinking, persuading them to completely change their opinions several times!

I thoroughly recommend the story of 'Can I Jump in the Same River Twice?' This story never fails to generate extremely deep thinking and *justification* of thinking and is an example of *philosophical questions that do not have an answer*. The main idea that is considered through this story is the concept that 'if something changes, can it still be the same?' In the case of the story, the thing that changes all the time is the river, but it is very interesting to ask the class, what else, apart from a river, is changing all the time? Their answers are always so creative. They think about time, the world and people. In terms of people and more specifically themselves, it is so interesting to then discuss how they are also changing all the time; blood constantly flows around our body (exactly like the river), our bodies are constantly producing new cells, having new thoughts, and so on. It is then fascinating to ask them 'Does the fact that we are also changing all the time mean that when you go home today, you can say to your families that you are a completely different person from the person who left for school in the morning?'

CASE STUDY

The Philosophy Files

Regular sessions based on *The Philosophy Files* had a very significant impact on a child who at the beginning of the year was at risk of exclusion. By the end of the academic year, the child had written and added to the class library her fifth volume of her own version of the *Philosophy Files* book (Staricoff, 2006).

Philosophy sessions also offer the opportunity to present children (and adults) with *moral dilemmas*, which require children to think about the relative value to individuals and society of different scenarios as well as about the consequences of the decisions that they may make. In these situations, the children become skilled at thinking innovatively, creatively and strategically. With time, they become experts at problem solving and at seeing and considering things from different points of views. As these moral situations invariably deal with human emotions, they also help children to develop a sense of social awareness and empathy, two key ingredients in developing as individuals who are able to create harmony in society.

Young children love to take part in the acting out of the 'receiving a present I don't like' conundrum. This scenario describes a child welcoming to their home their grandparents, who have come a long way to be with them to celebrate their birthday. Before handing over their present, the grandparents spend a little bit of time telling the child how much time, effort, thought and love they put into this year's present that they have brought for them. The child very excitedly opens the present. But as they open the present, they start to realise that they 'really don't like it'. What should the child say to the grandparents?

The responses that children offer when placed in this scenario tend to cover a very broad range of thinking. Some children would be very honest and say 'Thank you, but I don't like it'. Some children would say they like it, not to hurt their grandparent's feelings. Some children are amazing at finding a compromise or look for solutions that neither upset anyone nor require them to 'lie'. For example, some say that they would say 'Thank you so much, but maybe next year, could I have something different?' or 'Thank you so much, but I think I will not wear it now, I will save it for special occasions'. This is a fabulous scenario to model to the children the idea that sometimes things do not have a simple solution, even for adults, and that all of their thoughts and ideas are equally valid, especially as they all tend to be so well-meaning.

With older children, a similar depth of response, empathy and social awareness can be elicited by the question of 'What should happen to someone who steals a car?' As children offer their thoughts, the excitement begins. Usually, this takes the form of considering whether they should go to prison or not, whether community service is a good alternative, or whether there could ever be situations in which it is *justified* to steal a car (if there were an emergency, for example).

CASE STUDY

Stealing a car

K, a Year 4 child, said: 'I know what should happen to someone who steals a car; they should be given one'. After asking K to explain her reasoning a little bit further, she said: 'Well, it is obvious. If someone steals a car, it's because they must need one'. K's thinking was extraordinary. Rather than thinking about the consequences of when things go wrong, she was trying to find a solution that would stop things going wrong in the first place.

As the discussion invariably moves onto prisons, it is very interesting to pose the question of how people who go to prison should feel and should be treated. Should prisons be places of hardship and punishment or should they be places of reconciliation and reflection where people are treated humanely? Which of these alternatives leads to people being able to re-integrate into society more successfully? Children are very quick to point out that if prison were a really 'nice' place, then people would commit crimes on purpose to go there. It is extremely interesting to research with children examples of how different countries approach this conundrum. In a follow-up session, the question of whether it's possible to have a society without crime is fascinating to discuss.

Philosophical discussions allow children to develop a deep sense of *social consciousness, social responsibility and social awareness*. Considering the way that society functions from a philosophical perspective provides practitioners with a wealth of material. Should certain things be banned, for example? Should smoking be banned? Should boxing be banned? These real-life scenarios prompt a very broad set of connections to be made, justifications to be constructed and implications of the justifications to be considered. For example, if smoking were banned, what would happen to all the people who are employed globally in the various stages of the industry? Would a new product with the same health implications as tobacco be allowed on the market today? If boxing were banned, would this lead to bouts being set up 'illegally' without adequate medical protections and controls? What happened during Prohibition when alcohol was banned?

These moral and social scenarios represent a great way of discussing issues that are pertinent to children's lives and the world they are growing up in and helping to shape. Climate change, gender equality, international conflict, the coronavirus pandemic – the list is endless. Bringing the world into the classroom through a philosophical approach equips children to interact with the world as informed citizens and citizens who are able to formulate reasoned and considered judgements. As Barrell (2003) states, 'inquisitive minds are the safeguards of our democracy, now and forever … the promise of living enriching lives … the energisers of our growing and thriving civilisations'.

Feedback and metacognition

Philosophical discussions also ensure that children are able to develop a rich vocabulary and a means of structuring their thinking coherently, which has a very powerful impact on the way they are able to engage in *feedback* conversations with adults and peers. Thinking philosophically is also a great way of encouraging children to think metacognitively. How well do they understand particular concepts? How well can they explain concepts that they have understood? How does their metacognitive thinking lead them to become curious about finding out more? The contribution that philosophy makes to these last two sectors of the MEEE model stems from the fact that philosophy places children in situations that require them to think *metacognitively* about concepts that they already have a good understanding of but from a very different or angle. These last two sectors of the MEEE model, which focus on *thinking for understanding*, are ideal beneficiaries of a philosophical approach that develops children's strategic thinking and ability to make connections that lead to them making considered explanations.

 **CASE STUDY**

Thinking for understanding: Why can't babies talk?

As part of an inspection, the inspectors were very keen to see a philosophy session in action. I managed to persuade one of our mums to lend me her baby for a few minutes in the morning. The inspector and the mum joined the children in Reception for what proved to be a very memorable experience. I started talking to the baby and then asked the class: 'Why is he not chatting back? He is just sitting there staring at me!'

The class found this whole scenario hilarious and, amongst the laughter, went on to contribute the most fabulous thinking: 'babies don't have teeth', 'babies need to learn to talk', 'they can't make sounds'. Each suggestion led to further and more in-depth discussion. This question, not necessarily done with a live baby (a doll works perfectly well), is a fabulous way of developing children's thinking about human development and similarities and differences between babies, children and adults. The session finished by considering the advantages and disadvantages of being a baby, a child or an adult.

 **CASE STUDY**

Thinking for understanding: Who paints the rainbows?

On entering a Year 1/2 classroom for a philosophy session, I noticed that whilst they were waiting for the session to start, they were practicing their mindfulness by moving their arms to the rhythm of a rainbow, which kept appearing and disappearing on their whiteboard. This prompted me to ask them: 'Who paints the rainbow? I never see anyone doing it!'

Although children are very familiar with rainbows, they had never considered it from this angle! The responses, within seconds, were truly amazing. It was a privilege to experience the depth of thought, the poetic choice of words and the readiness with which they agreed and disagreed with each other.

'No one paints it', commented one child, 'rainbows are illusions of our eyes', which prompted a response from another child: 'They are not illusions; they happen when sunlight hits water droplets in the air'.

The thinking *for* understanding that this question prompted allowed us to discuss a great number of related scientific concepts and make lots of links to their topics.

These last two sectors of the MEEE Model also encourage children to think about what *is possible next* and to reflect and think about the boundaries of what they have learnt and the opportunities and possibilities that arise as a result of having learnt something new. Philosophy helps children to determine what is possible and what is impossible. This next set of philosophical questions are called Fermi Questions, which require the student to construct a *reasonable* answer or argument in response to an *impossible* scenario.

Enrico Fermi (1901–1954) was a Nobel Prize–winning physicist who took great delight in asking his audiences questions that are impossible to answer. He is most renowned for asking 'How many piano tuners are there in New York?' This question is the stuff of folklore amongst lecturers and their students throughout the world. What is so interesting about asking children a Fermi question is that they don't have to worry about *an exact answer*. It doesn't exist. The question of how many people there are in the world, for example, is impossible to know exactly at any point in time, but at the same time, it is essential to come to a reasonable approximation. The processes by which one arrives at these approximations are what make Fermi questions so valuable, training the children to think logically and strategically to arrive at an answer that makes sense.

 CASE STUDY

Fermi questions: Children round the world

In this scenario, the children are asked to work out how many children would be needed to hold hands all the way round the world. At first, this seems like a totally impossible concept to contemplate, but by starting to ask the right questions, the problem begins to seem much more manageable. How long is it all the way round the earth? How much does one child with outstretched arms measure? Asking the children to have a go at estimating an answer before working the problem out is very useful. It is interesting to note how age-dependent this estimation becomes, according to each child's perception of number. Estimates often range from 14 to 14 trillion! The children then set about trying to calculate the problem. They lined themselves up in the playground, worked out how many 30 children measured, then used this to multiply until they reached 40,000,000 metres, which is the circumference of the earth. These Fermi open-ended investigations enable children to become experts at problem solving, estimating, deducting, researching, analysing, thinking sequentially, communicating, linking understanding and connecting the classroom to the real world.

The concept of discussing what is 'possible' and what is 'impossible' is very interesting. Many things that seemed impossible not so long ago are now commonplace. Who would have imagined in the Seventies that 30 years later we would be able to speak to and see a person on a screen on the other side of the world? Asking the children to think about things that are currently impossible but may one day be possible is a great way of promoting creative thinking and raising aspirations. These types of discussions often lead to children saying that they would love to work in a certain field or help make something happen that changes the world. The current debate on climate change is a great example. Is it possible or impossible to completely stop using fossil fuels? These discussions enable children to create realistic arguments for and *against the cases being discussed and then think of professions they may follow that could help the world achieve those goals.*

The sections below describe four examples of the impact that philosophy and a philosophical approach to the curriculum have on the depth and breadth of school life:

1   **Families thinking together philosophically**

   ■ *Strengthening the child–school–family learning partnership*

2   **Reducing the word gap**

   ■ *Transforming children's life chances*

3   **Pupils as Philosophy Leaders**

   ■ *Children at the heart of school initiatives, improvement and change*

4   **Pupils' views and thoughts about philosophy in school**

   ■ *Philosophy as a unique motivational tool for all*

Families thinking together philosophically

Strengthening the child–school–family learning partnership

Philosophy provides a range of opportunities with which to inspire families to think philosophically together at home, at school and on their way to school. The Philosophy Question of the Week as an integral part of the newsletters for families works very well, as does dedicating a philosophy corner to the school's website. It is always so rewarding to hear families arriving at school still discussing the philosophical conversations they had had at home. It is very poignant that promoting philosophical thinking at home has a tremendous impact on adults too and can really transform their perception of education and schooling, especially if they have not been left with a very positive experience of their own schooling. The Thinking Together in Playground Blackboard (Chapter 7) offers a further opportunity to engage the families in philosophical thinking. Philosophical discussions started at home tend to continue amongst families in the playground as they gather around the blackboard!

CASE STUDY

Philosophy at home

Promoting philosophical thinking at home and involving families in their children's learning can be accomplished by setting up a *'Whole Class Philosophy Book'*. As with the Early Years idea of the teddy bear and its diary going to a different child's home every day, the Philosophy Book can do the same but with a philosophical question for families to consider. The book *But Why* (Stanley and Bowkett, 2004) comes with a Philosophy Bear, which becomes the perfect accompaniment for the book going home. The question 'Is it ever right to do something wrong?' is a good one to launch the concept with. It is very interesting to read and share with the class what the children and their families had contributed about the question but also about the thoughts that other families had contributed.

Philosophy as a means of reducing the *word gap*

Transforming children's life chances from an early age

Philosophy from a very early age has tremendous benefits in terms of developing children's vocabulary, love of talk and ability to speak in public with confidence. The *Why Closing the Word Gap Matters Report* (Oxford Language Report, 2018) highlights the disadvantage that children face when they start their school life with a significant 'word gap' and how hard it is for them to close this gap during their time at school. Philosophy ensures that children from a very young age develop the key skills that enable them to thrive as individuals and as members of society who make decisions to ensure a prosperous future for our world.

CASE STUDY

Philosophy in the nursery

On a hot summer's day, I took a bowl with ice cubes into the Nursery and said to them that I would be leaving them on the shelf and coming back later, after assembly. We could then use them for our weekly philosophy session. When I returned, the ice cubes had, of course, all melted. 'Where are the ice cubes that I left with you earlier? Who has taken them?'

These two questions led to the most wonderful discussion, full of talk, creative thinking and scientific reasoning. The thinking and discussion that ensued from the philosophy sessions with the Nursery children had a significant impact on reducing the word gap for a great number of children, who then were able to thrive throughout their time at school.

Pupils as philosophy leaders

Children at the heart of school initiatives, improvement and change

In Chapter 4, we saw how children can contribute to the strategic leadership of the school by working closely with senior leaders. Philosophy, through the concept of Philosophy Leaders, offers a similar opportunity for children to be involved in and contribute to whole-school improvement. Philosophy Leaders are elected representatives from each class, whose role is to set the whole-school 'Philosophy Questions of the Week'. These are displayed prominently in the classrooms, corridors, school newsletters and website. At any time, anyone can contemplate the question and offer a thought, which they post into the 'philosophy box'. The Philosophy Leaders then look through and discuss all the contributions for that week and award their own Philosophy Certificates during celebration assemblies. The Philosophy Leaders can also set up a box that encourages others to think of the philosophical questions that could be used by the school in successive weeks.

Pupils' views and thoughts about philosophy in school

Philosophy as a unique motivational tool for every child

This section offers examples of the thoughts of children when asked to describe how philosophy and all it brings to the values-led culture *for* learning feel to them. The thoughts from children in the example below are from a Key Stage 1 class (Staricoff, 2006) (Figure 8.7):

- I think philosophy is fun and nice. We learn from it.
- It helps me to think.
- Philosophy is a good and fun thing.
- Philosophy helps me with my learning.
- Philosophy helps me think a lot. I like starting new branches.
- Philosophy is fun because we can say our own words.
- It is fun because we got to chat.
- I like philosophy because we listen to each other's stories.
- I like to disagree with my friends.
- Philosophy is relaxing.
- I like philosophy because I get to know what people are thinking and I like to tell other people what I'm thinking.
- Philosophy is very thinkable!
- Philosophy is fun.
- Philosophy is listening, fun, learning and gives you advice.
- I like philosophy because it is interesting and it keeps me thinking.
- I like philosophy because we do it in all the subjects.
- I like philosophy and it is a fun way to think.
- I like it so much that I bought my own philosophy files. I like to disagree with my friends and it makes me think.
- Philospohy is exciting.
- I like philosophy because it answers great questions.

FIGURE 8.7 Year 2 Pupil Quotes on Philosophy

The thoughts below are from a Year 5 class after conducting a PMI exercise which was introduced to the reader as part of the second day of the Learning to Learn Week and which is designed to help children to structure their thinking. On this occasion (Figure 8.7), the children were asked to think about everything that they thought was positive about Philosophy (P), everything that was negative or 'minus' (M) and everything that they found interesting (I) about the subject and approach:

- Focuses your mind
- Allows your thoughts and feelings to come out
- Develops my imagination
- It starts my brain working
- We respect each other's points of views
- We learn how to debate politely
- Makes you *really* think
- You can't be wrong
- Makes lots of connections with the outside world
- It's fun
- It's interesting
- Makes you a good questioner
- You can express yourself without feeling embarrassed
- There's no right answer
- We learn to discuss rather than argue
- It helps me make the right decisions
- It helps me fight for what I believe in, my rights
- There's no winning
- We socialise
- You get to learn lots of new things
- Sets your mind free
- You get to think about things not in school
- We talk to each other rather than through the teacher
- There are no limits
- We don't need to prepare
- You can change your own views
- We can all have different points of view
- We can express our opinions
- It's great for discussing everyday news
- You find out what other people think
- We link it to so many things
- Helps you become a critical thinker
- We become better at discussing issues
- Brings outside issues
- It's so easy to contribute
- It can be very persuasive!
- It makes you think so deeply
- It stops us worrying since there's no right or wrong answer
- You can keep on going and going

- It's very difficult to end
- Our minds can't think as deeply as adults
- You sometimes don't succeed in persuading someone of your view
- You feel left out if you have nothing to say
- You might talk about things which some people have no knowledge of
- We have to stop!
- You could get into an argument if you really disagree
- It can seem that sometimes we are discussing things that are 'meaningless'
- If people argue back, you have to keep it going!

I

- Helps you learn so much and so many new things
- So exciting to be doing it at this age
- How sometimes none of us knows about something
- Helps me think
- So many people who haven't had the chance to do it as children
- No right or wrong
- We'll know so much when we are grown up
- You get to find things out
- It will help so much when we are older
- All the issues we discuss
- Having fun and learning!
- Helps us become better learners
- We are like the Prime Minister, making so many decisions
- Makes us better people
- You learn more than at university
- That we do it in school!
- Children have different ideas from adults
- It can be about anything
- That people actually change their views during a lesson
- How many open-ended questions there are!
- How people take so much for granted
- Adults learning from children!
- How we start with something and end with something completely different
- Great training for a lawyer
- Encourages you to take up new things
- We learn to respect each other
- We can find out what is in the news
- It leads to other questions and links to all our other subjects

- Lets us understand how to value things
- Gives us so much experience
- Makes thinking fun and helps to make you creative

These thoughts, feelings, emotions and opinions are a wonderful testimony to the benefits and impact that philosophy and a philosophical approach have on all individuals: socially, emotionally and academically as well as on all aspects of school life.

Lifelong learning and the lifelong learning dispositions

Learning at school is a catalyst for life
Marcelo Staricoff

This chapter introduces the reader to the principles that underpin lifelong learning in schools, where students acquire the skills and dispositions of successful lifelong learners by incorporating the *characteristics of effective learning* as part of the curriculum.

The concept of lifelong learning at school is introduced to the class as part of the fifth and final day of the Learning to Learn Week (Chapter 6). Embedding a lifelong learning approach to the curriculum equips students with the means by which they are able to navigate through the complexities of life, thrive as individuals and make positive contributions as citizens of our ever-changing world.

The lifelong learning dispositions are integral and distinct components of the JONK school's culture *for* learning, which was introduced in Chapter 3 and is shown in Figure 9.1:

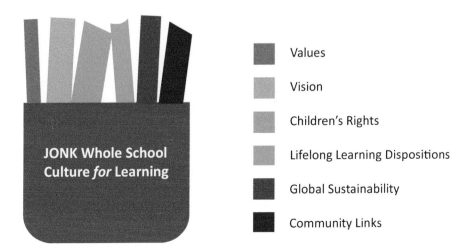

JONK Whole School Culture *for* Learning

- Values
- Vision
- Children's Rights
- Lifelong Learning Dispositions
- Global Sustainability
- Community Links

FIGURE 9.1 The Six Key Areas of Influence of the JONK School Culture *for* Learning

The involvement in the Effective Lifelong Learning Inventory research programme (Ruth Deaking-Crick, 2006), also known as 'ELLI', led to the identification of a series of *dispositions* that are associated with *effective lifelong learning*, namely creative thinking, critical curiosity, meaning making, strategic awareness, learning relationships, resilience and adaptability whilst changing and learning. The section below discusses the terminology that accompanies each of these terms (Figure 9.2):

FIGURE 9.2 The Lifelong Learning Dispositions and their Definitions

The seven dispositions that emerged from the ELLI project are excellent starting points for discussion at school and can act as a springboard for acquiring a bespoke set of lifelong learning characteristics for schools, derived from the thoughts and ideas of the *whole school* community, as explained below. The ELLI project found that if they are associated with an animal that tends to portray that trait (the resilient tortoise or snail, for example), the dispositions become much more meaningful for children.

SUGGESTED READING

The ELLI project led to the publication of the book *Learning Power in Practice* (Ruth-Deaking Crick, 2006), a useful resource for background reading, professional development meetings and informing practice in your school.

As soon as the dispositions are obtained, they begin to form an integral part of all that happens at school, as illustrated in the chart (Figure 9.3), which is a self-evaluative guide that enables schools to ascertain what is already in place in terms of lifelong learning and to decide on a strategy for possible next steps.

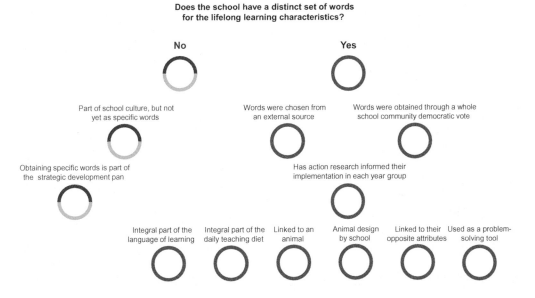

FIGURE 9.3 Self Evaluation Guide for the Lifelong Learning Dispositions

The sections that follow provide a guide to how each of these steps can be accomplished using a series of Headteacher Challenges, the principle of which was introduced in Chapter 3, as part of a two-year strategic plan.

Obtaining a set of lifelong learning dispositions for the school

The first step in acquiring a bespoke set of lifelong learning dispositions specific to the school is to set the first of three Headteacher Challenges, known as the 'Recipe for a Lifelong Learner'.

 THE FIRST HEADTEACHER CHALLENGE

A Recipe for a Lifelong Learner

Main Aims of this Challenge

1   To obtain a list of words from the whole school community that they associate with being successful as a lifelong learner

2   To prepare the school for a 'general election'

3   To analyse the results of the election

4   To announce the words that will become the school's lifelong learning dispositions (resilience, curiosity, etc.)

This challenge, which is known as the 'Recipe for a Lifelong Learner', offers every family and every member of the school community the opportunity to create a *recipe*, in all its splendour, that creates a *successful lifelong learner*.

In setting the task, it is a good idea to encourage everyone to be as creative as possible when deciding how much of each ingredient they wish to add (500 g of resilience, 2 L of curiosity, etc.), how the ingredients will be used, how long they will need to cook for, what the end product should look like and how best it should be served.

The ideas that this open-ended challenge promotes tend to be extraordinary and invariably range from a wide range of artistic interpretations to some very delicious and edible cakes, as was the case with these Year 6 children as they created their recipes for a lifelong learner (Figures 9.4, 9.5 and 9.6):

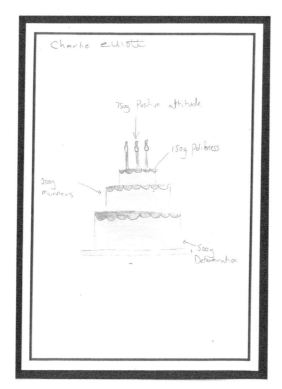

FIGURE 9.4 Recipes for a Lifelong Learner

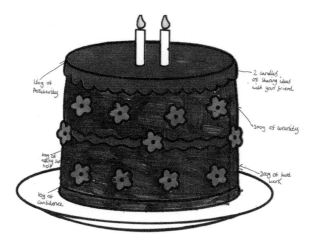

FIGURE 9.5 Recipes for a Lifelong Learner

FIGURE 9.6 Recipes for a Lifelong Learner

The reason that this challenge is so valuable in helping to launch the process that generates the dispositions for the school is that it encourages the participants to think of the 'ingredients' needed for this recipe. Collating the list of ingredients from every recipe received allows the school to obtain a pool of ideas for the dispositions which is representative of the ideas of the whole school community.

Once the whole school pool of ideas has been collated, the Learning Leaders, who are elected representatives from each class, are tasked with the process of analysing all the ideas in the pool, grouping them into six main themes and finally choosing two representative words from each theme to end up with a list of 12 possible dispositions for the school. For example, there may be several words that are grouped around the theme of curiosity: curious, inquisitive and questioning. The Learning Leaders choose the words that appear most frequently for their short list or the words that they feel will best portray the meaning of that theme to the children at the school. Some schools also use the 'wordle' principle at this stage to help them identify the words that come up with the greatest frequency. As always with the work of the Learning Leaders, they may wish to seek the views of their peers as they undertake this process, going back to their classes and seeking a majority view for the decisions that they are taking as a committee.

Having sought the views of the whole school community and having condensed these into a representative selection, the whole school community is invited to vote on these as part of a whole-school 'general election process' that will lead to six dispositions obtaining the highest votes becoming the dispositions for the school.

There are enormous benefits to be gained from setting up a *School General Election* (Staricoff, Times Educational Supplement, 2017) process at the school that mimics the actual democratic National General Election (NGE) process as closely as possible.

As soon as a date for the School General Election (SGE) is set, families are informed of the date, the purpose of the SGE and the arrangements that will be organised to ensure that all families, staff, governors and linked community members are able to cast their votes.

The School General Election process requires if at all possible:

■   Organising for the school to be open from 7 a.m. to 7 p.m. to maximise the opportunity for all family members to come to school and vote, which may be before, during or after school.

- Organising for each child to take home a Polling Card, mimicking the real cards as closely as possible and containing all the relevant details for the families and asking them to bring the card in on the day of the vote

- Organising for the school to source or create a number of ballot boxes. If the SGE is not close to an NGE, it may be possible to contact the local election commission and obtain real ballot boxes. If the SGE and NGE are close in dates, real ballot boxes will not be available.

- Organise for the school to be devoted to the voting process for the whole day and for the hall to contain 'voting booths' so that families and children are able to vote in privacy

- Organise for members of the Governing Body or the Local Community or the Learning Leaders to form a rota on the day and for them to act as Returning Officers

- Organise and communicate to everyone the means by which individuals will be able to vote even if they are not able to come to school; families and family members around the world may vote by post, by email, on the website, by text, by telephoning the school office, etc.

- Once the final shortlist of things to be voted has been decided, it is really interesting to place these on a very realistic looking ballot paper and produce enough for every child and family to vote with on the day of the SGE.

- On the day of the SGE, it is a good idea to formulate a timetable that allows every class to come to the Hall and take every child through the voting process; this is a good time to explain that if they have already voted with their families, they should not now vote again, as is dictated by the democratic election process.

- It is also a very good idea to have a 'Comments Book' available for anyone to contribute to during the day. This book can become very special. Indeed, I remember one parent writing in the book and feeling very emotional, explaining that she had been living in this country for over 12 years and this was the first time she had been able to vote! The book can be very useful for capturing comments that are shared or overheard during the day. I will never forget the child who had come to vote with his family, the date of which coincidentally fell on the day that families found out which school their child would be going to, saying: 'I've just voted for my future'.

- Organise for the Learning Leaders or the Year 2 or Year 6 children to count the votes the following day. This can be a fascinating and logistically complicated Maths Investigation exercise, and thinking about a 'strategy' for counting the votes beforehand is very useful.

- Arriving at a final count for each item on the ballot paper is also a complex task as the children will have to take into account the votes received for each item and by every means that the school has facilitated as a way of casting a vote. Figure 9.7 shows an example of how a school summarised its final count of votes:

FIGURE 9.7 A School's Ballot Paper as part of their School's Democratic Election Voting Process

- Ensure that there are rapid and efficient ways of communicating the outcome of the election process as soon as the results are in and have been verified by members of staff
- Explain to everyone what the outcome of the election will mean for the school and what the next steps of the process for the lifelong learning dispositions entail

Having obtained a set of lifelong learning dispositions for the school and communicated to everyone what these are, it is very interesting to launch the process by which all children begin to conceptualise how each of the dispositions will help them to learn and to thrive with everything they encounter at school and beyond. Deriving definitions that are age-appropriate can form the basis of great discussions amongst staff and the children themselves.

Once the children develop a conceptual understanding of the characteristics that accompany each of the dispositions, it is very beneficial to enrich this conceptual understanding by linking each of the dispositions to something that the children can relate to and that for them reflects what the disposition is all about. The scope for linking them is varied: some schools choose animals, some choose fictitious characters, some choose characters with superpowers that they design, and some choose famous people that children can relate to.

The process for associating the dispositions with something of the school's choice is accomplished by engaging the whole school community in a second Headteacher Challenge. In the example illustrated below, each process allowed each disposition to be linked to an animal.

 The Second Headteacher Challenge

Which animals shall we choose?

Main Aims of this Challenge

1   To obtain a list of suggestions from the whole school community of which animals they think best characterise each of the dispositions

2   To prepare the school for a second 'general election'

3   To analyse the results of the second election

4   To announce the animals that will become associated with each of the school's lifelong learning dispositions (the resilient tortoise or snail, for example)

This challenge asks the families and community to think of the qualities that each disposition brings to an individual and then propose an animal that they think best exemplifies those qualities. When this second Headteacher Challenge is being set, it is useful to remind the families of the definitions that the school has generated for each disposition.

Once all the ideas are received, it is fascinating to find a way of celebrating all the contributions and ideas submitted. The children will contribute these ideas in a range of ways: drawings, presentations, cartoons, films, models and invariably some edible ones too! In order to acknowledge each one, the schools can celebrate them in assembly or in the school newsletter, make a book of them and display them for all to enjoy. Once the celebration of all the contributions has taken place, the next step is handed over to the Learning Leaders again.

This time, the Learning Leaders have the job of collating all the suggestions submitted for each disposition and then choosing, as before, three animals that they think best represent the ideas submitted. For example, for resilience, the list may contain snail, tortoise or sloth. The three 'finalists' for each disposition are placed on a ballot paper, and the whole school community is invited to come and vote for the preferred choice of animal for each disposition at another School General Election.

Once the animals are chosen, the scope for using them as part of the daily routine becomes very exciting indeed. Having them physically in the classroom, as cuddly toys or puppets, is very powerful. Children love to have the animal with them as they learn; it makes the disposition really come alive for them. The animals act as a representation of the disposition across all areas of school life. Children who see the animals in the school office or the canteen, for example, will immediately associate them with all other adults also acquiring the skills of effective lifelong learners.

The next step in the process involves choosing the 'design' that will represent the animal for the school. At this stage, schools may choose to select an arbitrary, freely available design or they may choose to hold a third Headteacher Challenge to generate designs from the children themselves.

 The Third Headteacher Challenge

What should our animals look like?

Main Aims of this Challenge

1 To obtain a list of suggestions for the design for each of the animals from the whole school community

2 To prepare the school for a third 'general election'

3 To analyse the results of the third election

4 To incorporate the designs voted in within the infrastructure of the school

This challenge tends to produce some magnificent results as children really enjoy experimenting with a wide variety of media as a way of representing their ideas. The Learning Leaders are again tasked with condensing every idea submitted into a selection that can be voted on through the general election process and that they feel will be practical to reproduce and use widely across all areas of school life.

If the designs are submitted as three-dimensional works (sculptures, ceramics, wire constructions, Lego models, etc.), it is important to take photographs that will do them justice when they are placed on the ballot paper shortlist. This, of course, applies to all designs that make the ballot paper shortlist. As all the designs received are wonderful in their own right, it is also a great idea to use all the designs submitted to create an annotated bound book, possibly A3, which can be left on permanent display in the school's reception area for all families and visitors to enjoy. In this way, every child feels that their idea has been valued and celebrated.

Increasing the versatility of how the dispositions are used by deriving the *opposite characteristics* of each

As soon as the lifelong learning dispositions have been introduced and the students have become familiar with what each one signifies, it is very interesting to acquire an additional set of words to represent an *opposite* trait of each disposition. Deriving a set of opposite words and discussing their meaning explicitly with the students can be extremely useful, as often these opposites traits are the ones to pose barriers to the learning process (Figure 9.8):

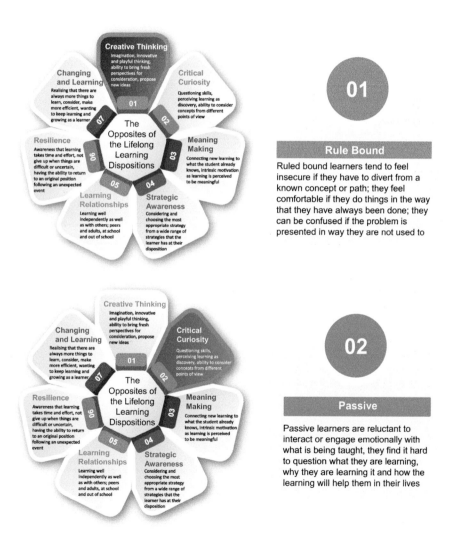

Rule Bound

Ruled bound learners tend to feel insecure if they have to divert from a known concept or path; they feel comfortable if they do things in the way that they have always been done; they can be confused if the problem is presented in way they are not used to

Passive

Passive learners are reluctant to interact or engage emotionally with what is being taught, they find it hard to question what they are learning, why they are learning it and how the learning will help them in their lives

FIGURE 9.8 The Lifelong Learning Dispositions

Fragmented

Fragmented learners tend to learn things in isolation, they are unable to connect what they are learning to what they already know; they find it hard to find purpose or personal value in what is being learnt

Robotic

Robotic learners rely on one strategy to engage with concepts, they feel comfortable following instructions and they find it hard to adapt or use different strategies to solve problems or appreciate situations from different perspectives

Dependent

Dependent learners find it difficult to launch into the learning process ndependently, they tend to always need help, guidance and reassurance from others before they are able to engage with their learning; they are reluctant to 'have a go' by themselves

FIGURE 9.8 (CONTINUED) The Lifelong Learning Dispositions

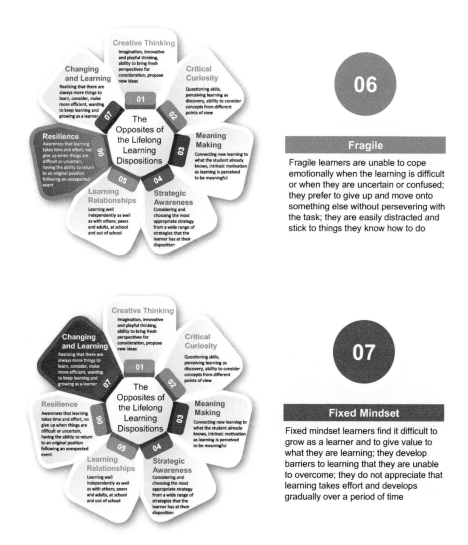

Fragile learners are unable to cope emotionally when the learning is difficult or when they are uncertain or confused; they prefer to give up and move onto something else without persevering with the task; they are easily distracted and stick to things they know how to do

Fixed mindset learners find it difficult to grow as a learner and to give value to what they are learning; they develop barriers to learning that they are unable to overcome; they do not appreciate that learning takes effort and develops gradually over a period of time

FIGURE 9.8 (CONTINUED) The Lifelong Learning Dispositions

Deriving a set of opposite words for each disposition broadens the way that the lifelong learning dispositions can be used. For example, the dispositions and their opposite traits can be placed at either end of a concept line. Concept lines, which were introduced in Chapter 6 as part of the third day of the Learning to Learn Week, are continuums that contain opposite characteristics at either end. This makes them a perfect vehicle for the dispositions, enabling them to become an integral feature of the classroom and of the way the curriculum is delivered and enjoyed by the students.

The diagram (Figure 9.9) illustrates how these concept lines can be constructed and illustrated to use in practice:

FIGURE 9.9 The Lifelong Learning Dispositions as Concept Lines

Once created, these concept lines can be used in a variety of ways. As soon as they are introduced and discussed with the class as part of the fifth day of the Learning to Learn Week, the children can be asked to map themselves on each of the lines as a baseline of how they view themselves as learners at the start of the academic year (Figure 9.10):

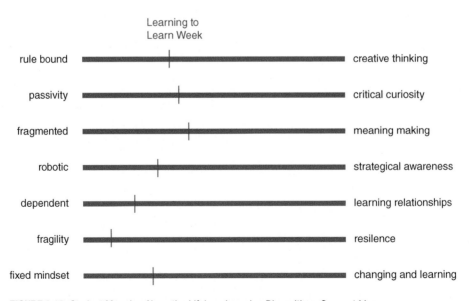

FIGURE 9.10 Student Mapping Along the Lifelong Learning Dispositions Concept Lines

These can be revisited regularly during the year, providing children with an excellent opportunity to self-reflect. They are very useful to revisit before parent consultation evenings, where they can be used as the basis for discussion with the families, and at the end of the year, when they can be used as part of the end-of-year report to parents and as part of teachers' handover conversations with the teacher inheriting the class (Figure 9.11):

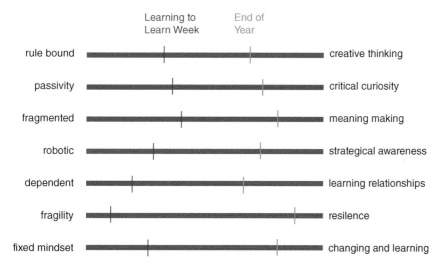

FIGURE 9.11 Student Mapping Along the Lifelong Learning Dispositions Concept Lines

Children feel very proud that their end-of-year report illustrates how they have progressed as a lifelong learner and it enables them to promote the language of lifelong learning with their families at home.

In order to make the lifelong learning dimensions integral to the daily life of the classroom, it is very useful to construct a large whole-class display of the concept lines. The class can then design a system by which the concept lines can be transformed into an 'interactive' display. For this, it is necessary to produce 'markers' that are able to be moved up and down the lines (little cars or trains, for example) (Figure 9.12):

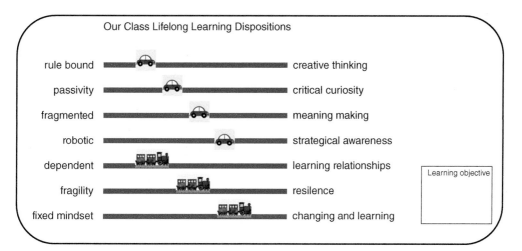

FIGURE 9.12 Lifelong Learning Dispositions Concept Lines Whole Class Display

At the start of a topic or lesson, each child can go up to the display and place the markers where they feel they are at that moment as a learner on the basis of the particular learning objective being set. A photograph can be taken with the child next to the dated learning objective that forms part of the display. At the end of the lesson or topic, the children can revisit their photograph and use this to map themselves again, this time reflecting how much they feel they have progressed after having completed the lesson or topic. A second photograph is taken and the before and after photographs can be displayed for all to see.

This process can also be used with the whole class. If a learning objective is being discussed, the whole class can reach a consensus of where the class is in terms of the challenge that awaits them. Making the dispositions so visible and so interactive ensures that they become part of the everyday language across all areas of the curriculum.

 CASE STUDY

The opposites of the Lifelong Learning Dispositions: 'Goat JONK'

The lifelong learning dispositions are very useful as a tool for communication with secondary schools in terms of transition. The learning ambassadors from the secondary school responsible for helping the primary pupils prepare for a smooth transition to secondary school became fascinated by the concept of the lifelong learning dispositions. They noticed that there were animals associated with the dispositions but not with the 'opposite characteristics'. A Headteacher Challenge was set for the secondary school learning ambassadors to try to think of the animals that could best be associated with each of the opposite characteristics. This is when the secondary pupils sought the help of their goats! The school is very well known for keeping goats and using them to promote learning and the well-being of students. The students realised that the goats were brilliant at being *all the opposites!* They named this *Goat JONK!*

The dispositions across the age ranges and across partnerships of schools, an action research–based approach

The non-prescriptive nature of the JONK approach and philosophy of education takes on a very significant role when considering the concept of lifelong learning and lifelong learning dispositions. We have already seen how each school is able to obtain their own unique set of dispositions, including *an opposite* characteristic for each. It is now important to consider how to make the dispositions accessible and relevant to children of all ages across a school, early years setting or higher education. There are two principal aspects to this process:

1   Is the terminology used for each disposition accessible to all age groups?

2   Are the implementation strategies for the dispositions as part of the everyday life of the classroom designed specifically to meet the needs of each age group?

The terminology aspect is very interesting, and each setting needs to decide whether the same sets of words can be used by the whole school or whether they need adapting according to age groups or phases. The example below illustrates how the ELLI wording was adapted to make it more meaningful for children in the Early Years and Key Stage 1 (3- to 7-year-olds) (Figure 9.13):

Enthusiastic		squirrel		Creative
Caring		badger		Connecting
Ambitious		snail		Persevering
Thoughtful		bat		Planner
Respectful		bee		Communicating
Friendly		mouse		Questioning

FIGURE 9.13 Lifelong Learning Dispositions Early Years and KS1 Version

In this example, each of the dispositions was linked to an animal and a school value rather than an *opposite*, so the snail became associated with being persevering *and* ambitious.

The actual *implementation* of the dispositions as part of the everyday practice also varies substantially according to the age group. Once the concept of the dispositions is in place in a school, it is very interesting to devote a period of one or two terms to using the dispositions as the basis of ongoing classroom action research. In this way, every teacher has the freedom to experiment with them and see how best to embed their use with the age group that they are teaching. Chapter 4 described how the concept of Enquiry Teams helps the action research process to become integral to the teaching and learning routine and to the school's use of self-generated evidence to inform and drive practice.

The example below is a summary of how practitioners from different year groups have used action research to make the dispositions specific to their year groups (Figure 9.14):

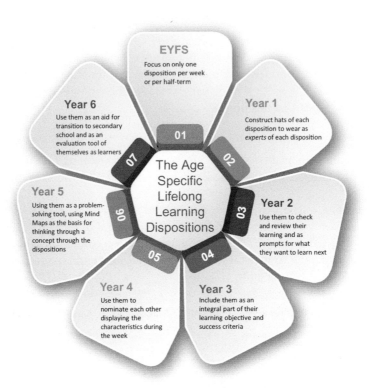

FIGURE 9.14 Considerations for Year Specific Lifelong Learning Dispositions

It can be seen from the diagram above that the lifelong learning dispositions are very versatile in supporting the teaching and learning process and ensuring that pupils develop what Dweck (2012) refers to as a *growth mindset*. Figure 9.14 shows how the dispositions play such an important role for students in terms of transition, both within each of the year groups at school and by providing students with a *toolkit for learning* when transitioning to their next phase of education. In her book entitled *Mindset* (2012), Dweck states that *transition is a time of great challenge for many students* and that in studies students with a growth mindset were actually able to increase their grades over the first two years in their new schools.

Figure 9.15 demonstrates how the dispositions can also be very powerful when used as a problem-solving tool, constituting each of the branches of a Mind Map. This works particularly well in science, when planning or evaluating an investigation. If the dispositions are made to represent each branch of a Mind Map, this prompts the children to think and analyse their work in a thought-provoking and strategic way (Figure 9.15):

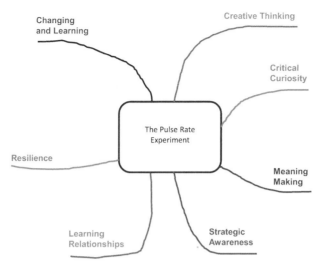

FIGURE 9.15 The Lifelong Learning Dispositions as a Problem Solving Tool

 Discussion Opportunities

It is very interesting at this stage to explore as a staff team the versatility of the dispositions and the different opportunities that arise for using them to support and enrich each of the eight sectors that make up the teaching Model of Excellence, Engagement and Enjoyment Model (MEEE) first discussed in Chapter 4.

The lifelong learning dispositions can also be used to great effect if they become the basis for inter-school collaborative action research projects, as illustrated in the case study below:

 **CASE STUDY**

The Better to Best Excellent Learner Project

The lifelong learning dispositions were used by schools that form part of the Viscount Nelson Educational Trust as the basis for a JONK inter-school collaborative action research initiative. The cohorts involved in these projects introduced either (i) a common set of dispositions across each of the schools or (ii) the principle of the dispositions that enabled every school to generate their own bespoke sets of dispositions in regard to terminology and how the dispositions were associated (some choosing animals, others superheroes, etc.). The value of the Excellent Learner Project was evidenced in terms of standards and professional collaboration, inter-phase dialogue, and the wealth of ideas exchanged between practitioners across and within each school as the projects involved regular dissemination sessions. An additional very powerful outcome of the project was seen with the impact that it had on children's motivation, self-esteem and the partnership of learning with families as each project culminated in a celebration event of *effective lifelong learners* attended by children, their families and staff at a large conference centre. This research project set the foundations for each school to continue their journey of innovation as an integral and sustainable part of their strategic plans and their philosophies of education (www.viscountnelson.net).

A strategic guide for planning the process that leads to obtaining a set of lifelong learning dispositions and embedding them in practice

The processes described thus far use a series of Headteacher Challenges that help the school to generate a set of lifelong learning dispositions and to embed them as an integral part of the teaching and learning process and life of the school. The diagrams below illustrate how these processes may be achieved as part of a two-year strategic plan for the school (Figures 9.16, 9.17 and 9.18):

Terms 1 and 2

What words should we use as our Lifelong Learning Dispositions (LLDs)?

- Headteacher Challenge One (HC1) generates these words for the school

- The title of the HC1 is: 'A Recipe for a Lifelong Learner'

- The Learning Leaders analyse all the ideas generated

- The Learning Leaders and SLT group ideas received into main categories

- The Learning Leaders and SLT choose twelve representative words

- These twelve words are placed on a ballot paper

- The school holds a 'General Election'

- The six words with the most votes become the LLDs for the school

How should we use our LLDs as part of our Teaching and Learning process?

- LLD action research is launched in each class

- LLD whole school approach adopted and communicated

- LLD opposites are generated

- LLDs introduced during Learning to Learn Week

- LLDs used for assessment, rewards, links with the community and home

FIGURE 9.16 The First Two Terms of the Headteacher Challenge

What animal or character should we associate with each LLDs?

- Headteacher Challenge Two (HC2) generates the association of the each

- LLD to an animal or character?

- The title of HC2 is: 'Which animal do you think best demonstrates in their

  way of being the characteristics of each of our LLDs?'

- The Learning Leaders analyse all the ideas generated

- The Learning Leaders and SLT group all suggestions for each LLDs

- The Leaning Leaders and SLT select three animals for each LDD

- All the animal choices selected are placed on a ballot paper

- The school holds a 'General Election'

- The animal with the highest vote within each LLD category is selected

- LLD and associated animal action research is launched in each class

- LLDs and their animals are integrated across all areas of the curriculum

Terms 3 and 4

FIGURE 9.17 The Third and Fourth Terms of the Headteacher Challenge

What should our 'animals' or 'characters' look like in our school?

- Headteacher Challenge 3 (HC3) generates the school specific design of

  each animal or character

- The title of HC3 is: 'Can you create a design for each of our animals or

  characters?'

- The Learning Leaders group the designs received for each LDD

- The Learning Leaders choose three designs to represent each LLD

- These designs are placed on a ballot paper

- The school holds a 'General Election'

- The designs with the highest votes are adopted by the school

- The adopted designs are visible in each class, on website, letter heads, etc

Terms 5 and 6

FIGURE 9.18 The Fifth and Sixth Terms of the Headteacher Challenge

The dispositions beyond the classroom, into the home and for life

The dispositions provide a fabulous way of celebrating, as a whole school, the learning behaviours and attitudes that the dispositions instil. The language of the dispositions provides a great source of inspiration for the teachers to use when writing children's certificates of achievement that are presented in whole-school assemblies. Using the dispositions in this way enables them to be at the forefront of what the school values as a place of learning whilst helping all children to develop the qualities of empathy for and pride in others.

The end of the academic year provides a further opportunity to focus on the life-long learning dispositions, using them as the basis for the last home-learning task. The task challenges children to 'think of famous people or people they know who have succeeded in life because they have excelled in one of the lifelong learning disposi-tions'. Setting the task at the end of the year allows the children to:

1   Appreciate the value of becoming a *master* of the dispositions, not just in school but for life

2   Engage in conversations about the dispositions at home and give families the opportunity to develop these dispositions at home

The examples above (Figure 9.19) highlight how the dispositions can become so well established within the understanding of a child and how the child can use this under-standing to think so creatively and so imaginatively, celebrating individuals across a wide area of disciplines, from ground-breaking scientific and technological discov-eries to the world of comedy and one of the greatest feats of human endurance in recent times.

For Learning Relationships I have chosen Dawn French and Jennifer Saunders because they have been at the top of their profession in Comedy for the past 20+ years. Each one of them gave work exceptionally well both with other people and on their own. They are particularly brilliant and exiting when working together in a they find off each other. Apparently when they do comedy sketches they don't even have a script, they improvise and ad-lib. To me they are the perfect role models of this learning dimension.

For Critical Curiosity I have chosen Stephen Hawking because he is a world famous Professor and he shows remarkable Curiosity in his theories and discoveries. To discover Black holes without any knoledge that we have now about space is quite extraordinary! Another thing is he can do extreanly complex Maths sums in his hedd because he has a muscle disease and therefore can't use his limbs to use a computer or pen and paper!

Hawking's Curiosity has led him to question the nature of our universe. For those who are clever enough to understand his work have benifited enormously!

For Resilience I have chosen Nelson Mandela. He was born into a society where black people were second class citizens. He decided to challenge the government. Though this did mean setting up an illegal group, the A.N.C. After protesting for rights in 1964 he was arrested and imprisoned. All over the world people were putting pressure on the South African government to release Mandela. Finally he was released after 26 years!!!

Nelson Mandela never lost heart in his own failor in his beleifs that one day black people would be equal to white. In his resilience he recieved the election to be president and the Nobel Peace prize with President de Klerk.

For Meaning Making I have chosen Sigmond Freud (1856-1939). He started out as an Austrian Physician studying in Veena. He is now much more famous his contribution to our understanding of Human Nature. He discovered the unconscious effect of thought and fears of behaviour. e.g If someone really really wanted to go to a funfair and when the day finally came the person hesitate when they were about to and then actually didn't want to go Freud took this and madde a meaning of it, it being the person didn't want to be disapointed. He developed theorys to the interpretation of dreams. When people today want to make sence of their lives they may go and see a therapist, Sigmond Freud is a founding father of this.

FIGURE 9.19 The Lifelong Learning Dispositions as Role Models

10 Thinking and learning at home

Start thinking and learning at school, keep thinking and learning at home
Marcelo Staricoff

This chapter introduces the reader to an innovative approach to setting and engaging children with homework tasks, known as the 'JONK home-learning' approach. The tasks are presented to the students as a series of weekly open-ended challenges that promote creative, critical and philosophical thinking at home.

The ideas presented in this chapter illustrate how these tasks can be used to support and enrich all areas of the curriculum as well as representing excellent vehicles with which to celebrate global events and multicultural traditions. The home-learning ideas presented in this chapter form part of a forthcoming book entitled *Keep Thinking* (in press, Imaginative Minds).

The JONK home-learning philosophy

The JONK home-learning philosophy and approach grew out of the success of the Thinking Skills Starters (Chapter 7). How could the motivational impact that the Thinking Skills Starters promote at school be replicated at home for *all* children? Could tasks be designed for the home in a way that motivates the children *and* their families? Could this approach to home learning serve as an opportunity to further foster a strong school–pupil–family triangular partnership? Could these tasks present opportunities for children to explain certain concepts to their families? Could these open-ended tasks promote cultural richness and global awareness at home? Could the tasks also promote active interaction of the families with their local communities? Could this approach to 'home learning' lead to children being intrinsically motivated to *want* to engage with each task?

Strategic considerations and benefits of the approach

As with all the JONK strategies, this chapter is designed to enable practitioners and senior leaders to use the home-learning concept and approach as part of a *non-prescriptive* framework that can be moulded by each school. The questions below are designed to promote the initial discussions that will lead to a whole-school approach:

- Does the school wish to incorporate this as a whole-school approach?
- If this is a whole-school approach, could weekly themes be adapted for different age groups?
- Will each year group set them at the same time for the same period of time?
- How will the tasks vary for children as they move from year to year?
- Could the same tasks be presented to the children again in other years but with a new adaptation?
- Has a convenient moment been identified within the Learning to Learn Week to introduce the concept to the class and provide each child with a Home Learning Thinking Skills Book?
- Have the principles, protocols and value of the approach been shared with the families?

Table 10.1 below summarises the key benefits that the home-learning approach brings to the child, the families and the school's culture for learning:

Table 10.1

- As with the Starters, the Home Learning Thinking Skills Books become a source for very special creative and innovative thinking.
- The routine and high expectations are a great way to build self-discipline and develop the child's ability to manage their time and meet deadlines.
- The nature of the tasks encourages children to work collaboratively with their families and their local communities.
- The tasks enable children to connect their learning at school with their lives outside of school and to give meaning to that learning.
- The tasks provide a never-ending means of celebrating world events and all cultures throughout the world.
- The tasks allow children to 'master' the learning introduced at school by using the concepts learnt in a different context.
- The nature of the tasks is an excellent way of promoting all the dispositions of lifelong learning at home.
- The home-learning tasks let the child act as an 'expert' at home, introducing family members to new concepts and ideas.
- The routine allows all children to develop a high level of self-esteem and a can-do positive mindset approach without the worry of its being competitive in any way.
- The tasks enable children to develop a wide range of problem-solving skills, and at all times they promote a love of challenge, achievable complexity and momentary uncertainty.
- The timing of the challenges gives children plenty of time to encourage thoroughness and effort.
- Home learning begins to be perceived as a natural and motivational extension of their lives rather than something that is perceived as a chore that needs to be completed for *school.*

The JONK home-learning approach induces extraordinary levels of engagement, dedication, creativity, imagination, collaboration and innovation for all children. The challenges help the children to extend the application of the dispositions of effective lifelong learning (Chapter 9) beyond the classroom and into the home. When the tasks are presented in this way, the process of home learning also proves to be quite transformational for families, helping them, regardless of their own experiences, to develop a very positive view of schooling, education and the processes of thinking and learning.

The JONK home-learning approach in practice

The end of the second day of the Learning to Learn Week (Chapter 6) introduces the home-learning process to the class and explains that the tasks are:

- Open-ended, thought-provoking, creative thinking challenges that they can enjoy at home with their families
- Completed in a dedicated Home Learning book
- Designed to be carried out and presented in any way that the child chooses
- Created to span one, two or three weeks, depending on the task

The sections below offer suggestions for a first and last task of the year as well as a range of ideas that can be offered in the autumn, spring and summer terms as one-, two- or three-week tasks.

The First Home-Learning Task of the Year | A Child's Life as a Mind Map

This task is recommended to be the first task in the academic year as it takes advantage of the skills that the children have been taught during the Learning to Learn Week (LTLW). On Day 3 of the LTLW, the students are introduced to the concept of Mind Mapping and how to Mind Map. This first home-learning task invites the children to create a Mind Map of their lives, including their families, hobbies, likes, travels and friends – anything at all. As part of the process, they are also tasked with having to teach a member of their family how to Mind Map, using the instructions that accompany this challenge and included in each child's Home Learning book. The examples below illustrate:

1   How the instructions of how to Mind Map can be provided for the children to include in their books. The list contains a box bullet point that they can use to tick as they complete or teach each step, as shown in Figure 10.1:

Mind Mapping
'Accelerated Learning Through Visible Thinking'

☑   Draw the first draft in pencil
❑   Create a central image that sums up the topic for YOU
☑   Brainstorm ideas
❑   Divide topic into sub-topics, creating one branch for each
❑   Make your branches grow and organise ideas brainstormed
❑   Make your map personal- use pictures, images, diagrams, icons
❑   Use a different colour for each branch
❑   Use size of word to reflect importance
❑   Make connections using icons
❑   Add to it at any time, they are never finished!

FIGURE 10.1 Instructions for Mind Mapping

2   How the task can be set (note that the date coincides with the first week of the academic year)

3   How the child in the example below planned the Mind Map by first making a list of all the main themes she wanted to include, as shown in Figure 10.2:

FIGURE 10.2 Planning for Constructing a Mind Map

4   How the motivational aspect of the task has led to these children *wanting* to present their Mind Maps in such an attractive and informative way (Figure 10.3):

FIGURE 10.3 A Personal Mind Map

Setting this task as the first home-learning task enables:

1   The children to practice and master a skill taught during the LTLW and apply it to their own lives, contributing to the 'Meaning Making' lifelong learning disposition

2   The children to cement their knowledge of how to Mind Map by teaching the skill to others

3   The children to feel that, right from the outset of the year, they have been able to communicate all that is valuable to them to the teacher and feel that this has been appreciated and valued

4   The teacher to gain an enormous amount of knowledge about each child. This can be so helpful in being able to personalise the learning experiences for each child during the year.

Ideas for the Autumn term I One-, two- and three-week tasks

One-week example

The *Odd One Out Grid* task uses mathematics to inspire a love of critical, creative, philosophical and playful thinking. This task works well if set as the second home-learning task of the year.

The *Odd One Out Grid* invites children to:

- Play with numbers in an enjoyable way
- Make meaningful links between numbers, the world and their lives
- Develop their ability to think about mathematical patterns
- Develop their creative thinking
- Source ideas from their siblings and adults at home

The Odd One Out Grid Task (Figure 10.4) is based on providing the children with a four-by-four grid populated with a set of random numbers (see example below). The children are challenged to find which numbers are *the odd ones out* in each column and row.

Thinking Skills Maths Investigation

The 'odd one out' grid !

column / row	A	B	C	D
1	5	6	7	3
2	11	12	9	13
3	15	24	11	30
4	10	50	40	33

Using your skills of Reasoning, Understanding and Creative Thinking, can you find numbers that are 'the odd ones out' in each row and in each column?

FIGURE 10.4 The Odd One Out Challenge

The children's answers could be related to anything. By being asked to explain the reasoning behind each of their choices, the children develop their ability to communicate, explain and justify their reasoning. The example below (Figure 10.5) illustrates how this task can be presented to the class and it includes an example of what one ten-year-old child created in response. It is interesting to note that, in this instance, the child has:

- Made connections that relate to mathematical sequence and pattern
- Made connections that relate to mathematical operations
- Made connections related to place value

- Used mathematical knowledge (prime numbers)
- Made connections that show how numbers can act as labels (age, in this case)
- Included an idea from one of her younger brothers (2a below). Even though it was only the second task of the year, this child was already enjoying engaging with it as a family.

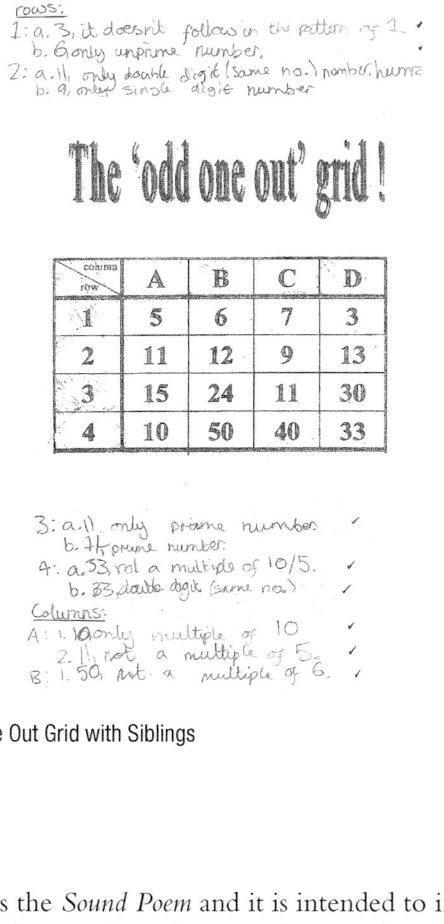

rows:
1: a. 3, it doesn't follow in the pattern of 1.
   b. 6 only unprime number.
2: a. 11, only double digit (same no.) number, hmmm
   b. 9, only single digit number

The 'odd one out' grid !

column / row	A	B	C	D
1	5	6	7	3
2	11	12	9	13
3	15	24	11	30
4	10	50	40	33

3: a. 11 only prime number ✓
   b. 7 prime number.
4: a. 33 not a multiple of 10/5. ✓
   b. 33 double digit (same no.) ✓
Columns:
A: 1. 10 only multiple of 10 ✓
   2. 11 not a multiple of 5. ✓
B: 1. 50 not a multiple of 6. ✓

FIGURE 10.5 The Odd One Out Grid with Siblings

Two-week example

This task is known as the *Sound Poem* and it is intended to inspire children and their families with a love of poetry by using everyday sounds as a stimulus. The timing of this task could be linked to a school focus on poetry or sound or to accompany the celebration of events such as National Poetry Day. The poems in Figure 10.6 illustrate a number of the benefits that are often seen as part of the creative thinking and open-ended approach to home-learning tasks:

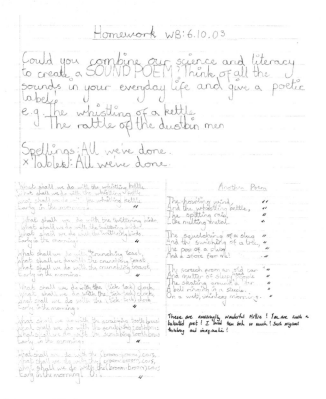

FIGURE 10.6 Science and Poetry

- Without being asked or prompted in the instructions, this child has used a Mind Map to plan her writing and structure her ideas (Figure 10.7):

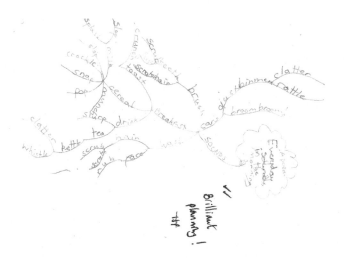

FIGURE 10.7 Using Mind Maps Across the Curriculum

- You may recall that teaching them to Mind Map is part of the third day of the Learning to Learn Week and features explicitly in the first home-learning task set. In this case, the use of the Mind Map shows that this tool has already become an integral part of the child's learning toolkit and repertoire which will remain a skill for life.

- This child has made connections between science, literacy and a theme that was familiar to her as a child. By using a nursery rhyme as the basis for one of her poems, she has been able to create something very special and original.

- This child has used the time productively and realised that with two weeks she had enough time to produce two poems. What is fascinating about this is that she wanted to produce more than the 'minimum required', illustrating how the JONK approach fosters intrinsic motivation both at school and at home.

Three-week example

The approach of the autumn half-term is an opportunity to introduce the concept of the three-week 'extended project', which spans the week before half-term, the half-term break itself and the week after half-term.

This is a fantastic opportunity to bring the humanities to the fore and to give history, geography, citizenship and religious education centre stage. Using these projects as a stimulus to invent games works very well; board games are excellent vehicles for promoting creativity and focused research. The example (Figures 10.8) shows a wonderful set of Top Trumps cards created as part of a three-week task set on the Victorians, which when submitted provided the children with many hours of entertainment in class, especially during wet play times!

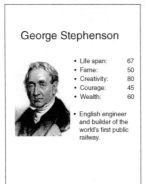

George Stephenson

- Life span: 67
- Fame: 50
- Creativity: 80
- Courage: 45
- Wealth: 60

- English engineer and builder of the world's first public railway.

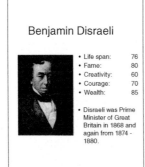

Benjamin Disraeli

- Life span: 76
- Fame: 80
- Creativity: 60
- Courage: 70
- Wealth: 85

- Disraeli was Prime Minister of Great Britain in 1868 and again from 1874 - 1880.

Florence Nightingale

- Life span: 90
- Fame: 100
- Creativity: 80
- Courage: 85
- Wealth: 54

- Florence Nightingale was an English founder of modern nursing.

FIGURE 10.8 A Home-Learning Set of 'Top Trumps' Box and Playing Cards

It is extraordinary how creative and artistic children can be with the presentation of these three-week tasks. Their contributions and inventiveness never cease to amaze, covering an incredibly broad spectrum: 3D models, sculptures, paintings, websites, videos, podcasts, radio programmes, and PowerPoint presentations – the list is endless. In the example (Figure 10.9), a nine-year-old child was inspired to create this most wonderful puppet in response to a family member who was travelling in India around the time that a three-week project task on India was set:

FIGURE 10.9 A Home-Learning Homemade Puppet

Ideas for the Spring term I One-, two- and three-week tasks

One-week example

The start of the spring term provides a great opportunity to return to a maths-based theme encouraging the children to apply their knowledge of mathematical concepts within the context of everyday life.

This task challenges the children to create a family data set that they represent diagrammatically as a table, a graph, a pie chart or (as in the example below) a bar chart. The prompt for generating the data could be anything at all, and the way they generate their data can vary according to the task set. The example below is from a six-year-old child whose family all carried out a 'jumping activity', which the child measured to obtain a data set, which was represented as a bar chart (Figure 10.10):

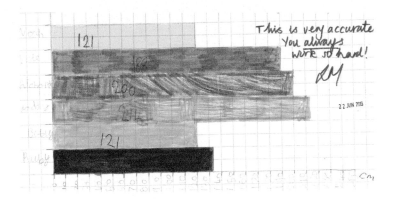

FIGURE 10.10 Family Jumping Activity Chart

The teacher was able to use the home-learning task to challenge the child's thinking further (Figure 10.11):

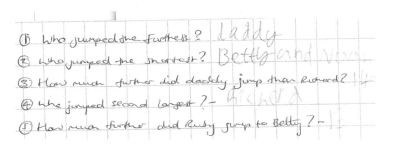

FIGURE 10.11 Family Jumping Activity Chart Follow-up Questions

An alternative idea to promote maths at home and in the context of the real world is to ask the children to illustrate, discuss and comment on all the 'shapes' that they can find at home and in the outside world. This task promotes a wide range of mathematical discussions at home: Is the shape 2D or 3D? Is it a shape we know the name of? Is it a regular or irregular shape? Is there a reason *why* that shape was chosen to make specific objects or parts of objects, such as tiles, plates, clocks, windows or wheels? Could the same object be made from a different shape? Are some shapes more efficient than others for certain objects or certain jobs? For example, could patio tiles be any shape? What if they were round? This task can also promote philosophical discussions at home. Do 2D shapes exist or not? By focusing on shapes in such detail, children begin to perceive the world in more curious ways and will tend to ask lots more 'why' and 'could' questions: Why do buildings, in general, have a rectangular base? Could buildings be circular? What shape can sustain the most weight? What shape is less likely to break?

Two-week example

This task inspires the children to create a *Chinese New Year Card* to coincide with the celebrations of the Chinese New Year, which is celebrated during the first month of the lunar calendar and falls in either January or February. This task works very well when set over a two-week period as it gives the children and their families plenty of time to enjoy researching all the traditions that accompany the festival as well as providing them with enough time to create the card. This may be one of those occasions where offering children a piece of red card is hugely beneficial (Figure 10.12):

FIGURE 10.12 Chinese New Year Cards

These cards make for a wonderful display in the classroom and they can also be used by the children to give to their families as a way of celebrating the Chinese New Year at home. Every month of the year provides an opportunity for schools to celebrate world events, international festivals and customs as a way of enriching the curriculum, promoting multicultural awareness and celebrating the wonders of our diverse universe.

Two-week example

National Science Week also tends to fall during the spring term and this gives us the opportunity to introduce the challenge of playing Science Scrabble at home as a family. The idea is that the players have to follow Scrabble rules in terms of how the letters and words are placed on the playing grid, but they are allowed to use words related only to a given topic. In Figure 10.13, the topic was the celebration of National Science Week. Each family member is asked to play with a different coloured pen as the following week's task turns the outcome of this game into a mathematical

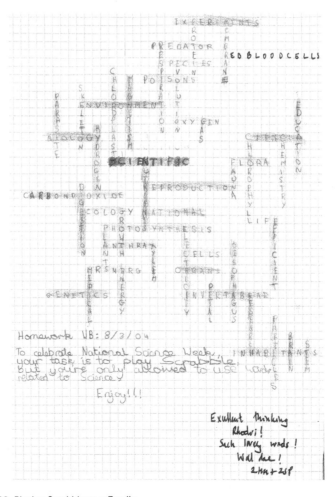

FIGURE 10.13 Playing Scrabble as a Family

challenge in which the children are asked to score each person's contributions using the real value of each of the letters as used in the real game of Scrabble:

The child below really enjoyed the mathematical perspective of this challenge (Figure 10.14):

player 2				
mr.s	globalwarming	2+1+1+3+1+1+4+1+1+3+1+1+2	22	
			22	22
player 3				
jenny	cold	3+1+1+2	7	
	heat	4+1+1+1	7	
			14	14
player 4				
liz	premafrost	3+1+1+3+1+4+1+1+1	17	
	thermoregulation	1+4+1+1+3+1+1+2+1+1+1+1+1+1	21	
			38	38
player 5				
mum	hot toddy	4+1+1+1+1+2+2+4	16	
	equator	1+10+1+1+1+1+1	16	
	shivering	1+4+1+4+1+1+1+1+2	16	
	sunshine	1+1+1+1+4+1+1+1	11	
	pyrexia	3+4+1+1+8+1+1	19	
	longjohns	1+1+1+2+8+1+4+1+1	20	
	hypothermia	4+4+3+1+1+4+1+1+3+1+1	24	
	gloves	2+1+1+4+1+1	10	
	scarf	1+3+1+1+4	10	
	slippers	1+1+1+3+3+1+1+1	12	
	incubator	1+1+1+1+3+1+1+1+1	11	
	thermostat	1+4+1+1+3+1+1+1+1+1	15	
	wetsuit	4+1+1+1+1+1+1	10	
	tropic	1+1+1+1+1+3	8	
	simering	1+1+3+1+1+1+1+2	12	
	stringvest	1+1+1+1+1+2+4+1+1+1	14	
			224	224
player 6				
dad	hotchocolate	4+1+1+3+1+3+1+1+1+1+1	18	
	fleece	4+1+1+1+3+1	11	
	blanket	3+1+1+1+5+1+1	13	
	vest	4+1+1+1	7	
	boiler	3+1+1+1+1+1	8	
	soup	1+1+1+3	6	
	duvet	2+1+4+1+1	9	
	insulation	1+1+1+1+1+1+1+1+1+1	10	
	centralheating	2+1+1+1+1+1+4+1+1+1+1+1+2	19	
	globalwarming	2+1+1+3+1+1+4+1+1+3+1+1+2	22	
	poridge	3+1+1+1+2+2+1	11	
	green house	2+1+1+1+1+4+1+1+1+1	14	
			148	148
player 7				
granny	northpole	1+1+1+1+4+3+1+1+1	14	
	trap	1+1+1+3	6	
	antartic	1+1+1+1+1+1+1+3	10	
			30	30
1st	Lizzie		640	1116
2nd	mum		224	
3rd	dad		148	
4th	Liz		38	
5th	granny		30	
6th	Mr.s		22	
last	jenny		14	

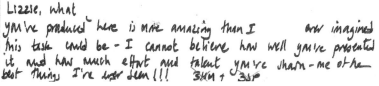

Lizzie, what you've produced here is more amazing than I ever imagined this task could be – I cannot believe how well you've presented it and how much effort and talent you've shown – me other best thing I've ever seen!!! 3×M + 3½P

FIGURE 10.14 Scoring a Family Scrabble Game

The outcome of this challenge led to a very inspirational moment for the class as they saw the letter that we wrote as a whole class published in the *Times Educational Supplement* (Staricoff, 2005) (Figure 10.15):

Letter published in the TES 11 March 2005

I was fascinated to read that Samantha Cooper is using Scrabble as a cross-curricular tool to raise standards in the primary classroom [Feb 25th]. At Westbury Park, we use a thinking-skills approach to our curriculum and we have found that Scrabble is a fantastic tool for stimulating children's learning.
We often use it at the beginning or end of a topic to assess current understanding- children playing against each other, using words that relate to the topic in question.
This playing with the curriculum has proved very popular in homework tasks, where children and parents can all enjoy playing together.

FIGURE 10.15 Letter Published in the TES

Three-week example

The three-week example task for the spring half-term is entitled *Why do People Read Fiction?* For this task, the children are asked to create a questionnaire, which could be produced at home or in class and which they then use to interview three people of different generations.

This task provides a great opportunity to focus on why reading is so important, how it offers people so much enjoyment and how it enriches our lives in so many ways. It is extraordinary how much insight children gain about a subject if they are the person doing the questioning. This task prompts children to present their information in a variety of ways: as filled questionnaires, a resume of the information gathered, a chart to show the types of responses obtained, etc.

This task is also really valuable as children will notice that the person being interviewed offers a different length and depth of response according to how the question is worded. Some questions will lead to only a 'yes' or 'no' response or to single-word answers, but others will lead to more detailed answers, deep in explanation and commentary. The three-week timeline for this task is very useful, as was illustrated once when a child sent the questionnaire to her grandmother in Australia and received her reply – all by post. The examples below in Figure 10.16 correspond to a child, adult and grandparent respectively:

Survey to find out why people read fiction   Rachel

1.   Who is your favourite author? *(handwritten)*

2.   Do you think fiction is more fun to read than non-fiction? yes

    Why?

3.   What is your favourite book or set of books? MIZ WIZ

4.   Have you read a well-known story in different genres? yes

    Which story? little red riding *(hood)*

5.   How long do you think it takes a good author to write a book? one year

6.   Do you like adventure stories? yes

    Why? make you feel like your there

7.   Do you think that the books you have read are based on a certain genre or are they mixed? *(handwritten)* Adventure

8.   Do you like stories based on animals? yes   — Adventure

9.   Do you like comedy books? yes

    Why? they're funny

10.   What is your favourite book at the moment? Horrid Henry

Why? there is four realy good stories   Great answers! ☺

Survey to find out why people read fiction   Daddy

1.   Who is your favourite author? Nick Hornby

2.   Do you think fiction is more fun to read than non-fiction? Non-fiction

    Why? Stories are pointless

3.   What is your favourite book or set of books? The Blind Watchmaker

4.   Have you read a well-known story in different genres?

    Which story?   NO

5.   How long do you think it takes a good author to write a book? 18 monthes

6.   Do you like adventure stories? NO

    Why? Too scary

7.   Do you think that the books you have read are based on a certain genre or are they mixed? How to be Good — comedy

8.   Do you like stories based on animals? No

9.   Do you like comedy books? yes

    Why? they make me laugh

10.   What is your favourite book at the moment?

Why?   ✓ Thanks Daddy I like Nick Hornby too!

FIGURE 10.16 A Home-Learning Task Involving Three Generations of the Family

Survey to find out why people read fiction Granpa

1.   Who is your favourite author? No one

2.   Do you think fiction is more fun to read than non-fiction? Non fiction

     Why? Non-fiction is true

3.   What is your favourite book or set of books? Hasn't got any

4.   Have you read a well-known story in different genres? yes

     Which story? 3 men in a boat

5.   How long do you think it takes a good author to write a book? 3 months

6.   Do you like adventure stories? No

     Why? Not true

7.   Do you think that the books you have read are based on a certain genre or are they mixed? Generaly

8.   Do you like stories based on animals? NO   Non-fiction

9.   Do you like comedy books? NO

     Why? Not realistic

10. What is your favourite book at the moment? Blood and fire

     Why?

                                    ✓ Thanks Granpa!

FIGURE 10.16 (CONTINUED) A Home-Learning Task Involving Three Generations of the Family

The task can be enriched by asking the children, as a follow-up, to create a summary of their findings. Do they notice any patterns in the responses they received? Are there differences and similarities between the responses from individuals of different generations? Did they find out anything surprising? Has it inspired them to read more or experiment with different genres? How would they answer the questionnaire themselves? It is also a good idea to follow this task up by encouraging the children to choose their own fiction book and to prepare a brief summary of why they chose that particular book to share with the class at the end of the week.

As an alternative three-week task at this stage of the year, the children could be set the *Living as an Artist* challenge. This task encourages the children to create a space in their homes which acts as their studio and which is not disturbed for the duration of the task. This task works very well if the children are given a theme or an artist to focus on. Equally, it could be set as an open task for the children to choose the style and type of artwork and artist they would most like to explore. The task can be accompanied by asking the children to include a piece of research on the artist they are focusing on and the artistic genre they have chosen. This task makes the children feel like 'experts of art', and having their own 'studio' for the three weeks makes them feel very special indeed. Children cannot wait to get home to keep working on their piece. Many families have recounted how the fact that the task covers a half-term has also inspired them to visit museums and art galleries, in some cases for the very first time.

The task also provides children with an excellent model of how, in real life, things take time and one may need to have several attempts at the same thing before being satisfied with the final product. The task also makes it possible for the Arts to be given real prominence within the curriculum and encourages children to feel that they can all be artists. In this example (Figure 10.17), the child chose to focus on Picasso and Still Life, adapting the 'studio' as she worked on her piece.

Name: Pablo Picasso

Life Span: 1881-1973

Born: Malaga, Spain

General Facts:

- He was the son of a drawing teacher
- After several years in Paris, Picasso moved permanently to the 'capital of arts' in 1904. There, he met many more famous artists. People admired him and he developed a life-long friendship with the master of the French Fauvism.

His Periods:
Picasso drew in many different ways as you probably know and these were his different periods.

- Blue Period = 1900-1904
- Rose Period = 1905-1906

Pictures of my Product.

FIGURE 10.17 Being an Artist at Home

Ideas for the Summer term | One-, two- and three-week tasks

One-week example

The summer term launches with a focus on democracy, citizenship and the Personal, Social, Health Education (PSHE) curriculum. The task asks the children to consider: '*If you were Prime Minister, how would you improve the lives of people of different ages: babies, toddlers, primary-age children, secondary-age children, young adults, adults and the older generation?*' The day before this task is set, it is a good idea to present the children with the *Wishes for our World* Thinking Skills Starter, where children are asked to grant the world wishes to make it a better place. In the example (Figure 10.18), the child has used a very well-presented set of cards to communicate her thinking.

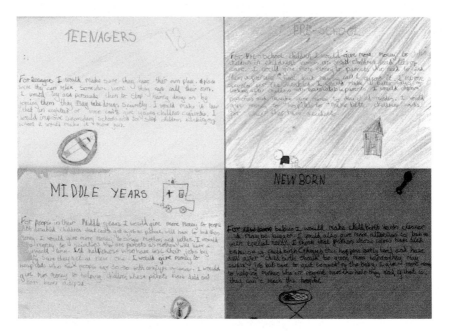

FIGURE 10.18 Improving the Lives of Others

This task is particularly powerful if it is set in the weeks prior to local or national general elections, a Ministerial Budget Statement or one of the school's general elections (Chapter 3). Linking this task to these more formal events encourages children to take an interest in world events and to compare their own thoughts with the proposals being made by election candidates. The example (Figure 10.19) illustrates how a pre-general election moment encouraged this child to produce his own Prime Ministerial brief!

FIGURE 10.19 The Child as Prime Minister

This task can also be adapted to take an international dimension as children can be asked to think about improving the lives of people in different parts of the world. It can also be set so as to challenge children with their thinking of the past and the future: '*How would you have improved the lives of people in the Victorian times?*' is a perfect companion to the study of the Victorians. *How would you improve the lives of people in the distant future* can lead to some highly creative ideas in terms of global sustainability and climate change?

Two-week example

The summer term is often the time when children go on school trips and overnight stays. The *Maps, Maps, Maps* (Figure 10.20) task works well prior to an outing or a trip and supports the geography and maths curriculum. The task challenges children to find, illustrate and describe as many different types of maps as possible.

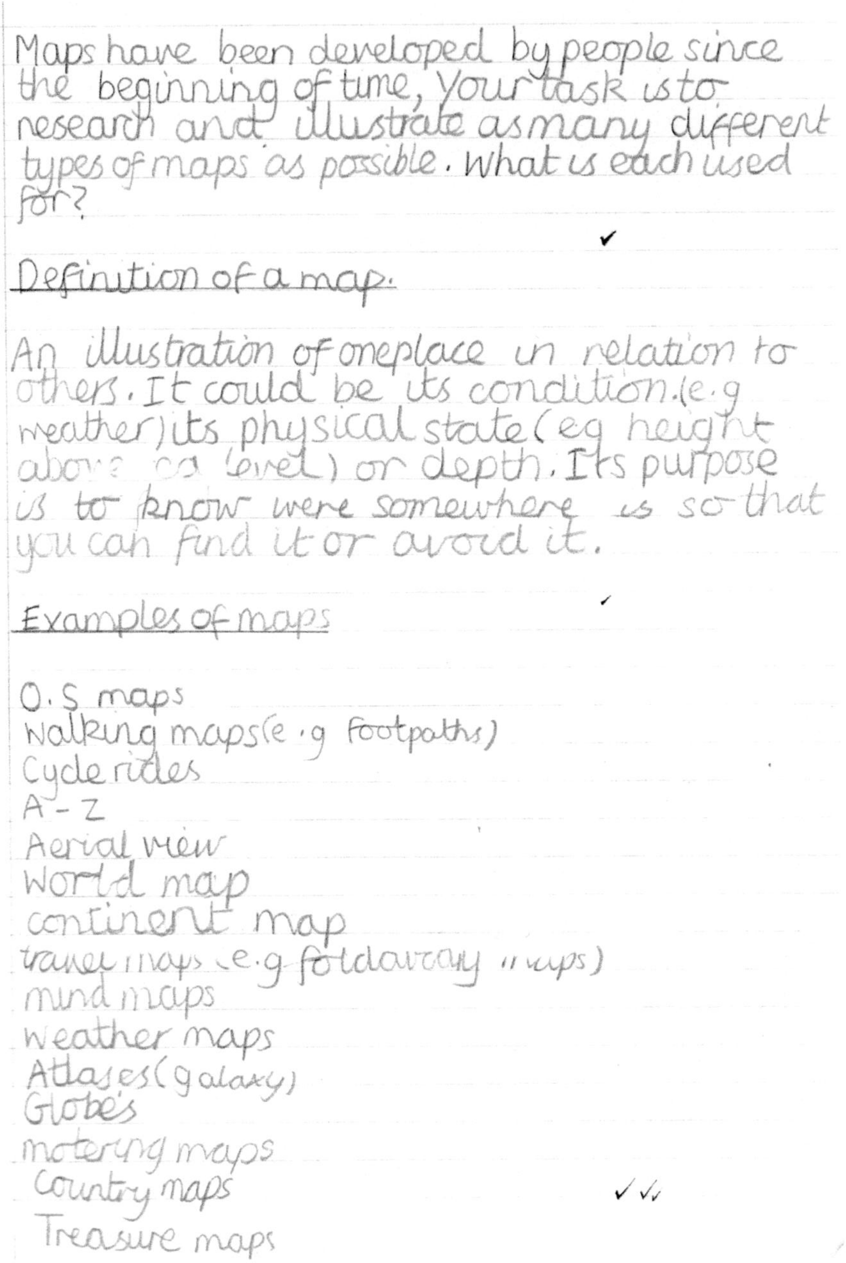

Maps have been developed by people since the beginning of time. Your task is to research and illustrate as many different types of maps as possible. What is each used for? ✔

Definition of a map.

An illustration of one place in relation to others. It could be its condition. (e.g weather) its physical state (eg height above sea level) or depth. Its purpose is to know were somewhere is so that you can find it or avoid it. ✔

Examples of maps

O.S maps
Walking maps (e.g footpaths)
Cycle rides
A - Z
Aerial view
World map
continent map
travel maps (e.g foldaway maps)
mind maps
weather maps
Atlases (galaxy)
Globe's
motoring maps
Country maps   ✔ ✔✔
Treasure maps

FIGURE 10.20 Investigating Maps

This task encourages children to look at the world through a very creative lens. In the example (Figure 10.21), the child has interpreted the concept of maps in its broadest sense and included examples ranging from a map of the solar system to a map of the family's favourite football ground!

FIGURE 10.21 Examples from an Investigating Maps Challenge

Three-week example

Healthy Eating and Healthy Lifestyles often feature as part of the topics for the summer term. This task requires children to *create their own menu for a restaurant of their choice*. This is a wonderful task that combines creativity, family life, science, art, maths and interaction with the local community. The task provides an opportunity for families to celebrate their heritage and for this to enrich the lives of all at school. The task suggests that the choices on their menus should reflect a healthy diet and that their menus should look as professional as possible – as if they were to be used in a real restaurant. Providing children with three weeks to do this one works well as this gives them time to walk around their local community as a family, looking at and examining real menus from real restaurants. Families often comment on how much they enjoy walking around their local community together with a specific task to accomplish. The task can be accompanied with some prompts as it is set:

- What route can they plan with a grown-up? How far will they go? Will they explore new areas? Are there areas with specific cuisines they can visit?

- How can the menu be designed so that it looks really attractive and appealing to all?

- What sections do menus usually include?

- What choices of dishes would make it a healthy restaurant?

- What would the price for each dish be?

- Would there be a special section for children? Could this be smaller portions of adult dishes or specific choices for children?

- Does the menu cater to different dietary preferences and cultural needs?

- Does the menu need to include other details, such as history of the food, telephone numbers, websites, addresses, allergy information, special offers, etc.?

As with all these tasks, the freedom to be able to present their work in their preferred way sparks a great amount of creativity and humour. *We are healthy to help* is such a great example of this in the menu entitled *Taverna Hay*, shown in Figure 10.22:

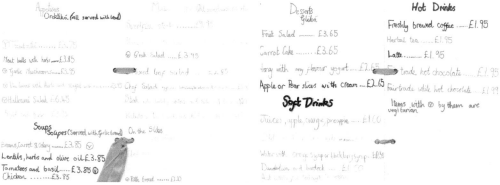

FIGURE 10.22 Creating Menus

This child has written the menu using a *bilingual approach* (Figure 10.23), which is the focus of Chapter 11:

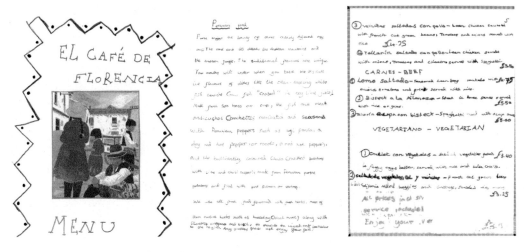

FIGURE 10.23 Creating Menus Bilingually

This child has created something professional with so much attention to detail and so well presented (Figure 10.24):

DRINKS

GREEN TEA....................£1.20
BLACK TEA....................£1.20
WULONG TEA....................£1.20
SCENTED TEA....................£1.20

PURE ORANGE JUICE....................£1.50*
VOLVIC TOUCH OF FRUIT
(STRAWBERRY/LEMON&LIME)....................£1.20*

All teas come half price with a meal.
*Comes free with one kid's meal.

TRADITIONAL CHINESE
FOOD

5 PORK &CHINESE LEAF
DUMPLINGS....................£6.99
5 SHRIMP&FUNGUS
DUMPLINGS....................£7.99
5 CHINESE CHIVE
DUMPLINGS....................£6.99 V

CHICKEN STIR FRY....................£5.99
CHINESE RICE WITH
EGG&TOMATO SAUCE....................£5.99 V

V=Suitable for Vegetarians.

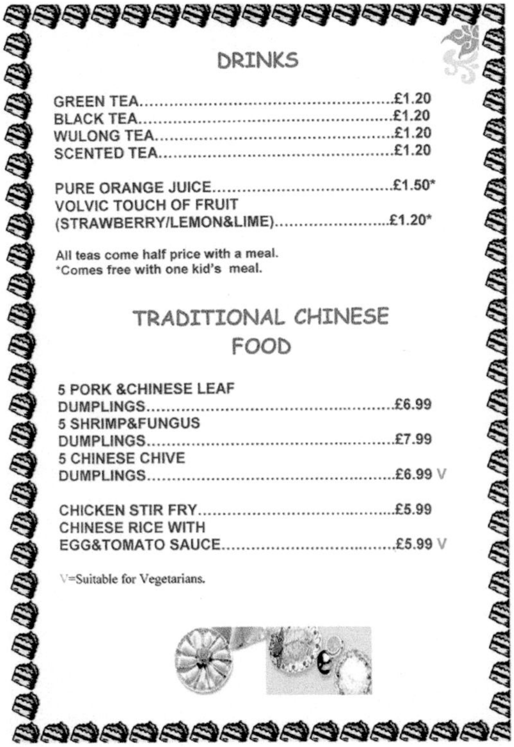

FIGURE 10.24 Creating Menus Multiculturally

DISCUSSION OPPORTUNITIES

How many of the points for consideration listed at the outset of this task can you spot in the examples above?

Once all the menus have been received, it is a really good idea to create a whole-class interactive display, where the children can access and enjoy looking through them. Having them on display also allows the menus to be used as the basis of a maths Investigation. As all the dishes are priced, the maths investigation challenges the children, depending on the age group, with investigating what they would choose if they had, for example, a £10 or £50 voucher to spend, how much change would they get, how much would the service charge be if it were set at 10%, 12%, etc. The menus provide great scope for mathematical investigations, and the children really enjoy using everyone's menus.

The final home-learning task of the year | Children as lifelong learners

The end of the academic year provides a great opportunity to focus back on the life-long learning dispositions (Chapter 9) which they have been developing during year. This task combines the idea (described in Chapter 9) of relating the lifelong learning dispositions to success in others to now think *about themselves as lifelong learners.*

The task asks them to map themselves along the same lifelong learning disposi-tions concept lines that they used at the beginning of the academic year (Chapter 9) and that featured as part of the fifth day of the Learning to Learn Week (Chapter 6) (Figure 10.25):

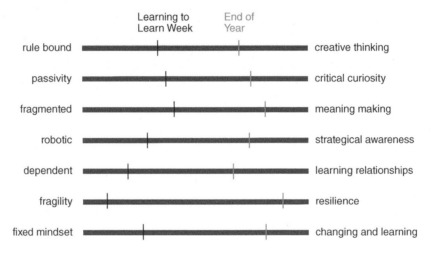

FIGURE 10.25 Final Home Learning Task

As part of this task, it is very useful to encourage the children to describe their thinking and reasoning that led them to map themselves along new positions on each line. Do they feel they have progressed along each line? What can they attribute this progress to? What examples can they give to demonstrate that they are now more 'resilient', for example? What do they think they need to work on most as a lifelong learner?

Once children have completed this task and provided a metacognitive explanation of their year as a lifelong learner, it is very valuable to include both their line chart and explanations as part of their contribution towards their end-of-year report to their families. Families find it fascinating to receive an end-of-year report with such a specific and interesting focus of their child as a lifelong learner.

This task can also be adapted to incorporate different contexts and different peri-ods in history by setting it in the context of different parameters. For example, the children could be asked to think of people who have succeeded in their lives because they demonstrated effectiveness in these dispositions, such as:

■ Romans
■ Characters in a book

- Actors in a film or play
- Friends in their class
- Members of their families
- Members of an orchestra or sports team
- Superheroes in cartoon characters
- People in the school
- Members of their local community

The ideas presented in this chapter are designed to act as prompts for schools to generate their own bespoke collection of open-ended home-learning tasks through-out the year. In order to maintain a whole-school strategic perspective of the tasks that each year group sets as one-, two- or three-week activities during the year, schools can create an overarching diagram of provision, as shown in Figure 10.26:

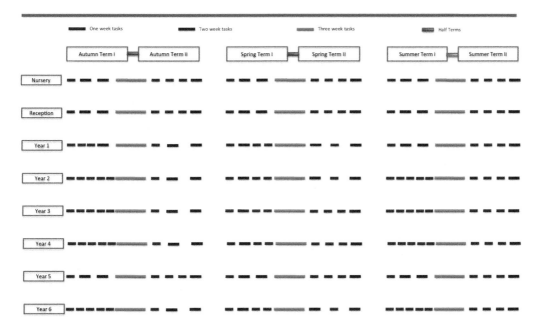

FIGURE 10.26 Whole School Strategic Map of Home Learning Tasks for Each Academic Year

Creating these whole-school strategic plans for the home-learning process and reviewing their relative success each year allow continuity and progression and ensure that the children experience a very rich, varied and age-related menu of provision throughout their time at the school.

11

Bilingual and multilingual thinking in multicultural classrooms

Embracing the richness that every child brings enriches the lives of all
Marcelo Staricoff

This chapter introduces the reader to the concept of *JONK Bilingual and Multilingual Thinking (BMT)* and how a BMT approach to teaching and learning can enrich the lives of all students. The examples included in this chapter demonstrate how the JONK BMT approach can be incorporated within the school's culture for learning and its philosophy of education and daily routines.

The chapter demonstrates how the universality of the concepts, principles, philosophies and methodologies that underpin the JONK approach can be used to *teach multiculturally*, embracing the richness of cultural heritage that exists within each classroom and school.

JONK and the multilingual multicultural classroom

We live in a multicultural world and in a multicultural society. The multicultural classroom approach helps to bring this multicultural world into the classroom. The JONK approach sets up a learning and social environment that reflects the multiculturality of every individual, the home and society, so that children do not perceive being at school as something that is different, unrelated or additional but rather as something that is an integral and natural component of their lives. The quote by Nelson Mandela that '*If you talk to a man in a language that he understands, that goes to his head. If you talk to him in his language, that goes to his heart*' illustrates perfectly the link that enables a child to feel that their language of heritage is being valued and embraced within the everyday teaching and learning philosophy of the classroom. As Mandela's quote indicates, this chapter discusses how embracing the multilingualism and multiculturality of a child allows them to engage with the curriculum, emotionally as well as academically.

Lind King (2018) quotes David Crystal, a world authority on language, who states that multilingualism is the 'normal human condition and that speaking two or more languages is the natural way of life for three quarters of the human race'. Marian and Shook (2012) state that 'today *more of the world's population is bilingual than monolingual*' and note that this trend not only facilitates 'cross-cultural communication' but also has a positive impact on an individual's cognitive ability. In their paper 'The Cognitive Benefits of Being Bilingual' (Cerebrum, 2012), the authors explain that 'the bilingual brain can have better attention and task-switching capacities than the monolingual brain' and that bilingualism 'has positive effects across the whole age spectrum'. The authors also describe how managing multiple languages appears to have 'broad effects on neurological function' and 'leads to enriched cognitive control, improved metalinguistic awareness (ability to recognise and be playful with language), better memory, visual-spatial skills and creativity'.

It is very interesting to note that establishing a multilingual classroom benefits *all* children. In an interview published on the Erasmus+ online platform (2016), Dina Mehmedbegovic, a lecturer at the Institute of Education, University College, UK, discusses the importance of communicating to children and their families that every language a child speaks is important, part of the teaching and learning process and also part of the thinking about the future, their employability, enabling them to convert their linguistic capital into economic capital in the future. Marian and Shook (2012) conclude that the cognitive and neurological benefits they observed from bilingualism are 'not exclusive to people who were raised bilingual; they are also seen in people who learn a second language later in life'. This observation is further supported by a collaborative study between Katherine Kinzler and the psychologists Boaz Keysar, Zoe Liberman and Samantha Fan that was published in the *Journal of Psychological Science* in which the authors showed that 'the social advantage we have identified appears to emerge from merely being raised in an environment in which multiple languages are experienced, not from being bilingual per se'.

 DISCUSSION OPPORTUNITIES

Chapter 7 discussed the importance of being able to diagnose, address and work towards closing the *word gap* that some children begin school with and that is so detrimental to their progress in school and their life chances. It is very interesting to consider the children who are presenting with a *word gap* in English. Is this also the case in their mother tongue? In other words, is the child able to function cognitively well in their mother tongue but not in English yet? If so, what opportunities can the child have to succeed using a multilingual approach?

Promoting bilingual and multilingual thinking in the classroom

In a study conducted by Fraser Lauchlan at the University of Strathclyde (2012), the researchers found that bilingualism had a positive effect on children's ability to think creatively and to problem-solve. It is interesting to note that in Ariadne de Villa's (2017) article entitled 'Critical Thinking in Language Learning and Teaching', critical thinking is seen as an essential tool for second-language acquisition. The ability to thrive in a multilingual learning environment is increased if the children are able to develop their critical thinking skills. These studies show that there is a symbiotic relationship between critical thinking and a multilingual learning environment; that is, they complement each other.

Is there a way, therefore, of using the JONK BMT approach to promote children's critical thinking skills as part of the daily routine? This chapter illustrates how this can be achieved by using the *Thinking Skills Starters*[1] (Chapter 7) from a multilingual perspective.

The multicultural ethos that this beginning to the day creates influences all that happens during the rest of the day and helps the children to use the entirety of their multilingual and multicultural repertoire to succeed as learners and metacognitive thinkers at each of the six stages of the learning process that were introduced using the diagram below in Chapter 2. In the diagram, situations 1 to 6 define the process that learners go through as they move *from a position of not knowing to one of knowing* (Figure 11.1):

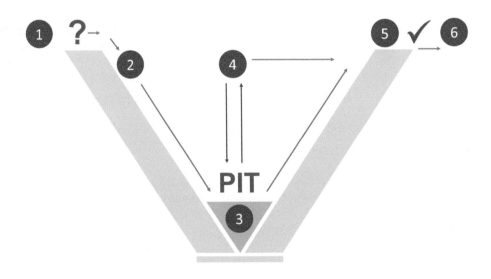

FIGURE 11.1 The JONK Model of Learning *how* to Learn (JMOLL)

The *Bilingual and Multilingual Thinking* approach is also very beneficial in:

1   Promoting children's ability to play intellectually (MEEE Model, Chapter 4):
    Inspiring children with a task that requires them to think bilingually offers them the opportunity to engage in extension tasks that promote the use of Higher-Order Thinking Skills (HOTS) rather than engaging in activities that involve doing More Of the Same (MOTS). For example, once they have solved a problem and climbed out of the Pit, the child is offered the opportunity to go back into the Pit and emerge from the Pit for a second time, this time having used a different language to problem-solve.

2   Enriching children's ability to engage with a task:
    Inspiring children with the opportunity to launch into a task using their language of preference. If the task is writing poetry, for example, it may be wonderful for the child to first explore thoughts and feelings that contribute to writing in the language closest to their heart. This principle can be extended to all areas of the curriculum within a JONK multilingual and multicultural thinking and learning classroom environment.

3   Setting of multilingual home-learning tasks (Chapter 10):
    The example of the home-learning task (Chapter 10) where a child produced her menu in Spanish and English illustrates how multilingualism can have such a powerful impact beyond the classroom and into the home.

 DISCUSSION OPPORTUNITIES

An interesting exercise at this point is to see how, as a staff, this multilingual and multicultural approach can be developed to embrace all areas of the curriculum. Is it possible to offer children the opportunity to think bilingually across all subjects? Is it possible to incorporate the teaching of a second language as part of the Modern Foreign Languages (MFL) curriculum into the multilingual approach to teaching and learning proposed in this chapter?

JONK bilingual and multilingual thinking | Identifying three key aspects of the approach

The JONK BMT approach defines three distinct aspects to promote multilingual thinking: using languages independently of each other, combining the languages with certain structures defined or combining the use of languages without any predetermined conditions (Figure 11.2):

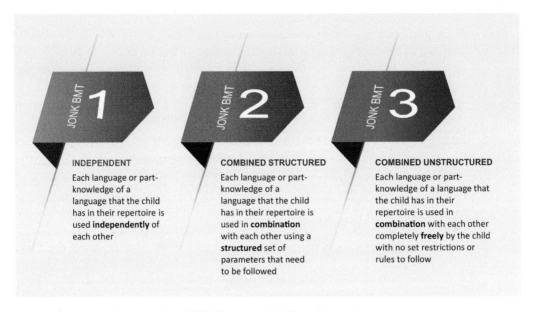

INDEPENDENT

Each language or part-knowledge of a language that the child has in their repertoire is used **independently** of each other

COMBINED STRUCTURED

Each language or part-knowledge of a language that the child has in their repertoire is used in **combination** with each other using a **structured** set of parameters that need to be followed

COMBINED UNSTRUCTURED

Each language or part-knowledge of a language that the child has in their repertoire is used in **combination** with each other completely **freely** by the child with no set restrictions or rules to follow

FIGURE 11.2 Three Key Aspects of the JONK Bilingual and Multilingual Approach

The three key aspects of the JONK BMT approach | Theory into practice

Using languages independently of each other

The independent BMT aspect uses a multilingual approach to the Thinking Skills Starters (Chapter 7) where children are presented with the opportunity to complete the same task in more than one language.

Let us take the challenge of creating an 'A–Z of a particular topic' as an example of the opportunities that this approach to multilingual creative thinking can offer:

■ Child A completes the Challenge in Language A as it is the only language that they are familiar with.

■ Child B completes the Challenge in Language B or any other language that they are familiar with.

■ If Child A and Child B are in the same class, the sharing of their ideas will enrich the cultural awareness of each other and the whole class.

■ Child C completes the task in one language and is encouraged to have another go at the same challenge using a different language (or languages), which they either are fluent in or are in the process of learning.

■ When Children A, B and C share the ideas generated whilst performing the task using each of the languages separately, all children develop a greater awareness of an additional language and its vocabulary, which can be particularly valuable if this is the language they are all learning at school as part of the MFL entitlement.

In completing the task using one language and then another, the child has the opportunity to benefit from all that bilingualism or exposure to a bilingual environment brings – cognitively, socially and neurologically. If we take 'Creating an A–Z of Healthy Living' as our example in which the class are encouraged to engage with the Starter using the variety of approaches described by Children A, B and C above, the sharing of the outcomes may result in an A–Z list compiled in English and additional A–Z lists compiled in other languages. When these lists created in more than one language are analysed, some very interesting observations may arise which can be used to promote and develop children's critical curiosity and ability to think creatively:

■ Similarities between the languages may be spotted. For example, *tomate* in Spanish and *tomato* in English seem to have originated from the same root word; this is a great opportunity to explore the etymology of these words in greater detail.

■ Spotting similarities may also lead to some 'playful' thinking. For example, children may spot that *lettuce* in English and *lechuga* in Spanish start with the same two letters and may or may not have originated from a common root word.

■ Distinctions made when comparing sets of answers produced in different languages can give us fascinating insight into different cultures and traditions. For example, one of the versions may contain an example of a type of food that is found in only a particular area or part of the world.

DISCUSSION OPPORTUNITIES

This a good opportunity to see whether any of the challenges can be translated into other languages that are spoken by children in your class. Could a child or a family member have a go at translating them?

Combining the use of languages using a structured approach

The second approach to BMT is based on encouraging children to pool all of their language repertoire and use it simultaneously. Using more than one language interchangeably to solve a problem allows the learner to draw upon the particular perspectives and nuances that each language offers and enables them to benefit from the 'accumulative' effect that this creates. This process is described in the literature as 'translanguaging'. The examples in this section and in the section below demonstrate how translanguaging can be presented to the children by using a structured approach.

In this scenario of the translingual approach, the children are presented with certain parameters or instructions to follow. For example, in a bilingual or multilingual version of the A-Z challenge where the children are asked to create an A-Z of Animals, they are also asked to alternate the language in which they respond. For example, A needs to be in Spanish, B in English, C in Spanish, D in English and so on:

A	**Alpacas**
B	Badger
C	**Cocodrilos**
D	Dog

As with the previous section, this example can be adapted for use with any language or languages. A trilingual approach may require children to use different languages for each of A, B and C, for example, with this pattern repeating for D, E and F and so on.

Combining the use of languages using an unstructured approach

In this third scenario, the children use a multilingual approach without having any preset parameters or restrictions in how they use their entire repertoire of language. Their multilingual knowledge just becomes a 'pool' of knowledge that they use without making distinctions of which language a particular word they are using belongs to, yet the child retains an accurate understanding of how each language in itself is used correctly as an independent entity.

It is interesting to note that Garrity, Aquino-Sterling and Day (2015) describe how translanguaging emerged as a powerful tool that helped them document the first year of a Spanish/English program in an infant classroom. They explain that in their study, as with the example illustrated below, 'the infants were not bound by implicit or explicit rules about what language to use when, with whom, or in what context'. They explain how in their multilingual classroom 'both children and teachers used language fluidly as they went about their daily lives'.

In the example (Figure 11.3), the child who worked on the 'Adding one letter at a time to the previous word to make a new word' challenge demonstrates this non-restrictive use of multilingualism very well. The child has chosen to switch from one language to another according to what works best, starting with *cat* in English but carrying on the list with words in Spanish.

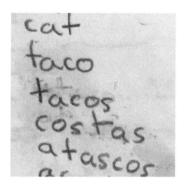

FIGURE 11.3 Using More than One Language Freely to Complete as Task

Language can also be combined with mathematics to promote creative thinking using a fluid multilingual approach. For example, in the challenge below, the children have to define each number using words or phrases that define that number, but they are allowed to use only the number of letters in their words or phrases of the number that they are defining:

'1' can be defined as '*a*' as '*a*' means one and uses one letter.
'2' can be defined as '*bi*' as 'bi' means two and uses two letters.
'3' can be defined as '*tri*' as 'tri' means three and uses three letters.
'4' can be defined as '*quad*' or '*four*' as both mean four and use four letters.
'5' can take on a multilingual approach if defined using the word '*cinco*', which means
    five in Spanish.
'6' can be defined as '*one six*' as this means six and uses six letters.
'7' can take us back to Spanish as this can be defined as '*un siete*' which means 'one
    seven' and uses seven letters.

It is interesting to see how far children can get with this challenge and how many languages they are able to use as they define each number. Mehnedbegovic (2016) states that children who use two languages are able to focus better on tasks and ignore irrelevant disruptions. Mehmedbegovic argues that this is particularly relevant in subjects like maths 'where you need to use more of your abstract thinking, because two languages develop abstract thinking and also metalinguistic skills as well which are useful for learning further languages'.

The multilingual fluid classroom, school and society

> *'A society's fate in the end depends on the quality of the schooling its children get in language.*
>
> John Amos Comenius, Czech philosopher (1657)

In this chapter, we have seen how beneficial a multilingual and multicultural approach to teaching and learning and to life at school can be for all children, whether they are proficient in another language, are in the process of learning another language or are monolingual but are benefitting from being exposed to a multilingual learning environment.

In an interview with the Erasmus Online Platform (2019), Nell Foster, from the University of Ghent's Centre for Diversity and Learning, states that 'research indicates that the use of home languages in the classroom helps children to make better progress and contributes to feelings of well-being in school, helps children engage with the curriculum in a more meaningful way and to be positioned as competent learners. When we allow children to use their home language in the classroom, it allows them to become confident, to have positive participation and it means that they can be valued for who they are now rather than who they will become once they have learned the language of instruction'.

This sentiment links in wonderfully with all the principles that underpin the JONK approach and the establishment of its culture *for* learning that enables all children to flourish *now* and *in their futures*.

 DISCUSSION OPPORTUNITIES

It is interesting to discuss as a staff team the possibility of developing a whole-school translanguaging approach to teaching and learning.

 DISCUSSION OPPORTUNITIES

Could the use of more than one language be accomplished in certain areas of the curriculum with greater ease than in others? Can this be achieved without compromising a child's understanding of the skills being taught?

 DISCUSSION OPPORTUNITIES

It is very interesting to consider using the BMT approach as a theme for a round of whole-school action research, enabling practitioners to explore:

DISCUSSION OPPORTUNITIES

How the various pedagogical methods that bilingual schools use (transitional, full, part and dual language immersion programmes, for example) help those schools to promote a multilingual approach to teaching and learning and explore elements of these approaches that can be incorporated into the daily teaching and learning routine of your class.

 DISCUSSION OPPORTUNITIES

The practice at La Scuola d'Italia NYC, an Italian Bilingual Preschool in New York, USA, where, as they describe to prospective families, 'the learning of a new language is spontaneous in their setting as it is related to the children's everyday experiences. Children are exposed to the culture and language of both countries through a variety of activities including drama, art, music, science and psychomotor projects that infuse learning and play'.

 DISCUSSION OPPORTUNITIES

How best to adapt each of the ideas in his chapter to the age group and context of each school and class. As Mehnedbegovic (2016) suggests, 'can teachers develop the reflective practice where they frequently ask themselves, [do] my curriculum and my teaching reflect the linguistic capital of my learners?'

 DISCUSSION OPPORTUNITIES

The three pillars of functional multilingual learning, defined by Nell Foster (2019): a safe classroom environment, possibilities for children to interact in other languages and the creation of meaningful multilingual activities to achieve a real-life goal.

As a native Spanish speaker, I have explored the transferability of the Joy of Not Knowing (JONK) philosophy of education and school leadership to settings where the main language of instruction is Spanish. As a lecturer during a secondment to the University of Brighton, I had the opportunity to develop this international dimension of the JONK approach through a collaborative project with the University of Cantabria and schools in Santander, Spain. As an associate lecturer at the University of Sussex, I have developed this work further through a collaboration with teachers from the English-Spanish Bilingual Schools in Madrid, Spain and Buenos Aires, Argentina.

In Spanish, the JONK approach has become known as the '*Placer De No Saber*' (PDNS), which translates as the 'Pleasure of Not Knowing'. The international collaborations that led to the PDNS approach demonstrate that the ideas and principles which underpin the JONK approach can be applied universally. The non-prescriptive and open-ended nature of the JONK ideology opens up the opportunity for all practitioners around the world to interpret the methodology and mould the ideas in a way that augments and enriches their practice and philosophy of education.

The book starts by describing that the JONK approach evolved from a desire to allay the fears we face when in situations of uncertainty or of not knowing and replace these with an intrinsic sense of attitudinal positivity and enthusiasm for *wanting* to know. It is very fitting to conclude the book by sharing how this concept was interpreted so beautifully and so meaningfully in one of the partner schools in Madrid by a seven-year-old child (Figure 11.4), who made a direct connection between the '*Placer De No Saber*' and his *emotional well-being*.

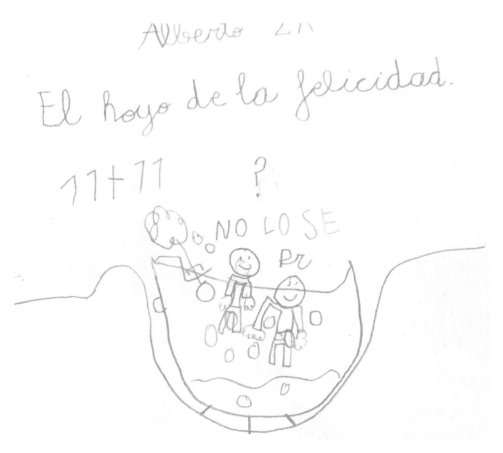

FIGURE 11.4 El Hoyo De La Felicidad

The child's diagram is entitled '*El Hoyo De La Felicidad*', which translates as *The Pit of Happiness*! In it, he depicts himself and his friend, in the JONK Pit, with huge smiles, even though they find themselves in a situation of *not knowing*: *NO LO SE – I DON'T KNOW.*

The link that this child has made between *happiness*, *not knowing* and *wanting to know* defines the purpose of this book wonderfully and illustrates how the JONK philosophy and approach can have such a transformational impact on children's lives.

Note

1   In order for children to be offered the opportunity of engaging with the Thinking Skills Starters bilingually, the book *Start Thinking* has been translated into Spanish, *Empezar Pensando* (Staricoff, in press, Imaginative Minds).

References

Alexander, R. (ed.) (2010). *Children, their World, their Education, Final Report and Recommendations of the Cambridge Primary Review.* Abingdon, Oxon, UK: Routledge.

Barrell, J. (2003). *Developing More Curious Minds.* Alexandria, VA, USA: Association for Supervision and Curriculum Development.

Bartlett, A. and Johnson, R. (2012). *Once a Pond of Slime.* Brighton, UK: Hertford Infant and Nursery School.

Bloom, B. S. (1956). *Taxonomy of Educational Objectives, Handbook I: The Cognitive Domain.* New York: David McKay Co. Inc.

Briggs, R. (2002). *Ug: Boy Genius of the Stone Age.* London: Red Fox Publishers.

Buzan, T. (2003). *Mind Maps for Kids.* London: Harper Thorsons.

Carpenter, S. and Toftness, A. (2017). The Effect of Prequestions on Learning from Video Presentations, *Journal of Applied Research in Memory and Cognition*, 6, 104–109.

De Bono, E. (1987). *Letters to Thinkers, Further Thoughts on Lateral Thinking.* London: Harrap Ltd.

De Bono, E. (2004). *How to Have a Beautiful Mind.* London: Vermillion.

De Bono, E. (2016). *I am Right, You are Wrong.* London: Penguin, Random House.

De Villa, A. (2017). Critical Thinking in Language Learning and Teaching, *History Research*, 7, 73–77.

Deakin-Crick, R. (ed.) (2006). *Powerful Learning in Practice.* London: SAGE-Chapman.

Dweck, C. (2017). *Mindset, Changing the Way you Think to Fulfil your Potential.* London: Robinson.

Eyre, D. and McClure, L. (2001). *Curriculum Provision for the Gifted and Talented in the Primary School.* Oxon, UK: David Foulton Publishers.

Eyre, D. (2011). *Room at the Top, Inclusive Education for High Performance.* London: Policy Exchange.

Eyre, D. (2013). *Able Children in Ordinary Schools* (2nd ed.). Oxon, UK: David Foulton Publishers.

Eyre, D. and Staricoff, M. (2014). Gifted and Talented, Chapter in *Learning to Teach in the Primary Classroom* (3rd ed.). James Arthur (ed.). Teresa Cremin. Abingdon, Oxon, UK: Routledge.

Eyre, D. (2016). *JONK Citation in High Performance Learning.* Abingdon, Oxon, UK: Routledge.

Fisher, R. and Williams, M. (eds.) (2004). *Case Study in Unlocking Creativity, Teaching Across the Curriculum*, 12. London: David Fulton Publishers.

Foster, N. (2019). Education Talks: Multilingual Classrooms: The New Reality in Urban Schools, *Erasmus Interviews Online Platform.*

Garrity, S., Aquino-Sterling, C.R., and Day, A. (2015). Translanguaging in an Infant Classroom: Using Multiple Languages to Make Meaning, *International Multilingual Research Journal*, 9, 177–196.

Groves, M. and West-Burnham J. (2020). *Flipping Schools*. Woodbridge, UK: John Catt Educational.

Hart, S. (2004). *Learning Without Limits*. Buckingham, UK: Open University Press.

Hattie, J. (2008). *Visible Learning*. Abingdon, Oxon, UK: Routledge.

Honoré, S. and Porter, M. (2018). *Education for Humanity*. Tunbridge Wells, UK: Spirit of the Rainbow™.

Hutchin, V. (2012). *Case Study in Assessing and Supporting Young Children's Learning: For the Early Years Foundation Stage Profile*. Oxon, UK: Hodder Education.

James, M., Renowden, J., West-Burnham, J. (eds.) (2013). *Rethinking the Curriculum; Embedding Moral and Spiritual Growth in Teaching and Learning*. Bath, UK: Brown Dog Books.

Johnson, R. (2020). *The People's Republic of Neverland: State Education Vs. the Child*. Oakland, CA, USA: PM Press.

Keith, M. (2010). *Not A Wake: A Dream Embodying (pi)'s Digits Fully for 10000 Decimals*. Portland, OR, USA: Vinculum Press.

King, L. (2018). The Impact of Multilingualism on Global Education and Language Learning, *Cambridge Assessment English*, Cambridge, UK.

Kirby, P and Webb, R. (2018). Spaces to be Uncertain: New Initiative Calls for Conformity to be Challenged in the Classroom, *Education Today*, Kent, UK.

Lauchlan, F., Parisi, M., and Fadda, R. (2012). Bilingualism in Sardinia and Scotland: Exploring the Cognitive Benefits of Speaking a 'Minority' Language. *International Journal of Bilingualism*, 17, 43–56.

Law, S. (2000). *The Philosophy Files*. London: Orion Publishing Group.

Lipman, M. (2003). *Thinking in Education*. Cambridge, UK: Cambridge University Press.

Lorio, J.M. (2016). Reggio Emilia Approach in *The SAGE Encyclopaedia of Contemporary early Childhood Education*, Donna Couchenour & J. Kent Chrisman (eds.). London: SAGE.

MacGilchrist, B., Myers, K. and Reed, J. (1997). *The Intelligent School*. London: Paul Chapman Publishing Ltd.

Marian, V. and Shook, A. (2012). The Cognitive Benefits of Being Bilingual, *Cerebrum*, 13.

Mehnedbegovic, D. (2016). Education Talks: Bilingualism in Education, *Erasmus Interviews Online Platform*.

Naylor, S. and Keogh, B. (2000). *Concept Cartoons in Science Education*. Cheshire, UK: Millgate House Publishers.

Nottingham, J. A. (2017). *The Learning Challenge: How to Guide Your Students Through the Learning Pit*. Thousand Oaks, CA, USA: Corwin.

Nuthall, G. (2007). *The Hidden Lives of Learners*. Wellington, New Zealand: New Zealand Council for Educational Research.

Oxford Language Report (2018). *Why Closing the Word Gap Matters*. Oxford, UK: Oxford University Press.

Peacock, A. (2016). *Assessment for Learning Without Limits*. London: McGraw-Hill/Open University Press.

Robinson, K. and Aronica, L. (2015). *Creative Schools*. London: Penguin Books, Random House.

Sacchs, J. (2018). *Unsafe Thinking*. London: Random House Business Books.

Sharron, H. and Coulter, M. (2006). *Changing Children's Minds; Feuerstein's Revolution in the Teaching of Intelligence*. Birmingham, UK: Imaginative Minds.

Stanley, S. and Bowkett, S. (2004). *But Why? Teacher's Manual: Developing Philosophical Thinking in the Classroom*. London: Network Continuum Education.

Staricoff, M. (2001). Higher Order Thinking Skills in Science, *Flying High Project*, Bristol, UK.

Staricoff, M. and Rees, A. (2003a). Start The Day on a Thought, *Teaching Thinking*, 12, 40–44.

Staricoff, M. and Rees, A. (2003b). Thinking Skills Transform Our Day, *Teaching Thinking*, 10, 40–43.

Staricoff, M. (2003). Measuring the Speed of Sound, *CLEAPPS*, 25, 4–5.

Staricoff, M. and Rees, A. (2004). The Fours Four Challenge, *Teaching Thinking*, 15, 10–14.

Staricoff, M. and Rees, A. (2005). *Start Thinking*. Birmingham, UK: Imaginative Minds.

Staricoff, M. (2005). Word Play More Than Just Fun, Letter, *TES*, 11 March 2005, UK.

Staricoff, M. and Rees, A. (2006). *Start Thinking*, Australian Ed. Adelaide, Australia: ACER Press.

Staricoff, M. (2006a). Here Comes The Philosophy Man, *Teaching Thinking and Creativity*, 20, 10–14.

Staricoff, M. (2006b). Lifelong Learning in the Primary Classroom, Chapter 7 in *Powerful Learning in Practice*, Ruth Deakin-Crick (ed.). London: SAGE-Chapman.

Staricoff, M. (2007). Here Comes The Philosophy Man, Philosophising the Primary Curriculum, *Gifted Education International*, 22, 182–191.

Staricoff, M. (2009). Thinking in Playgrounds, *Leadership Focus*. Haywards Heath, UK: NAHT Publications.

Staricoff, M. (2013). The Joy of Not Knowing, *Creative Teaching and Learning*, 4.2, 45–53.

Staricoff, M. (2014). Nurturing Creative Thinking from an Early Age, *Creative Teaching and Learning*, 4.3, 16–24.

Staricoff, M. (2017). Children, Goats and Democracy, *Times Educational Supplement*, London.

Staricoff, M. (2018a). Laying the Foundations for Young Thinkers, *Creative Teaching and Learning*, 8.1, 18–26.

Staricoff, M. (2018b). Enjoying Not Knowing Even More, Children as Leaders of School Improvement, *Creative Teaching and Learning*, 7.4, 18–27.

Swann, M., Peacock, A., Hart, S., Drummond, M.J. (2012). *Creating Learning Without Limits*. Maidenhead, UK: McGraw-Hill/Open University Press.

Training and Development Agency for Schools (2010). *Impact Evaluation: A Model Guidance and Practical Examples*. Manchester, UK: TDA Publications.

UNICEF (1990). *The United Nations Convention on the Rights of the Child*. London: UNICEF UK.

Webb, R. and Kirby, P. (2019). Modelling Transformative Education, *FORUM*, 61(1), 89–103.

West-Burnham, J. (2010). *Leadership for Personalised Learning*. Nottingham, UK: National College Publications.

White, R. & Gunstone, R. (1992). *Probing Understanding*. London: Falmer Press.

Wood, D. (1998). *How Children Think and Learn* (2nd ed.). Oxford: Blackwell.